Ingmar Bergman

Ingmar Bergman

His Life and Films

by Jerry Vermilye

McFarland & Company, Inc., Publishers

Jefferson, North Carolina, and London

Frontispiece: Bergman directing in the fifties. Svensk Filmindustri.

The present work is a reprint of the illustrated case bound edition of Ingmar Bergman: His Life and Films, *first published in 2002 by McFarland.*

LIBRARY OF CONGRESS CATALOGUING-IN-PUBLICATION DATA

Vermilye, Jerry.
Ingmar Bergman : his life and films / by Jerry Vermilye.
p.   cm.
Includes bibliographical references and index.

ISBN-13: 978-0-7864-2959-2
ISBN-10: 0-7864-2959-3
(softcover : 50# alkaline paper) ∞

1. Bergman, Ingmar, 1918–
2. Motion picture producers and directors — Sweden — Biography.
I. Title.
PN1998.3.B47V48   2007   791.43'0233'092 — dc21 [B]   2001055849

British Library cataloguing data are available

Cover photograph: Ingmar Bergman in the forties (*Svensk Filmindustri*)

Manufactured in the United States of America

*McFarland & Company, Inc., Publishers
Box 611, Jefferson, North Carolina 28640
www.mcfarlandpub.com*

For Debra
and
for Harvey
— Bergmaniacs both

Acknowledgments

The author wishes to thank the following individuals and organizations for helping with facts, photos, information and research assistance, without which no such project could be fully realized: Harriet Andersson, the British Film Institute, the Everett Collection, the late Henry Hart, Jane Klain, José Martinez, the Museum of Television and Radio, Donica O'Bradovich, Jay Ogletree, Jerry Ohlinger's Movie Material Store, Eve Povzea, the late Marc Ricci and his Memory Shop, Thom Toney, Allan Turner and the Film Society of Lincoln Center. With a salute to Bergman scholars Peter Cowie, Jörn Donner and Robert Emmet Long for laying the groundwork. And finally, a debt of gratitude is due the distributors and importers who gave us the films of Ingmar Bergman: Ajay Film Co.; Cinema 5; Cinerama Releasing Corp; Embassy Pictures; Film Classics; Gaston Hakim Productions, Inc.; ITC/ Associated Film Distribution; Janus Films; Lopert Pictures; New World Pictures; Nordisk Tonefilm; Paramount Pictures; Rank Film Distributors of America; Sandrews-Bauman; Surrogate Releasing; Svensk Filmindustri AB; Terrafilm; Times Film Corp.; Triumph Films and United Artists. And special thanks to Jamie Bohack for her invaluable help with manuscript preparation.

Contents

Liv Ullman on working with Ingmar Bergman:

"He hates to discuss and analyze. He believes that if you have chosen your profession as an actor, then you know a little how to act. He assumes that you are fairly intelligent. He feels that an analysis would take away the fantasy. He knows that is the way an actor creates. The actor has to use his own fantasy and imagination.

"He always is very, very close to the camera, and he is terribly inspiring. I don't know what his magic is, but it is something that makes you want to give everything you have. He has respect for actors and for everybody. A bad director very often doesn't have that respect."

I
Man and Artist

The Formative Years

As the motion-picture world greeted a second century of cinema, the international "art house" film has almost become ancient history on American movie screens. Few of the great foreign directors are still living or still *working*, and even fewer of the foreign-language stars who attracted U.S. filmgoers at mid-century remain more than memories today. In his early eighties, Ingmar Bergman stands apart with names like Federico Fellini, Akira Kurosawa, Satyajit Ray, François Truffaut, and Luchino Visconti—all lamentably departed—among those whose work is tirelessly studied in film schools, analyzed in print, and occasionally shown on educational and noncommercial TV channels.

Bergman has continued, past his "official" last theatrical film, 1983's *Fanny and Alexander*, to write and direct for the stage and for television. His screenplays are now entrusted to other, younger directors, like Billie August, Liv Ullmann, and the director's promising son, Daniel Bergman. In 1996, the filmmaker announced that he intended to cease *all* theatrical activity by the end of that year. Whatever Bergmanian remnants are yet to come, we can expect little to challenge the classic motion pictures of his peak years, encompassing such rare black-and-white gems as *The Naked Night*,

The Seventh Seal, Smiles of a Summer Night, Wild Strawberries, The Virgin Spring and *Through a Glass Darkly*. And as Bergman ventured further into areas of experiment, we were challenged by the revelations of *Persona, Winter Light, Cries and Whispers* and *Face to Face* as his critics increasingly chose words like "personal" and "chamber cinema" to describe — or *attempt* to describe — what Bergman may have been endeavoring to express. Whether adored or reviled, the filmmaker was difficult to ignore as an independent force who managed to write and direct *his* way, with little attempt at commercialization and long accompanied by the fiercely loyal band of actors and artisans whose careers would be defined by their work with him. Actresses, in particular, reflected his profound interest in their sex by realizing some of the greatest movie parts ever written for women, often with award-caliber results.

It has been said that Bergman is better appreciated in America than he is in his native Sweden, where his greatest hit was apparently that late masterpiece, *Fanny and Alexander*. If filmgoers in the rest of the world found some of his pictures too downbeat and too depressing to support, Swedes avoided them like the plague. Even today, there remains a sharp division between the

Ingmar Bergman in the forties. Svensk Filmindustri.

Bergmanites and those who'd gladly complete their lives without any further encounter with even the more acclaimed and accessible of his works. How many lifetime fans of the Oscar-winning *Ingrid* Bergman went to see her only collaboration with her fellow Swede, *Autumn Sonata*, and came away charmed by the encounter, perhaps for the first time, with a new cinematic "voice"? On the other hand, how many grumbled, "Never again; Bergman's too depressing!"? At the millennium, few movie buffs are undecided about Ingmar Bergman; either they like him or they don't. There's no middle of the road.

He was born at the Academic Hospital in Uppsala on July 14, 1918, and was christened Ernst Ingmar Bergman. The family was not well-to-do: his father, Erik

Bergman, was a chaplain, and his mother, the former Karin Åkerblom, was Erik's second cousin. Ingmar was the second of their three children. The first, Margareta, born in 1914, would become a successful novelist; another son, Dag, born in 1922, would enjoy a diplomatic career of some distinction. Although displaying a proper, controlled public facade, Erik and Karin suffered a conflict of personalities. He was the authoritarian, professional pastor who restrained any expression of emotion. From all reports, he was more comfortable in the pulpit than in his own home with his family. But his wife was a woman of underlying passions whose strong, wiry constitution was met with resistance by Erik. Years later it was revealed that during their marriage Karin had engaged in an extramarital affair and that Erik, as a result, had undergone a period of depression so serious that he had threatened her with suicide. But as Ingmar revealed in his 1987 autobiography, *The Magic Lantern,* "they were reconciled and decided to continue on 'for the sake of the children,' as was said at the time. We noticed nothing, or very little."

Among young Ingmar Bergman's strongest childhood memories are the visits to his grandmother's sprawling fourteen-room apartment in Uppsala, where he fondly remembers "lots of big rooms with ticking clocks, enormous carpets and massive furniture ... the combined furniture of two upper-middle-class families, pictures from Italy, palms." The boy's explorations in that apartment fired his young imagination: "I used to sit under the dining table there, 'listening' to the sunshine which came in through the cathedral windows. The cathedral bells went ding-dong, and the sunlight moved about and 'sounded' in a special way."

One day when he was five, the boy imagined a large picture of Venice coming to life as he listened to piano music from an apartment adjoining his grandmother's. On another, he believed he witnessed movement from a reproduction of the *Venus de Milo.* But most evocative of all was the window blind in the nursery, where light and shadow played strange tricks:

"No special little men or animals, or heads or faces, but *something for which no words existed.* In the fleeting darkness they crept out of the curtains and moved toward the green lampshade or to the table where the drinking water stood. They ... disappeared only if it became really dark or quite light, or when sleep came."

One Sunday in 1924 the Bergman family was struck with good fortune when Victoria, the wife of King Gustav V, heard Erik Bergman deliver an eloquent sermon that so impressed her that he was appointed to the Royal Hospital, Sophiahemmet. The immediate result was an improvement in the

family's living conditions, for they were given a spacious vicarage in the hospital's adjoining parkland. In that locale, little Ingmar found even more food for thought: "I played very much alone... There was a small chapel in the park, where the dead patients were brought and placed until they were taken for burial." Having made friends with the gardener, whose duties included transporting the bodies, he reflects, "I found it fascinating to go with him; it was my first contact with the human being in death, and the faces looked like those of dolls. It was scary but also very fascinating." On more gruesome occasions, he observed hospital workers disposing of surgical waste and limbs in the great coal furnaces. "For a child, it was traumatic, and I loved it!"

Sundays, of course, were for church, and all three Bergman children were obliged to attend their father's services. But young Ingmar never liked the traditions and dogma attached to Swedish Lutheranism, and as soon as they could each Sunday, he and his brother would escape to a matinee at the Stockholm cinemas. Erik Bergman was apparently a stern disciplinarian, but Margareta recalls her brother Ingmar's ability to charm and disarm his father when punishment was in order. And the boy did strive to win his father's approval: "I remember from early childhood a need to show what I had achieved; progress in drawing, the ability to bounce a ball against the wall, my first strokes in the water."

From the age of ten, Ingmar began frequenting the film showings at the Östermalm Grammar School, where he and his brother, Dag, enjoyed seeing the nature films, documentaries and dramatic features that had been especially edited for a young audience. But his lifelong addiction to film had begun four years earlier when he had been taken to see *Black Beauty.* Its frightening fire scenes had so impressed little Ingmar that he was confined to his bed with a temperature for three days.

At twelve, inspired by a stage production of the fairy tale *Big Klas and Little Klas*, Ingmar was moved to construct a puppet theater in the Bergman nursery, complete with moving scenery and a sophisticated lighting system. Working with dolls, he and Margareta would stage fantasy plays, utilizing phonograph records for mood music.

For a time, one childhood ambition was to be a projectionist; after all, what could be better than running movies all day? In a reflection of the 1988 Italian film *Cinema Paradiso,* young Ingmar was allowed in the projection booth at the Castle Cinema in Uppsala. But it seems that the child was eventually discouraged by that projectionist's undue display of affection for him.

In those days the increasing cost of movie tickets sometimes drove Ingmar to help pay for his admission by appropriating the needed coins from his father's pockets. And because his grandmother shared the lad's enthusiasm for moving pictures, she was frequently his companion at the cinema. He later admitted, "She was in every way my best friend."

One Christmas in the late 1920s, an aunt surprised Dag Bergman with a movie projector, for which the enterprising Ingmar traded virtually his entire army of lead soldiers. What has been described as "a rickety apparatus with a chimney and a lamp and a band of film that circulated endlessly" immediately became the object of the boy's obsession. He was soon making his own primitive films with makeshift plots. Eventually, he acquired a box camera, and as he would later describe in *Bergman on Bergman:* "[I] then made a cinema out of cardboard with a screen, on which I glued up the photos I'd taken. I made a whole series of feature films and ran them through on that screen, and made believe it was a cinema." One of those experimental, early movies became the inspiration for the silent farce viewed by the couple in *The Devil's Wanton/Prison.*

As a teenager, Ingmar Bergman attended Palmgren's School in Kommendörsgatan, near Storgaten, where the family moved in 1934 when Erik Bergman was appointed pastor of Hedvig Eleonora. The boy did not have an easy time of it at Palmgren's, for his inhibitions made him the target of unkind teachers. The experience would eventually provide the background and atmosphere for his first filmed screenplay, *Torment.*

By the early 1930s, Ingmar had become a genuine movie addict, sometimes frequenting cinemas several evenings in a row. Horror films, in particular, intrigued him, especially Boris Karloff in *Frankenstein* and *The Mummy.* And in the mid–1930s, young Hedy Kiesler (five years before she became Hedy "Lamarr") was a revelation in Gustav Machaty's *Extase.* ("There was that naked woman one saw suddenly, and that was beautiful and disturbing.")

In 1934, Ingmar paid his first visit to Germany as part of a summer exchange arrangement involving thousands of young people. It brought him into contact with a family whose son was a part of the Hitler youth movement. That summer, he was present at a Weimar rally celebrating the Nazi Party and attended by Adolf Hitler. A performance of Wagner's opera *Rienzi* followed. Young Ingmar had long since acquired a taste for classical music, and for a time he naively believed in the propaganda of Germany. Back in Sweden the Bergmans now had a summer villa on Smådalarö in the Stockholm archipelago.

After putting in two stretches of compulsory military service of five months each, he attended Stockholm High School and the University of Stockholm, where he majored in literature and the history of art. But he had trouble adhering to the requirements of the curriculum and failed to complete the degree course. A serious break with his family at this time may have had much to do with his academic failures. An altercation

with his increasingly disapproving father
had led Ingmar to not only return his father's slap but also to strike his intervening
mother. He immediately moved out of the
family home, and did not see Karin and
Erik Bergman again for four years.

Looking back on the breach years later,
Ingmar Bergman recalled: "It was as though
they were from another planet. I couldn't
draw, I couldn't sing … I couldn't dance. I
was shut in in every way." Remembering a
stifling atmosphere where punishments were
frequent and where discussions of topics like
money and sex were unthinkable, he wrote:
"That really was God's silence. Even today,
I can still lose my temper for no apparent
reason when someone consistently keeps
silent and turns away from me — then I kick
and keep at them until I get an answer."

Through the connections of Sven Hansson, a friend with whom he shared quarters
in Stockholm's Old Town, Ingmar was invited to teach a theater course at Mäster-
Olofsgården, a settlement community that
offered an opportunity for him to acquaint
himself with all aspects of theatrical activity. At the same time, he became a frequent
attendee at the opera and the Royal Dramatic Theater. Erland Josephson, later to
play important roles in many of Bergman's
films, recalls the young director staging a
production of *The Merchant of Venice* at
the Norra Real Högskola, in which Josephson played Antonio, and that even then
Bergman "was absolutely clear what he
wanted."

During the spring of 1938, Bergman
directed himself, as the Reverend Frank
Thomson, in the Mäster-Olofsgården production of *Outward Bound*. For two more
years he remained at the settlement, where
apparently his well-reputed directorial personality became fully developed. Although
he was much admired by his colleagues,
Bergman's demands were as hard on them as
on himself. When news came of the German invasion of Norway and Denmark on

April 9, 1940, he was playing Duncan in his
own production of *Macbeth*.

To make ends meet during those re-
bellious, bohemian years, the young director worked backstage at the opera. And he
shared quarters with a young woman whose
lust for life would inspire his 1947 screenplay for *Woman Without a Face*. But his nervous, moody personality and frequently
bizarre patterns of behavior often con-
founded his circle of friends.

In 1940, Bergman was not only continuing his theatrical activities at Mäster-
Olofsgården but also producing plays at
Stockholm's Student Theater, whose audi-
torium was a restaurant during the day. His
first production there was Strindberg's *Pel-
ican*. The following year, he was busy directing that author's *Ghost Sonata* and *A
Midsummer Night's Dream* at the Civic Center, where he also utilized the library to
mount plays for children.

In 1942, Bergman managed to stage a
play of his own, *The Death of Punch*, at the
Student Theater. Sten Selander's rave notice
in *Svenska Dagbladet* the day after the opening said, "No debut in Swedish has given such
unambiguous promise for the future," and
it so impressed Svensk Filmindustri's Stina
Bergman that she contacted her promising
young namesake and urged him to pay her a
visit. She remembers his being "shabby and
discourteous, coarse and unshaven." She adds:
" He seemed to emerge with a scornful laugh
from the darkest corner of Hell; a true clown,
with a charm so deadly that after a couple of
hours' conversation, I had to have three cups
of coffee to get back to normal."

Despite that first impression, Bergman
was offered a position as an assistant screenwriter. Unable to resist the challenge of
worlds to conquer and more money than he
had ever had before, he accepted. In that
exciting new atmosphere of a film studio,
he not only helped hone and polish the
work of other writers, but he also managed
to turn out a dozen plays of his own.

That October, Bergman became engaged to Else Fisher, an Australian born
Norwegian-Swede who had served as his
choreographer on *The Death of Punch*. They
were wed on March 25, 1943, at Hedvig
Eleonora Church, followed by a brief two-
day honeymoon in Gothenburg, after which
they settled into a two-room apartment.
Else continued with her dancing, and Ingmar suffered doubts about his professional
progress. Marriage apparently served to curb
some of the young Bergman's bohemian
habits; yet he maintained a small, pointed
beard and took to wearing his wife's beret (a
trademark which would last until his fourth
wife, Käbi Laretei, finally broke him of the
affectation).

During the war years, according to Ingmar's friend Birger Malmsten, who would
portray the hero in many early Bergman
films, the young writer-director is remembered as being "small and skinny, wearing a
pair of worn-out suede pants and a brown
shirt.... He directed the play holding a
hammer in his hand, and he threw it from
time to time at the young actors."

The Making of an Artist

In the spring of 1943, Bergman was elevated to scriptwriter at Svensk Filmindustri, with a year's contract. His first effort for the studio, a screenplay called *Scared to Live,* was considered quite promising. Another was his adaptation of *Katinka,* an Astrid Väring novel. Actor-director Victor Sjöström, who had been one of Sweden's great filmmakers in the silent era, had been appointed artistic director of Svensk Filmindustri in 1942. Sjöström liked Bergman, admired the young man's scenario for *Torment,* and was instrumental in getting the screenplay to director Alf Sjöberg, who responded to the shock of recognition brought on by reading the story of a sadistic schoolmaster and the young student and girl whose lives are affected by him. Sjöberg said: "I read the script and found that it mirrored exactly my own experience as a boy. The atmosphere at my school was very Germanic and full of spiritual pressure. Ingmar Bergman and I had had the same teacher — I for eight or nine years!"

Torment began shooting on February 31, 1944, a fascinating but curious experience for its author, who was assigned to serve in a position generally known as "script girl," since a female usually handled the chore of keeping track of the continuity from scene to scene. There's obviously much of Bergman's own experience in this story of a humiliated student (played by Alf Kjellin) who is victimized by his sadistic Latin master (Stig Järrel) and misunderstood by self-absorbed parents. The youth finds solace with a sympathetic shopgirl (Mai Zetterling), ignorant of the fact that she, too, is the object of a sinister obsession by the schoolmaster, who later kills her. The student brings charges against his master, but his behavior disqualifies him from taking his exams. And while his classmates pass, he retreats to his dead lover's room, where the headmaster pays him a visit, offering assistance. Significantly, the film's conclusion is scarcely uplifting. Indeed, its initial close was considered too downbeat, and Bergman was inspired to write another one, offering some hope for the future as the student walks out into the dawning city. Its realization afforded Ingmar Bergman his first opportunity to direct a bit of a theatrical motion picture when, because Alf Sjöberg was unavailable, Bergman himself was given the job.

"I was told to shoot these last exteriors, since Sjöberg was otherwise engaged. They were my first professionally filmed images. I was more excited than I can describe. The small film crew threatened to walk off the set and go home. I screamed and swore so loudly that people woke up and looked out their windows. It was four o'clock in the morning."

Torment enjoyed great success, initially in Scandinavia and later abroad, after the war's end. It didn't appear on American screens until 1947, when it marked a motion picture breakthrough for Swedish films, with both Alf Kjellin and Mai Zetterling receiving offers from British and American producers. She would enjoy considerable success in England, while he did some Hollywood acting and eventually became a successful TV director. In later years, Zetterling turned motion-picture director.

In April 1944, Bergman was made director of the Helsingborg City Theater, a three-hundred-seat facility in that coastal town, whose city fathers wished to detract some attention from the magnificent new theater in neighboring Malmö. That September, several months after Ingmar and Else had welcomed the birth of a daughter, whom they named Lena, Helsingborg witnessed the inauguration of Bergman's artistic direction with a production of *Mrs. Ascheberg from Witdskövle* by Brita von Horn. Bergman's work made a strong, positive impression on a company of young people whose salaries were as modest as the theater's subsidy. As Erland Josephson remembers, "Ingmar's productions were so good that it appeared as though there *were* a lot of facilities. His use of the stage, the actors, the music, the rhythm, was excellent."

In two Helsingborg seasons Bergman would produce ten plays, including such highlights as an anti–Nazi rendition of *Macbeth,* Olle Hedberg's *Rabies,* and *Requiem* by a promising new playwright, Björn-Erik Höijer.

The spring of 1945 marked the end of his marriage to Else Fisher; Bergman, separated from her by his work in the theater, had fallen for a dancer named Ellen Lundstrom. In time, as his second wife, she would bear him four children: Eva, Jan, and twins Anna and Mats. Three of those offsprings would eventually settle into show-business careers.

On the following July 4, Bergman began shooting *Crisis,* his first motion picture as a full-fledged director. It was based on his own adaptation of a Danish radio play, *The Mother Creature,* by Leck Fischer, and was made for Svensk Filmindustri, whose Carl Anders Dymling had sought out Bergman when none of their staff directors were interested in the project. As the novice filmmaker later admitted, "I'd have filmed the telephone book if anyone had asked me to at that point." But he held little respect for the material and did not much enjoy the making of *Crisis,* despite the luxury of his being able to cast actresses Dagny Lind and Inga Landgré, with whom he had worked in the theater. *Crisis* was not a success when it opened in early 1946, and Svensk Filmindustri was reluctant to furnish funding for a script Bergman had written entitled *Sentimental Journey* (four years later it would become *Summer Interlude*).

More receptive to working with Ingmar Bergman was Lorens Marmstedt, of the less prestigious company Terrafilm, for whom Bergman next filmed *It Rains on Our Love,* based on a play by the Norwegian writer Oskar Braathen. Barbro Kollberg and Birger Malmsten were cast as the star-crossed young lovers who meet in the rain, endure a series of challenging crises, and wind up facing an uncertain future together — in the rain. Gunnar Björnstrand, who had played the small part of a teacher in *Torment,* now played the small part of a bailiff. Much influenced by the movies of the French director Marcel Carné, Bergman allowed characteristics of that so-called school of "poetic realism," with its romantic fatalism, to infiltrate his own early filmmaking efforts. Twenty years later, writing in *Bergman on Bergman,* he would admit, "I just grabbed helplessly at any form that might save me, because I hadn't any of my own."

Bergman and cameraman Gösta Roosling on the set of *Crisis* (1946). Svensk Filmindustri.

The autumn of 1946 marked the start of Bergman's enduring association with the Gothenburg Civic Theater, where he discovered that he still had a lot to learn about actors and directing, by way of his association with "a hard, difficult man" named Torsten Hammarén. Whereas he had once been a virtual theatrical dictator, Bergman now began to discover that he could gain far better results by listening to the ideas of his cast members and trusting in their integrity and imagination. After first staging a production of *Caligula* by Albert Camus with Anders Ek in the title role, Bergman then mounted his own play, *The Day Ends Early,* an astringent allegory that, according to biographer Peter Cowie, "painted life as Hell on earth during an otherwise lusty Mid-

summer's Night." The critical reviews were negligible.

Bergman was anxious to be given the opportunity to direct one of the various movie scripts that he had been engaged in writing, but perhaps his lack of producing a winning box-office product accounted for the fact that producers were now more interested in his writing than his direction. Consequently, they bought his screenplay *Woman Without a Face* and assigned it to the veteran director Gustaf Molander, whose six films with Ingrid Bergman (notably the original 1936 *Intermezzo*) paved the way for her great Hollywood career. Bergman's extravagantly emotional script centered on a heartless young nymphomaniac (portrayed by Gunn Wållgren) and her effect on the men

Frustration (1947). Birger Malmsten. Nordisk Tonefilm.

in her orbit. Critics didn't much care for it, but the public did.

Lorens Marmstedt then engaged Bergman to adapt a play by Martin Söderhjelm, *A Ship Bound for India*, a moody tale of family conflicts within the setting of a waterfront and a salvage barge that echoes early Eugene O'Neill. Again, there were reverberating mirrors of Marcel Carné, especially of the 1938 *Quai des Brumes* (*Port of Shadows*). And again Birger Malmsten portrayed the young male protagonist, as he would continue to do as Bergman explored variations of youthful protest in his early films. Although little known today (and still unavailable on video), *A Ship Bound for India* remains an interesting remnant of Bergman's cinematic past. Outside of Scandinavia, it has been shown under the titles *Frustration*

and *The Land of Desire*, in an effort to exploit its low-key sexual elements. Some critics were impressed.

By way of elucidating the late-forties rationale behind his screenwriting, Bergman wrote in *Filmnyheter*: "I want to describe the universal activity of evil, made up of the tiniest and most secret methods of propagating itself, like something independently alive, like a germ or whatever, in a vast chain of cause and effect."

Bergman continued commuting between the stage and the screen in the autumn of 1947, splitting his creative forces between staging his new play, *To My Terror*, for the Gothenburg Civic Theater and directing his fourth movie, *Music in Darkness* (better known in English-speaking countries as *Night Is My Future*), which teamed

Birger Malmsten and *Torment*'s Mai Zetterling as, respectively, a blind pianist and the girl who embraces both him and his disability. This time the screenwriter was Dagmar Edqvist. Aside from his writing and his stage and screen activities, Bergman was also busy directing radio adaptations of Strindberg; namely, the plays *Dutchman* and *Playing with Fire*.

Based on a sentimental novel by Edqvist, *Night Is My Future* was deliberately aimed at the Swedish box office, and its resultant success marked an exciting new experience for Ingmar Bergman, who had begun subscribing to the Hitchcock-like indulgence of making brief on-screen appearances in his own films, beginning with *A Ship Bound for India*.

Bergman's name as a playwright began to attract a wider audience that year when stage versions of *Torment* were produced in Oslo and London, where Peter Ustinov directed it. In Gothenburg, Bergman again staged his concept of *Macbeth*, albeit this time with the more rewarding facilities provided by that theater. During the summer of 1948, while Gustaf Molander was directing Bergman's psychologically charged script *Eva* for Svensk Filmindustri — about a youth's efforts to come to terms with death — Bergman began shooting *Port of Call*, from a script he had worked on with Olle Länsberg, author of its original story "The Gold and the Walls." Again influenced by the waterfront settings so closely associated with Carné, *Port of Call*, focuses on a suicidal delinquent (Nine-Christine Jönsson) who is rehabilitated (after undergoing much stress) by a persistent seaman (Bengt Eklund). Much of it was filmed on location in Gothenburg, lending some of the continuity a documentary atmosphere. Bergman admits to also having been influenced during this period by the works of Roberto Rossellini: "Rossellini's films were a revelation — all that extreme simplicity and poverty, that grayness."

In the autumn of 1948, Hollywood's David O. Selznick, apparently impressed with the film *Torment*, attempted to set up an international co-production of Ibsen's classic *A Doll's House*, to be adapted by Bergman and directed by Alf Sjöberg, through an arrangement with Lorens Marmstedt. Bergman was paid for his work on the project, but the movie was never made. His explanation: "Sjöberg had too many ideas, and I had too few."

But Bergman was about to break free of the conventional movie script and shake up his audience. As he remarked in an interview: "I don't want to produce a work of art that the public can sit and suck aesthetically.... I want to give them a blow in the small of the back, to scorch their indifference, to startle them out of their complacency." And so he did, courtesy of the willing-to-gamble Lorens Marmstedt, who arranged to produce Bergman's experimental screenplay *Prison* (*The Devil's Wanton* in English-speaking countries). It was shot on a tiny budget in a mere eighteen days, and Bergman was challenged to use all his resources to create art out of what even Marmstedt predicted would be a failure. Among the personal questions that the filmmaker admits motivated him to create *Prison*: "Is earth Hell, and is there in that case also a God, and where is He, and where are the dead?" With its expressionist photography, echoing the celebrated German cinema of the 1920s, the downbeat film told of morose young people (Birger Malmsten, Eva Henning and Doris Svedlund) trying to find happiness amid the heavily symbolic twists and turns that life is dealing them. For the first time on film, Bergman deals in shock effects, and there are portents of things to come in his 1950s movies. Like it or hate it — and audiences were certainly divided — *Prison* is undeniably a major step forward in the progress of Ingmar Bergman the filmmaker. Following its production, he wrote a letter of deepest gratitude to Lorens

Marmstedt, expressing his appreciation for the moral and financial support that enabled the realization of such a deliberately non-commercial project. Upon its completion, he resumed his nonstop theatrical commitments, directing Anouilh's *Wild Bird* in Stockholm, Williams's *A Streetcar Named Desire* in Gothenburg, and also a production of Strindberg's *Mother Love* for Swedish radio. And as 1948 turned into 1949, he was busy planning his new motion picture, Herbert Grevenius's adaptation of short stories by Birgit Tengroth, to be called *Thirst* in Sweden (in the United States: *Three Strange Loves*), Bergman worked (uncredited) with Grevenius on this screen play, but because there were limits on his time, divided as it was between so much theatrical activity, it is difficult to sort out who did what. Certainly, some of the script's marital bitterness involving the dissenting couple, portrayed by Birger Malmsten and Eva Henning, bears signs of Bergman's personal experiences, for by now his second marriage was in shambles. And although certainly more conventionally told than *Prison*, *Thirst*'s multiplot structure employs flashbacks and the use of parallel action to explore several stories in one narrative. In the movie's secondary story line, a woman who had once been Malmsten's mistress (played by author Birgit Tengroth herself) teeters on the verge of entering into a lesbian relationship with an old friend (Mimi Nelson) before rejecting homosexuality for a leap into the harbor. Bergman here indulges in his lifetime love affair with mirrors as his characters literally reflect on their past lives (just as cinematographer Gunnar Fischer reflects on their present). By this time, the filmmaker's uncanny rapport with his female characters makes manifest Bergman's preferences; the men in his films are more often than not characterized as ineffectual, shadowy figures and objects of derision or disgust.

During the summer of 1949, Bergman filmed *To Joy* centering on the marriage between a previously wed girl and a violinist (Maj-Britt Nilsson and Stig Olin), told in a lengthy flashback. Those who question the melodramatic plot twist that kills off the wife with an exploding portable stove might not be informed that Bergman employed this only in desperation when he needed an ending for his story.

A notable sidebar involves the casting of Bergman's old Svensk Filmindustri production mentor, the great Swedish actor-director Victor Sjöström, as Olin's orchestral mentor, in a role that anticipates his ultimate performance as the elderly academic of Bergman's *Wild Strawberries*. *To Joy* also introduces a setting that Bergman would utilize as a favored location for several of his early–1950s works, the Stockholm archipelago in summer.

After the completion of *To Joy*, Bergman spent an extended vacation in Paris in late 1949 in the company of Gun Hagberg, a journalist who had interviewed him earlier that year and with whom he had found immediate rapport. Their sojourn in the French capital enabled Bergman to immerse himself in the French theater world as well as to write a play, which he called *Joakim Naked*.

As the 1950s dawned, Lorens Marmstedt noted that many of Ingmar Bergman's attention-getting bohemian affectations had fallen by the wayside, among them beard stubble and his dirty fingernails. "But," he noted, "the burning spirit is still there." Bergman now announced that in August he would begin directing at Marmstedt's Intima Theater in Odenplan, to commence on the heels of his next film, *Summer Interlude*. First, however, was his final work for the Gothenburg venue, Ramón Maria del Valle-Inclan's dark comedy *Divine Words*, which won him an accolade from screenwriting colleague and theatrical critic Herbert Grevenius, with whom he now collaborated again on the script for *Divorced*. Intended for the noted Swedish stage actress, Märta Ekström,

Three Strange Loves (1949). Birgit Tengroth and Mimi Nelson. Svensk Filmindustri.

this study of a middle-aged woman's life adjustments — and romantic affiliations — when her husband of twenty years tells her he now loves a younger woman and wants his freedom, eventually went to Inga Tidblad when illness prevented Ekström from taking the part. Gustaf Molander directed.

At about that time, *While the City Sleeps*, with which Bergman was only marginally affiliated, was filmed. An inferior study of juvenile delinquency in Stockholm, it was originally a novel by P. A. Fogelström entitled *Delinquents*. Bergman's only contribution to the project was an *adaptation*; the actual screenplay was coauthored by novelist Folgelström and Lars-Eric Kjellgren. The latter also directed.

Summer Interlude remains one of Bergman's favorite movies, perhaps because it had evolved from a story called "Marie" that

he had originally written in the 1930s, about a girl he knew who had contracted polio and died. About *Summer Interlude*, he commented: "This was my first film in which I felt I was functioning independently, with a style of my own, making a film all my own, with a particular appearance of its own, which no one could ape.... For sentimental reasons, too, it was also fun making it. Far back in the past there had been a love story, a romantic experience." In *Summer Interlude* the tragedy of a young woman's death becomes that of a young man's, while Bergman retains the name "Marie" for his heroine, an aging ballerina who recalls the blossoming of young love on a long-ago summer in the Stockholm archipelago. Again, much of the story involves flashbacks, occasioned by the delivery of a girlhood diary sent to the dancer by her lecherous old uncle, whose motivations

Summer Interlude (1951). **Birger Malmsten and Maj-Britt Nilsson. Svensk Filmindustri.**

are highly questionable. Again, Birger Malm-sten represents the youthful Bergman coun-terpart, with Maj-Britt Nilsson offering an exceptional performance as both the young and the older Marie. As Bergman's biogra-pher Peter Cowie has written, "No other film has caught so well the buoyant sensuality of high summer in Scandinavia." Because of a shutdown in Swedish film production, the picture was shelved for over a year and not released until 1951, at which time it was very well received.

Directly after the completion of *Sum-mer Interlude* in June 1950, Bergman plunged into the filming of *This Doesn't Happen Here*, a cold-war thriller that was never in-tended to be anything more than a quickly shot programmer. With reference to a mo-tion picture he has quite repudiated — and

which yet remains to be included in even the most comprehensive of Bergman retro-spectives in the United States — Bergman has said, "Only once has it happened that I've made something I've known from the beginning would be rubbish." Without as-sistance from Bergman, Herbert Grevenius adapted this screenplay from a Norwegian novel called *During Twelve Hours* by "Peter Valentin," a pseudonym for Waldemar Brøg-ger. Not unexpectedly, coming directly off work on *Summer Interlude*, Bergman was dejected and exhausted during the shooting of *This Doesn't Happen Here*. But with an impending standstill in Swedish movie pro-duction, he realized the need for income (there were now five children to support), and so he signed to direct this spy yarn, for which Swedish émigré Signe Hasso had returned from Hollywood to star opposite Ulf Palme. Because of Hasso, Svensk Filmindustri thought they had a potential worldwide box-office winner, and the film was shot simultaneously in both Swedish and English. But there were drawbacks during production. As Bergman has written in *Images — My Life in Film*: "Signe Hasso, a talented and warm person, unfortunately felt poorly during the entire filming. We were never sure from one day to the next whether she would be euphoric or depressed on the set." But there were various other factors amid filming that moved Bergman to call *This Doesn't Happen Here* "complete torture from beginning to end."

That autumn, Bergman's stage productions of *The Threepenny Opera* and a double bill of Hjalmar Bergman's *Shadow* and Anouilh's *Medea* met with critical disapproval at the Intima Theater, and there followed a rift in the friendship of the director and Lorens Marmstedt. Conflicting reports had it that Bergman either resigned or was fired form the Intima. Actor-director Hasse Ekman, Bergman's longtime rival, then replaced him.

Without any immediate means of income—and with the film industry about to shut down—Bergman found little source of solace except for his relationship with Gun Hagberg, whom he made his third wife early in 1951. Their union would not last very long, although she would become the mother of a son they named Ingmar, but they would remain friends until her death in an automobile crash twenty years later.

Eventually the studios closed in 1951 in protest against Sweden's high entertainment tax, a levy that was virtually crippling the industry. Because the film studios had anticipated the shutdown by stockpiling product, much of the moviegoing public was unaffected by this situation. It wasn't until the start of 1952 that government concessions allowed the turnover of a portion of the entertainment tax to benefit the film industry.

Unable to make a film for some eighteen months, Ingmar Bergman resorted to other creative means of financial survival: a series of one-minute Bris soap commercials for theatrical distribution and a radio play, *The City*, directed by a man he had always revered, Olof Molander. In April 1951, Bergman made his directorial debut on the Royal Dramatic Theater's small stage with *Light in the Hovel* by Björn-Erik Höijer, followed by a production of Tennessee Williams's *The Rose Tattoo* at Norrköping's Municipal Theater. In addition, he also directed a production of *The Murder in Barjärna*, a "passion play" of his own devising, at the Malmö Municipal Theater. Peter Cowie wrote: "its description of evil in a small community was as horrific and ghoulish as the wildest of film fantasies, and [critic] Henrik Sjögren thought it the most shocking of all Bergman's stage productions."

The settlement of the film strike predictably brought a flurry of production activity; Bergman immediately began filming *Secrets of Women* (April–June 1952) and then, with only a month in between for preparation, shot *Summer with Monika* (July–October). The director's original seriocomic screenplay for the former sprang from a story idea by Gun Hagberg that may have been suggested to her, in turn, from a viewing of Joseph L. Mankiewicz's clever American comedy *A Letter to Three Wives*, released three years earlier. In the Swedish film, three wives exchange marital tales from their own experience as they await the arrival of their husbands at a summer vacation home. Both of these necessarily episodic movies were told with wit and a sense of surprise. Mankiewicz's film won him Oscars for script and direction; Bergman's Scandinavian echo only proved that he could handle screen comedy as well as the more serious stuff. Its highlight, an episode in which bickering husband Gunnar Björnstrand and wife Eva Dahlbeck are trapped in their building's recalcitrant elevator, became the popular nucleus of the

Secrets of Women (1952). **Gunnar Björnstrand and Eva Dahlbeck. Svensk Filmindustri.**

1954 comedy *A Lesson in Love*, in which they teamed again. Bergman has said that *Secrets of Women* "was written in a mood of bad temper, sheer temper, and grim necessity," due to the need of readying a project to start the moment the film stoppage ended. The movie's success, his first significant one in the cinema, caused him such joy that he enjoyed visiting and revisiting Stockholm's most elegant movie theater just to hear the laughter engendered by that Dahlbeck-Björnstrand sequence.

Summer with Monika was an adaptation by Ingmar Bergman and Per Anders Folgelström of the latter's novel of that title, and its sexual frankness — including a nude bathing sequence, which was in the book — caused heated arguments behind the scenes at Svensk Filmindustri during production. Amid the summer of 1952, Bergman spent two months filming in the Stockholm archipelago, a protracted shoot that was apparently the result of the director's enthrallment with Harriet Andersson, his nubile, teen-aged leading lady. Though still relatively unknown — and admittedly engaged to young Swedish leading man Per Oscarsson (which might account for Oscarsson's never working in a Bergman film) — Andersson apparently quickened the pulse of *many* a male during *Summer with Monika*. Understating the situation in his *Bergman on Bergman*, the director wrote, "Making *Summer with Monika* was a lot of fun." This story of the summer affair between a naïve boy and a wanton girl results in pregnancy and a disastrous marriage. Because of its exploitation-worthy visual aspects, *Summer with Monika* would eventually draw worldwide attention to Harriet Andersson and her director.

Unfortunately, though a good film, its audiences would largely be drawn to *Monika*'s pleasures for reasons of prurience — and often, thus, in the less reputable cinemas of the larger cities, where censorship sometimes looked the other way and critical notices hardly mattered.

It has been said that Bergman's ongoing relationship with Andersson inspired him to greater creativity, onstage as well as on the screen, coinciding with his appointment as artistic director of Malmö's distinguished Municipal Theater. At that venue he soon established a pattern of directing one or two productions each year over a season that lasted from September until May, and then filming during the summer months. At the theater, Bergman's imaginative innovations attracted admiring attention: Faced with a cavernous stage area, he often kept his actors down front on the apron, utilizing the upstage area for projections. Moreover, in his ongoing mission to simplify the tendency of his colleagues to embrace clutter, Bergman would often remove the furniture altogether. He dealt with Molière's classic *The Misanthrope* by permitting the inclusion of but one chair, a carpet, and a painted dropcloth, while filling the stage with oversized costumes for his cast. Actors who relied at times on the "crutch" of furnishings would now find themselves utterly devoid of objects to sit on, lean against, or hide behind. Bergman found he had the luxury of staging musicals and operettas on the big stage, in addition to his regular choice of dramas, while Malmö's smaller, adjoining Intima Theater was ideal for the more experimental and offbeat fare.

Bergman's assistant during this period, Lennart Olsson, has described the master's unusual approach to directing at Malmö: "Ingmar was so far ahead of everyone in his understanding of the play that you never questioned him. During the first week of rehearsals, he would outline to you the basic arrangements he required on the stage. Then

he left you for two weeks. I had to take over the rehearsals for that period. Ingmar felt that if he was there all the time he would grow tired of hearing the lines over and over. So he preferred to come back fresh, with the groundwork already established."

Nor was it his habit to leave a production to the stage manager, once opening night had passed. Instead, he would appear at every performance, chatting with the cast and making certain that all was in order, as he had planned it. His reputation with his actors was apparently a very good one, and his celebrated outbursts were usually occasioned by frustrations over failure to achieve his theatrical goals. The very fact of Bergman's ability to maintain a loyal following of actors and technicians, both in theater and films, attests to his respect for their talents and their efforts.

Although still wed to Gun Hagberg, while supporting the offspring of his unions with both Else Fisher and Ellen Lundström, Bergman was now living openly with Harriet Andersson in a liaison that continued throughout his first three years in Malmö. She was also involved in his stage work, as were many, over those years, whom he employed in his films, including Max von Sydow, Ingrid Thulin, Gunnel Lindblom, Allan Edwall, Getrud Fridh, Bibi Andersson, Åke Fridell, and elderly Naima Wifstrand. With actors like these in his "stock company," Bergman often tailored his screenplays to their abilities and their appearances. And it was his custom during filmmaking to set up screenings for the entertainment of his casts at the Råsunda studios, outside Stockholm. With the help of Svensk Filmidustri, he would show films from all over the world, although his particular favorite director appeared to be Alfred Hitchcock.

Bergman's two 1953 films, *The Naked Night* and *A Lesson in Love*, were poles apart in every respect except one: Harriet Andersson was prominently cast in both, and fully justified her mentor's faith in her talent, as well as her sensuality. In the former, she's an aging circus owner's restless young mistress; in the latter, a teen tomboy eager to experience life and scarcely reconciled with her future as a girl. *Night* is a moody period piece, while *Lesson*'s farcical exploration of marital mores, as exemplified by that charmingly contentious couple from *Secrets of Women*, Eva Dahlbeck and Gunnar Björnstrand, for this is really an extension of their vignette in the earlier movie.

Although now considered by many as perhaps Ingmar Bergman's first great work for the cinema, *The Naked Night* (or *Sawdust and Tinsel*) was not generally well received in Scandinavia in 1953, and he was deeply stung by the condemnation of Sweden's most respected critics. But not all the criticism was negative, and the film intrigued and impressed distributors outside of Scandinavia.

That winter Bergman concentrated on Malmö's smaller stage, directing Kafka's *The Castle* and Pirandello's *Six Characters in Search of an Author,* as well as a major production of Strindberg's *Ghost Sonata* in the larger theater.

His only film that summer of 1954 was the minor but interesting *Dreams*, about the owner (Eva Dahlbeck) of a Stockholm fashion studio who journeys to Gothenburg with her star model (Harriet Andersson) for an ill-fated shoot that results in romantic complications of a sudsy nature when the businesswoman confronts her married lover (Ulf Palme). The Swedish public found little of general interest in *Dreams*, which marked the end of Bergman's liaison with Harriet Andersson.

For a radical change of pace, Bergman celebrated the Malmö Municipal Theater's tenth anniversary with a highly popular production of Franz Lehár's sparkling operetta *The Merry Widow*. An enormous hit with his public, this would be known for years to come as Bergman's *Widow*. Twenty years later, Lehár's perennial favorite would be se-

riously talked about as a vehicle for uniting the diverse talents of Bergman with no less than Barbra Streisand.

Bergman enjoyed a prolific first half of 1955 at Malmö. Starting off the year with Molière's *Don Juan* in the Intima Theater, he introduced touches that he would find worthy of recycling five years later in his film *The Devil's Eye*. A month later, on the larger stage, he momentarily abandoned the classics to embrace the contemporary with an uneasy production of the American comedy of clashing cultures *The Teahouse of the August Moon*. Not unexpectedly, it didn't appear to be quite Bergman's cup of tea. More congenial to his nature was his own one-act drama *Painting on Wood*, which followed in March, offering a foretaste of what would evolve into *The Seventh Seal*. But before that masterpiece, he would direct one of a different kind, *Smiles of a Summer Night*. Difficult as it is to believe, this delightful Gallic comedy of manners and mores was created during a "down" period in the filmmaker's life. But Svensk Filmindustri wanted a comedy from him, and as his finances were at a low point, necessity inspired invention. Its production transpired during one of the hottest Swedish summers on record, with all major shooting taking place between the end of June and the last day of August. And to make problems worse for Bergman, the pregnancy of Ulla Jacobsson, his young leading lady, necessitated subterfuge in both costuming and direction. *Smiles of a Summer Night* also marked the first appearance in a Bergman feature of young Bibi Andersson, an actress who had starred at fifteen in one of his commercials for Bris soap during the film strike. In *Smiles* she's glimpsed briefly as one of two supporting actresses with Eva Dahlbeck in the stage sequence when Jacobsson and her screen husband, Gunnar Björstrand, attend the theater. Actually, Bergman had met Bibi through her older sister, Gerd, and — with a thought to Jacobsson's condition — promised to give *her*

Smiles of a Summer Night (1955). Gunnar Björnstrand, Eva Dahlbeck and Jarl Kulle. Svensk Filmindustri.

the role of the young wife should his star not be able to fulfill her commitment. As it turned out, although she didn't get the *important* role, Bibi Andersson not only made an impression on her director that would lead to starring parts in his later movies, she also became a positive and inspiring force in his private life, creating a bond of love, admiration, and fierce, enduring loyalty.

Bergman had reason to feel insecure about *Smiles of a Summer Night*. At the time of its mixed critical reception, he wrote: "I went to it and sat there thinking this is the worst fiasco I've ever known. Not a soul seemed to laugh, nobody was enjoying it, they all sat grim and silent." But positive word about the film was beginning to circulate, and when it won a Special Jury Prize at the 1956 Cannes Film Festival, there was no

longer a question of its audiences being limited to Scandinavia; foreign interest accelerated. In the United States its late–1957 release would plant the seeds for what, in 1973, would become the hit Broadway musical *A Little Night Music*, which Stephen Sondheim would so cleverly fashion around Bergman's screenplay.

At about this time, Svensk Filmindustri resuscitated an old script, *For the Children's Sake*, that Bergman had written years before, and Alf Sjöberg agreed to direct it, with the casting of such Bergman-associated players as Eva Dahlbeck, Jarl Kulle, Björn Bjelvenstam, and the unrelated young Andersson ladies, Bibi and Harriet. The uncohesive outcome, released as *Last Couple Out*, represents a talented effort to conquer a problematic screenplay. The fault was Bergman's.

Painting on Wood had been written by Bergman expressly for performance by the ten students who formed his acting class at the Malmö Municipal Theater, including Gunnar Björnstrand and Toivo Pawlo. But its second production, at Stockholm's Royal Dramatic Theater in September 1955, was the more successful one. This time, Bengt Ekerot directed an entirely different cast, which included Bibi Andersson; Ekerot would attract far greater attention when he impersonated Death in the play's cinematic incarnation, *The Seventh Seal.*

Death in its many forms and certainties had consumed an important part of Ingmar Bergman's imagination and his ponderings since childhood, when the images in church frescoes haunted him and Erik Bergman's funeral orations offered him food for iconoclastic thought. As he would reveal years later: "My personal view is that when we die, we die, and we go from a state of something to a state of absolute nothingness, and I don't believe for a second that there's anything above or beyond, or anything like that, and this makes me enormously secure." However, in the mid–1950s these were thoughts yet unreconciled.

That Ingmar Bergman's two most-admired films, *The Seventh Seal* and *Wild Strawberries*, were filmed in 1956 and 1957 would seem to mark these as his most productive years. Following the delightfully saucy, sexual frolicking of *Smiles of a Summer Night*, *The Seventh Seal* offered such diverse elements — rich in symbolism and deeply reflective of man's destiny, viewed from the distance of its bare-boned medieval setting — that it's difficult to believe that both works emanated from the same man, such is the breadth and versatility of Bergman's style. Against the bleak and brooding backdrop of a plague-ridden landscape, a Crusades-weary knight (Max von Sydow) engages in a game of chess with Death (Bengt Ekerot), while a God-fearing couple (Bibi Andersson and Nils Poppe), the film's only hopeful el-ement, appear destined to be the tale's sole survivors, along with their little troupe of traveling players. As for the others, Death leads them in a giddy dance over the horizon — a brief but memorable final image — as the movie draws to a forceful close.

In an era far less fair with regard to the Academy Awards than the 1990s, *The Seventh Seal* won not even a single nomination: *The Bridge on the River Kwai* was voted Best Picture of 1957, while *Nights of Cabiria* won for Best Foreign Film. But *The Seventh Seal* won greater respect in Europe; it was awarded a Special Jury Prize at the 1957 Cannes Film Festival; the French Motion Picture Academy voted it the Grand Prix International de l'Académie du Cinéma the following year; and in 1960, it belatedly won the Golden Banner at Valladolid, Spain's religious film festival.

The Seventh Seal had been well received by the Swedish press when it opened there early in 1957, and Bergman was pleased that his father, Erik, was among its most supportive champions. The picture not only established a major new star in twenty-seven-year-old Max von Sydow; it finally elevated Ingmar Bergman to the first rank of the most respected contemporary film directors. By way of characterizing the impact of his mentor, Max von Sydow sums up Bergman's technique: "He never likes to analyze his own productions. But he managed to stimulate the imagination of his players by giving everyone a little tidbit of something. Bergman did not give you precise instructions about a scene; instead, he would give you a pace, a rhythm, or a musical score by which to be guided, so to speak. He'd say: 'This is a scene where people are indifferent to each other.' Or, 'Someone is letting out his aggressions at this point.'"

Those familiar with von Sydow's performance in *The Seventh Seal* may be hard put to imagine this imposing, mature-looking actor as Brick, the sexually confused, crutch-dependent hero of Tennessee Williams's *Cat on a Hot Tin Roof*; yet that is the role with

The Seventh Seal (1957). Bibi Andersson and Nils Poppe. Svensk Filmindustri.

which the actor concluded 1956, under Bergman's direction, at the Malmö Municipal Theater. Along with Vilhelm Moberg's biblical drama *Lea and Rakel* and Strindberg's *Erik XIV*, Williams's intense, heated drama of family conflicts proved an unexpected triumph for both Bergman and von Sydow.

In March 1957, Bergman enjoyed his greatest theatrical success up to that time with his production of Ibsen's challenging, full-length *Peer Gynt*, a four-hour epic with a large cast headed by Max von Sydow in the title role. Amid what must have been formidable challenges to the director presented by this play, he was already working on the nucleus of what would be the first of two 1957 film projects, *Wild Strawberries*.

That now-classic account of an elderly professor's introspective review of the regrets of his life — revealed in a complexity of dreams and flashbacks — afforded Bergman's old friend and mentor, Victor Sjöström, the valedictory role of his distinguished career. It was not an easy production, for Sjöström, at seventy-eight, was in failing health, often peevish and subject to memory lapses and mood swings following the death of his wife. But an unusual friendship developed between the elderly actor-director and young Bibi Andersson, who played a dual supporting role, and her harmless flirtatiousness probably helped him get through what could only have been a severe endurance test.

Wild Strawberries won the Golden Bear at the Berlin Film Festival in 1958 as well as the Grand Prize at Argentina's Mar del Plata Festival. And it took the Critic's Prize at Venice. In the United States it was named Best Foreign Film by the hard-to-impress National Board of Review but only received an

Wild Strawberries **(1957). Bibi Andersson, Gunnel Lindblom, Victor Sjöström and unidentified actors. Svensk Filmindustri.**

Oscar *nomination*— for Best Original Screenplay (*Pillow Talk* was that year's winner).

Commuting between the varying demands of stage and screen, Bergman remarked in the early 1950s, "The theater is like a loyal wife; film is the great adventure, the costly and demanding mistress — you worship both, each in its own way." Twenty years later, reassessing the rewards of his creativity, he allowed: "As a process of working, I actually prefer the stage." Indeed, long after ceasing to direct for the movies, he would continue to labor in the theater.

After the scope of *Wild Strawberries*, with its multiplicity of characters and settings, Bergman's other 1957 film was a virtual "chamber" work, confined chiefly to a single setting, the maternity ward of a small Stockholm hospital. Nor did *Brink of Life*

have many actors to deal with: Aside from a few nurses and husbands, the drama centers on three pregnant women, portrayed by Ingrid Thulin, Eva Dahlbeck, and Bibi Andersson — and the compassionate head nurse (Barbro Hiort af Ornäs) who helps them through their various crises. For a change, Bergman shared screenwriting credit with Ulla Isaksson, on whose short stories the film was based. Although well-made, beautifully acted, and fairly engrossing, *Brink of Life* is considered minor Bergman. But the film was the recipient of a special Cannes Festival Award for the excellence of its ensemble acting, for which all four of the picture's leading actresses were cited. It was the beginning of what would prove an ongoing series of citations directed at the women in Bergman films; if George Cukor deserved recognition as the American cinema's director of award-winning actresses, then Ingmar Bergman merited credit as his European counterpart, the more so since Bergman also *wrote* most of those female roles as well.

In December 1957, Bergman once again impressed the Malmö critics, this time with a production of Molière's *The Misanthrope* that one reviewer called "the brilliant climax of all Swedish theater in the fifties." And another went so far as to write, "Ingmar Bergman's production of *The Misanthrope* on the big Malmö stage is the finest Molière production we have ever seen in any Swedish theater."

In Hjalmar Bergman's *Saga*, which he directed at Malmö in early 1958, Bergman employed many of the actors familiar to his filmgoers — Ingrid Thulin, Max von Sydow, Gunnel Lindblom, Naima Wifstrand included — whose Malmö salaries only compensated them for that part of the year when the two theaters were operating. Loyalty to his company of players helped motivate Bergman to create roles for them in the screenplays he would habitually devise for summer production, a factor that accounts for the ensemble excellence of so many of his movies.

That year, from late June to the close of August, he worked on that bizarre but revered gothic period piece known variously as *The Face* (in Britain) or *The Magician* (in the United States). Told with cinematic legerdemain, this dark, provocative tale of a nineteenth-century theatrical troupe's eventful sojourn at a consul's home, where they are detained, pits a clever charlatan (Max von Sydow) against a distrustful doctor (Gunnar Björnstrand) who challenges the performer. In this unusual film, Bergman obviously enjoys playing tricks on his audience, even as his protagonist plays games with *his* opponent. *The Magician* is a film that continues to inspire controversy. Citing its "directing, poetic originality and style," 1958's Venice Film Festival jury awarded the movie a Spe-

cial Prize, while Italy's film critics gave *The Magician* the Pazinetti Prize as Best Foreign Film of 1959.

That winter in Malmö, Bergman directed Max von Sydow and Gunnel Lindlom in an acclaimed production of Goethe's *Urfaust* (his early, first version of what would be best known simply as *Faust*), a production notable for its imaginative deployment of lighting and pantomime. Rounding out the year were Bergman's production for television of Olle Hedberg's *Rabies* and the play that would mark the end of his association with the Malmö theater, F.A. Dahlgren's folk comedy *The People of Värmland*, which starred Max von Sydow and Bibi Andersson. Bergman's contract with Malmö was at an end, and so was his romantic relationship with Andersson, although their friendship would continue. Like many men of power and creativity, Ingmar Bergman appears never to have gone long without female companionship, and in the spring of 1959 he met the woman who would become the fourth Mrs. Bergman. This time, she was a person of intelligence, sophistication, and accomplishment in her own right, the distinguished, Estonian-born concert pianist Käbi Laretei, who was then married to the conductor Gunnar Staern and was the mother of a four-year-old daughter. Having first noticed her performing on TV, Bergman prompted a mutual friend to introduce them. Obviously, he was not about to let a mere marriage stand in his way. Their immediate rapport took them together to Dalarna that early spring, where she practiced her piano and Bergman worked with Ulla Isaksson on the screenplay of *The Virgin Spring*. Because it was considered by Svensk Filmindustri an iffy project commercially, he also worked simultaneously on a comedy, *The Devil's Eye*. Both projects would be filmed before the close of 1959, the former consuming Bergman's attention between May and August; the latter, from October until the end of December.

The Virgin Spring **(1960). Birgitta Pettersson and Tor Isedal. Svensk Filmindustri.**

The Virgin Spring was based on a medieval ballad and concerned an innocent maiden who was raped and killed by vagabonds, whereupon a spring wells forth from the ground where the crime took place. For Bergman, this was a happy shoot, although his regular cinematographer, Gunnar Fischer, was unable to work on the picture due to a prior commitment with Walt Disney Productions. This caused the director to seek out Sven Nykvist, one of three cameramen with whom he had worked on *The Naked* *Night* six years earlier. With the exception of the subsequent *Devil's Eye* (shot by Fischer), Nykvist's professional relationship with Bergman would continue throughout the remainder of the director's film career.

Bergman was less happy with the outcome of *The Virgin Spring* (1960), which he regards as "an aberration." In harsh self-appraisal, he has called it "touristic" and "a lousy imitation of Kurosawa." But it won him his first Oscar for Best Foreign-Language Film of 1960.

Another Beginning

On the first of September in 1959, Käbi Laretei, having shed her husband, and Bergman were wed in Dalarna. While in the midst of directing *The Devil's Eye*, with Jarl Kulle and Bibi Andersson — in a period during which he nursed self-doubts as to his theater skills — he was engaged as the director of Stockholm's Royal Dramatic Theater. This renewal of faith in his theatrical worth didn't help make his work on *The Devil's Eye* more felicitous; it was not a happy experience from any viewpoint, although he approved of his wife's choice (and performance) of the Scarlatti harpsichord music, with which the movie opens and closes (a credit which she requested not be acknowledged).

By now Ingmar Bergman was being lauded and hailed as a new cinematic genius in the American press by way of the critical "discovery" of the artistry of *The Seventh Seal*, *Wild Strawberries*, and *The Magician*. Oddly enough, the first important study of his art was published in Uruguay.

Early in 1960, Bergman directed Strindberg's *Storm Weather* for TV, and he completed the screenplay for *Through a Glass Darkly*, dedicating it to Käbi. Early in their marriage she made an effort to improve her husband's sense of personal style; the best she could do was to get him to abandon his trademark berets.

Bergman's love affair with the Baltic island of Fårö stems from this period, when, at the suggestion of a friend, he and his wife ventured there to scout possible locations for his upcoming film. In his words: "On a nasty, wet day we went over there on the ferry. It was pouring. But I don't know why, it was a kind of instant love. I just felt this was my landscape." And so *Through a Glass Darkly* was filmed there that summer. It would become the first installment in Bergman's "faith" trilogy, to be followed by *Winter Light* and *The Silence*, all chamber works in scope and containing small casts. The first is a moody tale of the effects of a young woman's insanity on her husband, her father, and her younger brother, all of whom share an isolated island home. As the central figure, Harriet Andersson returned to work for her early mentor, offering so impressive a delineation of schizophrenia that she helped Bergman win his second Oscar for the Best Foreign-Language Film of 1961. It also won the British Film Academy Award.

Winter Light, produced in the late autumn and early winter of 1961-62, is a far more austere film — perhaps Bergman's least accessible picture up to that time, dealing as it does with a village priest (played by

The Devil's Eye (1960). Bergman directing Bibi Andersson. Svensk Filmindustri.

Gunnar Björnstrand) and his disillusionment with his calling. Käbi Laretei's assessment may have been shared by many of the director's worldwide followers: "It's a masterpiece, but it's a dreary masterpiece." In the United States, the National Board of Review cited *Winter Light* as one of the five best foreign imports of 1963.

At the start of 1962, Bergman enjoyed a momentous meeting, in the privacy of his quarters at Svensk Filmindustri, with an illustrious fellow Swede, Greta Garbo, who had then been absent from the screen for more than twenty years. They had tea together, and Bergman later expressed how she had impressed him with her voice, her eyes, and her good humor. Rumors circulated that he had asked her to take a part in *The Silence*. But the actress was then fifty-

seven, and it's hardly conceivable that she might have played the role of the elder of the two pivotal sisters that went to thirty-three-year-old Ingrid Thulin. It was filmed in the late summer of that year, with Gunnel Lindblom as the younger, more sensual of the women who, with Lindblom's young son, are travelers who stop over at an old Eastern European hotel where the elder's repressed lesbianism contrasts with her sibling's sexual license. Heavy with symbolism and dark portent, *The Silence* achieved a measure of sensationalistic attention by dint of its scenes of sensuality, mild though they were. It raised a great deal of controversy in Sweden, and its notoriety continued to raise hackles elsewhere in Europe. All of which attracted the attention of filmgoers; in Britain and the United States it became a considerable

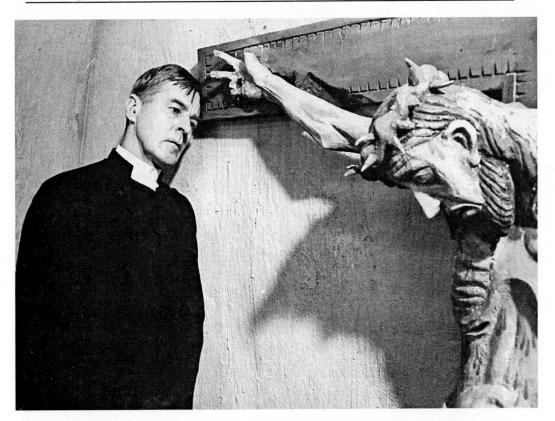

***Winter Light* (1962). Gunnar Björnstrand as Pastor Tomas Ericsson. Svensk Filmindustri.**

hit, perhaps for reason of prurience rather than art.

But his "faith" film trilogy didn't consume *all* of Bergman's creativity during those early years of the decade: There were also his production of Chekhov's *Sea Gull,* which marked his debut with the Royal Dramatic Theater in Stockholm, as well as Stravinsky's *Rake's Progress* at the city's Royal Opera. To help relieve a crisis at Svensk Filmindustri (production chief Carl Anders Dymling was dying of cancer), Bergman and Erland Josephson, employing the whimsical pseudonym "Buntel Eriksson," fashioned a comic vehicle for Gunnar Björnstrand, *The Pleasure Garden,* about the indiscretions of a turn-of-the-century Swedish schoolmaster. It was directed by Alf Kjellin, one of Bergman's earlier stars, and Bergman also helped with its production.

Ingmar Bergman was now a high-pro-

file celebrity, for better or worse, in Sweden, where his salary per film hovered in the vicinity of $35,000. By contrast, Simon and Schuster paid him an advance of $10,000 for the rights to publish in 1960 *Four Screenplays of Ingmar Bergman,* a volume which contained the texts of *Smiles of a Summer Night, The Seventh Seal, Wild Strawberries,* and *The Magician.*

At the beginning of 1963, Bergman was elevated to Sweden's most prestigious theatrical post: head of the royal Dramatic Theater, known more familiarly in that country as "Dramaten." For the noted director, this proved a frustrating and time-consuming job: "I started in the morning at eight o'-clock and was there until eleven at night; then I went home and slept. I was at it ten months a year, and there was no place left for demons and dreams." In the three years of his tenure at Dramaten, Bergman staged

Strindberg's *Ghost Sonata* and *A Dream Play* for Swedish TV, directed Edward Albee's *Who's Afraid of Virginia Woolf?* for Dramaten, and followed that with what has been termed a "brilliant" staging of Ibsen's *Hedda Gabler* with Gertrud Fridh in what was apparently "a magnificent performance," according to the *London Sunday Times*, when that production later toured there.

Bergman's only 1964 film, his first in color and an uncharacteristic piece of comic frippery, is variously known as *All These Women* and or *Now About These Women*. Like *The Pleasure Garden*, it bears the nom de plume of "Buntel Eriksson," representing a second collaboration of Bergman with Erland Josephson. In fact, they both enjoyed input from Käbi Laretei, who came up with the movie's inspiration by dint of an account of one of her music teachers, a virtual Don Juan. He, it seems, was wed to a successful violinist, a fact that didn't prevent his seeing many another lady on the sly. In their screenplay, the central figure is a renowned music critic (played with flamboyant style by Jarl Kulle), who's bent on writing the biography of a deceased cello virtuoso named Felix, a man of many mistresses, all of whom appear to populate the lavish country villa that is central to the film's action. The cast was further filled by many of Sweden's female stars who had previously worked for Bergman. But the end result was only intermittently diverting. It was as if Bergman had joined forces in a directorial collaboration with Britain's Ken Russell and America's Blake Edwards, all at their least inspired. Indeed, Bergman himself would later term the movie a "fiasco." *All These Women* was reviled by most of the critics who may have expected a like follow-up to *The Silence*, which earned its director a "Gold Bug" from the Swedish Film Institute on the occasion of their first annual awards ceremony, a Scandinavian equivalent of the Oscars.

As 1965 began, Bergman was struck down by a serious lung infection, compli-cated by antibiotic poisoning. It forced him to cancel an engagement to stage *The Magic Flute* in Germany, as well as preparations to make his first wide-screen film, a vehicle for Bibi Andersson, Liv Ullmann, and Anders Ek, to be called *The Cannibals*.

While recovering from his illness, the director had assuaged his boredom by a return to screenwriting; the result was *Persona*, perhaps the most experimental of all Bergman's films — and the most open to a variety of interpretations. Conceiving it as a work for only a pair of actors, he remarked. "I was lying there, half-dead, and suddenly I started to think of two faces, two intermingled faces, and that was the beginning, the place where it started." His cast, aside from three brief supporting roles, consisted of the two actresses he wasn't able to direct in the abandoned *Cannibals* — Bibi Andersson and her longtime friend Liv Ullmann. *Persona* was not only the initiation of an inspired collaboration between Bergman and Ullmann, but also the beginning of what would become the director's most intense and long-lasting personal relationship out of wedlock — one that would produce a daughter. Indeed, it would surround them in a scandal as widespread in their time as had been that of Ingrid Bergman and Roberto Rossellini some fifteen years earlier. During *Persona's* filming on Fårö, their initial rapport was seen to grow deeper despite Bergman's marriage to the concert-touring Käbi Laretei and Liv's to a husband in Norway. With the end of filming, Liv and Ingmar decided to live together, and he took steps to build a home for them on Fårö. Liv Ullmann was then twenty-five; Bergman was forty-six.

Bergman had not directed a play in 1965 when he was obliged to take over the staging, from an ailing Bengt Ekerot, of Edward Albee's enigmatic *Tiny Alice*. It somewhat delayed his overseeing the editing of *Persona*.

In what would become a period of extensive change for the director, he decided

Persona (1966). Bibi Andersson and Liv Ullman confer with Bergman. Svensk Filmindustri.

to cut short what was to have been a six-year sojourn at Dramaten. Due to almost overwhelming pressures and responsibilities, Bergman handed in his resignation early in 1966, after only half that term. Undoubtedly, inevitable alterations in his personal life had much to do with it: Bergman's marriage to Käbi Laretei drew to a close, and he took to cohabitation on Fårö with Liv Ullmann. On the positive side was his triumphant production of the Peter Weiss play *Auschwitz*; on the negative was the sudden death of his mother, following a third heart attack, at seventy-four. Erik Bergman was bereft. He would survive his wife, Karin, for four years.

In celebration of his son Daniel's second birthday, Bergman assembled a short film made up of home movies he'd taken of the child on various occasions, frequently with his mother, Käbi. In its edited form *Daniel* would eventually become one of the eight episodes by different directors that make up the 1967 anthology film *Stimulantia*.

The never-filmed Bergman screenplay he called *The Cannibals* now became the genesis of his 1968 *Hour of the Wolf*, the first of a trio (including 1968's *Shame* and 1969's *Passion of Anna*), in all of which Max von Sydow represents the director's alter ego. *Hour of the Wolf*'s murky nightmare drama owes something to Bergman's profound fear of birds, as well as his affection for the Dracula legend, especially as portrayed in the 1931 Bela Lugosi movie. There are also both visual and textual references to Mozart's *Magic Flute* as well as to Bergman's earlier film *The Magician* in a story centering on a painter (von Sydow) whose tortured dreams blend in his mind with his life experiences — much of which may have confused *Hour of the Wolf*'s audiences.

During the film's production, Liv Ullmann gave birth to their daughter, Linn. It was an event that Ullmann felt "was very right," later commenting: "We did not marry, because we were both married when we met and it was never needed. There was no lawyer, no priest in our relationship; it was our friendship, and our love."

In the autumn of 1966, Erland Josephson, who had succeeded Bergman as head of Dramaten, engaged his friend to return as guest director for Molière's *School for Wives*. It was not well received, encouraging Bergman to move his theatrical activities elsewhere. The following spring, he staged Pirandello's *Six Characters in Search of an Author*, with a cast that included Liv Ullmann, for Oslo's National Theater of Norway.

In *Shame* (originally entitled *The War*),

Max von Sydow is a violinist who, with his wife (Ullmann), survives a mysterious invasion by "enemy forces" that endanger their island home. It's a powerful, well-acted story with a large supporting cast of small-part players, one that employed a surprising amount of improvisational acting. In an interview Bergman once commented that *Shame* stemmed from his own conjecture, "How would I have behaved during the Nazi period if Sweden had been occupied and if I'd held some position of responsibility?" As he also told an interviewer, "*Shame* is not about bombs falling as much as the gradual infiltration of fear."

A far more accessible film than the unpopular *Hour of the Wolf*, *Shame* won praise from a number of Swedish critics while inviting condemnation from others, perhaps occasioned by America's then-much-criticized presence in Vietnam. *Shame* managed to win no Academy Awards, but it did get recognition from two other American groups: The National Board of Review cited Liv Ullmann as Best Actress for her work in both *Shame* and *Hour of the Wolf*, as did the National Society of Film Critics. The latter organization also named Ingmar Bergman 1968's Best Director for both works and called *Shame* the year's Best Picture!

In 1968, Bergman set up his own motion-picture company, which he called Cinematograph, centered in Stockholm. Their first effort, made in association with Swedish television — and released to cinemas elsewhere — was *The Ritual*, a strange and puzzling chamber piece for a cast of four (Ingrid Thulin, Gunnar Björnstrand, Erik Hell, and Anders Ek), which Bergman rehearsed for a month and shot in nine days, chiefly in a succession of close-ups. In *The Ritual*, in which three entertainers are detained for questioning over an obscenity charge, can be seen the filmmaker's retaliation against the critics and theatrical bureaucrats who had dampened his spirits in recent years. In a confessional sequence,

Bergman himself appears briefly as a hooded priest.

During a 1968 spring vacation in Rome, Bergman met Federico Fellini. They developed such an immediate and complete rapport that they made plans to direct jointly a movie to be called *Love Duet*. They were to shoot it in both Rome and Stockholm, under the aegis of producer Martin Poll. A contract was signed, and there were plans to cast Viveca Lindfors and Katharine Ross in it. But other commitments intervened, and eventually the project was abandoned.

Without theatrical assignments in the wake of his disillusionment over his Dramaten tenure, Bergman centered his creativity on writing a screenplay for *The Passion of Anna*. With Liv Ullmann and Max von Sydow in the leading roles, as they had been for both *Hour of the Wolf* and *Shame*, *Passion* marked the final chapter in another Bergman "trilogy," whose common linkage incorporated not only the ruggedly striking terrain of Fårö but also a continuity of theme.

With *The Passion of Anna*, Bergman returned to the use of color film, which he had previously employed only for the lighthearted frivolity of *All These Women*. This time, the mood is somber and mysterious, involving an emotionally unstable man (von Sydow) who is separated from his wife and living in barren isolation, only to cross paths with two women (Ullmann and Bibi Andersson), one a widow and the other a married lady not averse to cheating on her architect-husband (Erland Josephson). At the same time, an air of menace hangs over the rural setting, manifested by the senseless killing of animals by some unidentified madman. Ill-advisedly, Bergman punctuates his narrative from time to time by incorporating mini-interviews with his actors, who, one by one, discuss their characters for the camera. Rather than shed light on the proceedings, these puzzling interruptions only serve to confound the viewer.

For reasons of logistics and ill health,

The Passion of Anna was a difficult film to shoot and equally challenging to edit, and it was among the least congenial filmmaking experiences of Bergman's career.

Bergman began 1969 with a return to Dramaten, where he staged a liberal conception of Georg Büchner's *Woyzeck*. The play opened to a warm critical reception that March, just a few days before he began a TV documentary about his island home, *The Fårö Document*. His interest was to raise public awareness as to the plight of the seven hundred islanders whose lives were hampered by government apathy. Realizing the power of television to spread influence in a single hour or two, the filmmaker talked Sveriges Radio into backing this documentary, which was shot in both color and monochrome in cinéma-verité style on 16-mm film. When it aired on New Year's Day, 1970, *The Fårö Document* was estimated to have been seen by an audience of three million.

In the spring of that year, Bergman completed writing a Strinbergian TV drama about marital problems, reminiscent of *The Passion of Anna*. This he called *Reservatet* (The Sanctuary), which was consigned to Jan Molander, who directed a Swedish cast headed by Erland Josephson, and Gunnel Lindblom. An English-language version, retitled *The Lie*, was presented in the United States in 1973 by CBS's *Playhouse 90*, with George Segal and Shirley Knight Hopkins (as she was then known).

Bergman has never wanted to film adaptations of either Strindberg or Ibsen, since he considers them best suited to the stage. However, in March 1970 he turned out an austere but imaginative edited adaptation of Strindberg's normally daunting *Dream Play*. Staged for Dramaten's smaller facility, the production enjoyed considerable success, which was somewhat sobered by the death of Erik Bergman, the awe-inspiring father from whom Ingmar had eventually won respect and admiration in his later years. The passing of his parent also coincided with the end of Bergman's alliance with Liv Ullmann, whose burgeoning international career had been keeping her increasingly preoccupied elsewhere. However, their working friendship would continue, with their strongest collaborative efforts destined to come in the following decade. Their daughter, officially known as Linn Ullmann, stayed with Liv, who moved to Oslo. For a short time Bergman found consolation with *A Dream Play*'s young leading lady, Malin Ek.

That May in London, Bergman restaged his successful 1964 production of *Hedda Gabler*, but this time with an English-speaking cast featuring Maggie Smith. During its rehearsals, the director met with Morton Baum, of the American Broadcasting Company (ABC), to discuss the story of his next movie, *The Touch*, as a possible project for ABC's new feature-film division, ABC Pictures Corporation. The result was a contract by which Bergman would receive a million dollars for delivering the finished product, to be shot in English with an international male star of the filmmaker's own choice. First, he secured the services of an understandably flattered Elliott Gould, whom Bergman had admired in the American movie *Getting Straight*. And then he set about writing the actual screenplay. After shooting commenced that September 1970, Bergman first began to speak of retirement. At fifty-two, his twenty-six years of filmmaking were beginning to take their toll, both mentally and physically. At that time, he spoke of continuing "for another couple of years," during which period he envisioned turning out four or five more pictures — and then retire.

With Bibi Andersson and Max von Sydow in the two other leading roles, *The Touch* tells the triangular story of a fifteen-year-old marriage disrupted by the appearance of a romantic stranger (Gould), who soon enters into an ill-fated affair with the wife. Both Andersson and von Sydow found no difficulty performing in English, although his role offered few acting challenges — perhaps one reason why it was the actor's last part in a Bergman film. But Bibi Andersson attacked her assignment with a multi-faceted characterization that won her some of the most glowing notices of her career. *The Touch* failed to draw a majority of moviegoers upon its 1971 release, likely due to its obvious attempt at international appeal. Or perhaps it was a general aversion to Elliott Gould, whose then concentrated bid for stardom never quite captivated film audiences. Not even Ingmar Bergman's rare public appearance on TV's *Dick Cavett Show*, along with Bibi Andersson, could much help *The Touch*.

Bergman's next production for Dramaten seemed an odd choice for Stockholm — an irreverent new work by the Swedish playwright Lars Forssell called *Show* that centered on American entertainer Lenny Bruce and in which Allan Edwall and Harriet Andersson played the leads. It was followed by Bergman's production of *A Dream Play*, this time presented in London as part of the Aldwych's World Theatre season.

On April 15, 1971, Liv Ullmann accepted Hollywood's distinguished Irving T. Thalberg Award on behalf of Ingmar Bergman during the Oscars ceremony with these words: "He has asked me to say to you that he is sitting on his little island in the Baltic writing a new script ... and he believes that he shows his respect and gratefulness ... by staying home, finishing his script."

Preparations for the filmmaker's next movie, *Cries and Whispers*, coincided with a new love affair, once again with a married woman. Ingrid von Rosen was a forty-one-year-old mother of four when she began a relationship with the fifty-three-year-old Bergman. Their marriage that November 1971, following her divorce from Count Jan Carl von Rosen, would turn out to be the happiest and most enduring of all the director's emotional alliances.

Cries and Whispers sprang from a dream that had haunted Bergman: "I had a vision of a large red room, with three women in white whispering together. This picture came back again and again to me." Visualized as a costume drama taking place on a grand turn-of-the-century estate, it was a project that defied investor interest — until his chosen stars (Ingrid Thulin, Liv Ullmann, and Harriet Andersson) and faithful cameraman Sven Nykvist agreed to forgo salary payments until the "package" found a distributor. Meanwhile, Bergman induced the Swedish Film Institute to lend him its financial support to this characteristically noncommercial project. Its story centered on three affluent sisters, two of whom have gathered in a death watch for the cancer-stricken third sibling, whose faithful servant (Kari Sylwan) affords the patient more love and comfort than either self-centered blood relative.

The color red pervades *Cries and Whispers*, and as each scene ends, it fades out to red, the color of the soul, according to Bergman. In contrast to the film's essentially somber subject matter, *Cries and Whispers* was apparently an enjoyable filming experience for all concerned; and even Harriet Andersson's death scene was alleviated by practical joking and laughter, once the cameras had stopped.

After its completion, *Cries and Whispers* sat on the shelf for a year until Roger Corman's New World Pictures acquired it for U.S. distribution, and quickly set about releasing it in time to qualify for 1973 Oscar consideration. And a fortuitous thing, too, for the film garnered nominations for Best Picture, Director, Costume Design, and Original Story and Screenplay — all of which lost out to *The Sting*—while winning an Oscar, his first, for cinematographer Sven Nykvist. Not having enjoyed critical success in some time for his filmmaking, Bergman was astonished at the enthusiasm of both the press and public for *Cries and Whispers*.

In March 1972, Bergman's Dramaten production of Ibsen's *Wild Duck*, with Max von Sydow and Lena Nyman, drew favorable attention, particularly for the imaginative details of its staging.

With mounting difficulties surrounding the financing of his motion pictures at home, Bergman now turned his sights more positively than ever toward television, where he found a lucrative outlet for his multipart drama *Scenes from a Marriage*. In what U.S. TV circles would term a "miniseries," Bergman mapped out an economical, small-cast domestic drama, with Liv Ullmann and Erland Josephson shouldering the bulk of the acting load and with only a small crew, headed by the trusty Sven Nykvist, shooting in 16mm. The screenplay was completed in a month, and following ten days of rehearsals on Fårö, the *Scenes* were shot in an intensive forty-five days. Admittedly, Bergman drew heavily on his own marital experiences as well as those of friends and acquaintances. He deliberately made them and their circumstances both contemporary and typical so that his TV audiences could readily identify with the embattled protagonists and their behavior. In the first sequence, Marianne and Johan (Ullmann and Josephson) entertain another couple (Bibi Andersson and Jan Malmsjö), who reveal their contempt for one another, contrasting with their own ideal-seeming relationship. But change is in the wind when Marianne happily announces her unplanned pregnancy and Johan moodily retorts that he doesn't want any more children; she must undergo an abortion. Her doing so subsequently leads to a marital rift that appears irreparable. Bergman's script creates wonderful acting opportunities for Ullmann and Josephson in the expression of emotional truths, and both performances are superb.

Scenes from a Marriage originally aired in Sweden over a six-week period in April and May 1973, with less satisfactory, English-dubbed prints made for British and

Cries and Whispers (1972). **A moment of levity on the set with Bergman, Ingrid Thulin and Liv Ullmann. Cinematograph.**

American TV. Bergman also prepared a theatrical-release version that ran nearly three hours. Although enough material was excised to produce a separate full-length film, the theatrical print of *Scenes from a Marriage* stands very much on its own, equally strong in its total effect, if somewhat less rich in detail.

In every sense, *Scenes from a Marriage* was a success for Bergman's Cinematograph company, even providing the funds to finance works of other directors. And then Svensk Filmindustri startled the international movie world with the news that Ingmar Bergman would finally direct an adaptation of Lehár's operetta *The Merry Widow*, for which he had drafted a screenplay eigh-

teen years earlier. But most controversial of all was the announcement that this project would star Barbra Streisand, with filming to take place in the autumn of 1974. Bergman himself spent eight month preparing the production, which was to have been financed for $4 million by producer Dino De Laurentiis, in association with Svensk Filmindustri. But production costs were then rapidly rising, and unable to make the film he envisioned, Bergman finally canceled the agreement.

Redirecting his creative energies to the stage, he undertook a triumphant new production of *The Ghost Sonata*, followed by *The Misanthrope*, directed for the Danish Royal Theater in Copenhagen.

The Magic Flute (1975). Josef Köstlinger and Bergman on the set. Cinematograph.

Bergman created a sensation in May 1973 when he was persuaded to make a rare personal appearance at the Cannes Film Festival, where he spoke in halting English about directing for films versus theater. Back home, he was now pacing himself more deliberately, dividing his schedule between one motion picture a year and one play at Dramaten. He began 1974 by directing the combined first two parts of Strindberg's seldom-performed trilogy *To Damascus* at the Royal Dramatic Theater. And that year's film project, *The Magic Flute*, was made for television — and later shown in movie theaters.

Bergman's adaptation of the 1791 Mozart opera was commissioned by Swedish Radio as part of their 1975 golden jubilee; as planned, it was ready for telecast on New Year's Day of that year. Because Bergman

sought "natural voices," auditions were held as early as 1973, with leading roles finally assigned to Austrian-born Josef Köstlinger (Tamino), Finland's Irma Urrila (Pamina), the Royal Danish Opera's Ulrik Cold (Sarastro), and Sweden's internationally known Håken Hagegård (Papageno). With scenery deliberately theatrical and painted as it might have been in Mozart's day, this *Magic Flute* moves quickly, with its textual cuts and upbeat tempos, under the musical direction of Eric Ericson. And while Bergman never allows it to become merely a photographed stage performance of the work, neither does he make it completely cinematic; there are occasional backstage glimpses of the performers as well as intercut reaction shots of a viewing audience, chief among them the director's young daughter, Linn, whose lingering close-ups become *The Magic Flute's*

Face to Face (1976) Bergman rehearses Ulf Johanson and Liv Ullmann. Cinematograph.

greatest indulgence. But this is among Bergman's more acclaimed later films and a unique accomplishment.

Before embarking on his next picture, *Face to Face*, Bergman directed a popular Dramaten production of Shakespeare's *Twelfth Night* that managed to keep Bibi Andersson, as the cross-dressing Viola, attired as a male throughout the play.

Like *Scenes from a Marriage*, his 1976 film *Face to Face* is first and foremost a four-part TV miniseries that became more widely known outside Scandinavia as an edited feature film. Its production was made possible through the auspices of Dino De Laurentiis despite the earlier failure of his collaboration with Bergman on *The Merry Widow*. This time, the extravagant Italian producer visualized "an exciting entertainment that would attract large audiences all over the world." In view of the finished product, one can only wonder what fired De Laurentiis's enthusiasm.

Face to Face is truly a tour de force for the extraordinary Liv Ullmann, who could hardly have surrendered her acting resources more completely to any role than that of Dr. Jenny Isaksson, a psychiatrist who under-goes an agonizing nervous breakdown and a painstaking recovery. But an "exciting entertainment"? Even Ullmann had her doubts, to which Bergman responded: "Regard it as a surgeon's scalpel. Not everyone will welcome it." This effort should have won its deserving star a bundle of acting prizes. In Hollywood there were nominations for Ullmann's performance and Bergman's direction, but the Oscars went, respectively, to Faye Dunaway for *Network* and John G. Avildsen for *Rocky*. Like many a film that fails to find an audience, *Face to Face* showed briefly in theaters and then disappeared. It's among the few Bergman films unavailable on videocassette.

Just as the summer of 1975 moved into autumn, Stockholm University honored Ingmar Bergman with an honorary doctorate of philosophy. In an uncharacteristic expression of sentiment, he evinced the wish that his parents might have been able to share the moment with him. Before the year ended, he completed writing *The Petrified Prince*, a screenplay that was to have been part of a never-realized erotic trilogy whose other contributors were to be Mike Nichols and Federico Fellini.

Exile

On January 30, 1976, Bergman was rehearsing Strindberg's *Dance of Death* at Dramaten when he was rudely interrupted by tax police and taken in for questioning on a matter dating back some five years. In view of a statute of limitations, authorities moved swiftly to prevent any evasive act on Bergman's part. The director was questioned for nearly three hours before being escorted back to his home, where his passport was confiscated. The cause of all this oppression was one tax officer's assertion that in his business dealings Bergman had tried to defraud the Swedish government by liquidating the Swiss-based corporation Persona AG following the collapse of a possible collaboration with Italy's RAI. The filmmaker was now accused of evading the payment of several hundred thousand crowns in income tax, and faced either paying an enormous fine or imprisonment of up to two years. As he protested at the time: "I am an artist. I know nothing about money, and I know nothing about these charges." For the wholly dedicated writer-director, who followed his own muse and lived modestly, this was sufficient to induce what was announced as a "nervous breakdown."

With the aid of friends, his wife, Ingrid, secured Bergman a room at the Karolinska Hospital. By now, the director's plight was making news around the world. On March 24, Bergman and his lawyer, Harald Bauer, were suddenly cleared of all previous charges. Then, as if that were too miraculous to be true, the Swedish tax assessors focused on Bergman's earnings — and the dealings of Cinematograph — in 1974 and 1975. The result was that he was now found to be owing taxes in excess of $500,000, due to the unexpected worldwide success of both *Cries and Whispers* and *Scenes from a Marriage*. There were profits that Cinematograph had used to finance, among others, Gunnel Lindblom's debut feature *Paradise Place*, as well as a four-part TV adaptation of Strindberg's *Madman's Defense*, directed by Kjell Grede.

And as if their threats and assessments were not sufficiently confusing to the humiliated filmmaker, the authorities now presented him with a revised offer: Should he consent to pay the original fine levied that past January, then they would be willing to overlook Cinematograph's 1975 tax arrears.

At that time, *Face to Face* was about to air on Swedish TV, and Bergman was planning an ambitious film about 1920s Germany called *The Serpent's Egg*. Also, he was helping Gunnel Lindblom with the production problems of *Paradise Place,* as well as in renewed discussions regarding a collaboration with Fellini. But Bergman's astonishing answer to his embarrassing predicament was an extensive article published in the April 22 edition of Scandinavia's most popular evening newspaper, *Expressen*, entitled "Now I Am Leaving Sweden." In it, he attacked "a particular kind of bureaucracy, which grows like a galloping cancer," and naming names, he castigated his oppressors and announced that he would not be compromised by any under-the-counter deals with the tax authorities. He also blasted *Aftonbladet*, whose editors were among his severest tax critics.

A day earlier, the Bergmans had flown to Paris, for want of a better locale in which to reconnoiter. They next spent some time in Los Angeles, discussing plans for *The Serpent's Egg* with Dino De Laurentiis and Bergman's U.S. agent, Paul Kohner, who arranged a press conference. Characterizing his recent experiences in his homeland as "Kafkaesque," the visibly upset filmmaker remarked in English: "It was terrifying, but I can't blame my country for some clumsy individuals in the administration. I fell into a deep depression, the first real depression in my life, because I couldn't create."

The Bergmans now found themselves exiles in search of a country in which to settle. Finally, during a stay in Munich, where *The Serpent's Egg* was to be filmed at the Bavaria Film Studios, they decided to take an apartment and stay on in Germany. Their exile from Sweden would officially last three and a half years, until late November 1979, when Harald Bauer revealed to the press that the Bergman affair had been settled, with Cinematograph obliged to pay only about 7 percent of the original tax levy. The attendant court costs would be the responsibility of the Swedish government. But long before that decision, the Bergmans were often glimpsed in Sweden, whether visiting friends in Stockholm or summering on Fårö.

The Serpent's Egg, set in 1923 during a week of ominous political ferment, was not only an expensive German-American co-production but also Bergman's first filming experience outside Sweden. Moreover, it was shot in English, with only one familiar Bergman actor (Liv Ullmann) and one technician (Sven Nykvist) to comfort him. The filmmaker had the uneasy task of dealing with a sea of new faces, including that of leading man David Carradine, who replaced an ailing Richard Harris. Most of the movie's formidable budget went to pay for the huge, detailed period sets of Rolf Zehetbauer, who had won an Oscar for designing 1972's *Cabaret*. For those familiar with Bergman's tax struggles in Sweden, there are obvious parallels with the incipient Nazis of *The Serpent's Egg*. But its sinister melodramatics tend to become overwrought, and the film's eventual release failed to find a receptive audience. By that time, Bergman had already completed *Autumn Sonata*, which was filmed in Norway.

Aside from a common heritage, Ingmar and Ingrid Bergman, the actress, had only a shared participation in different sequences of one film, the multipart 1967 *Stimulantia*. But these two cinema giants had long talked about working together. Finally, he wrote for her the role of a self-centered concert-pianist mother who pays her daughter (Liv Ullmann) a long-overdue visit that develops into a major catharsis for them both. A lifetime of discreetly hidden accusations and recriminations are subtly revealed in Bergman's telling use of close-ups as the dueling words of the two women batter one another in compensation for the lost years of covert thoughts and sullen silences. Here Liv and Ingrid deliver beautifully modulated performances in a display of truthful acting perhaps unsurpassed in any of the director's works. This was Ingrid Bergman's last theatrical feature film, and it's a wonderfully courageous performance, delivered as she herself was battling cancer. The actress extolled her director to an interviewer: "I heard he was a beast, very temperamental, always yelling and screaming, but he never raised his voice to me. And he listens to actors; he's big enough to listen to your ideas, and if he likes them, he'll use them. He's very flexible and open, allowing his actors to feel they are creating, too, and not just marionettes in his hands."

Autumn Sonata was shot in Swedish, but an English-language version — well dubbed by its leading actors — later circulated successfully. Academy Award recognition included nominations for Best Actress Bergman and screenwriter Bergman, but no wins; *Coming Home* and Jane Fonda were the winners in both those categories.

While continuing to call Munich his home base, Bergman returned to directing at that city's Residenzteater, where, despite some difficulties communicating in German, he staged — for the third time in his career — *A Dream Play*. Characteristically, he would choose a fresh approach each time, avoiding any reference to his notes from a previous staging. "That's the most fascinating way to deal with a play" was Bergman's thinking. A year later, he would return to the Residenzteater with Chekhov's *Three Sisters*, for which he enjoyed the unusual luxury of fifteen weeks' rehearsal.

On July 14, 1978, Bergman celebrated his sixtieth birthday on Fårö in the rare company of his entire family, including all eight children, some of whom had not previously met one another. Later that summer, an attempt was made to resurrect the aborted Dramaten production of *The Dance of Death*, that had been so rudely interrupted two and a half years earlier. But this time the fatal illness of Anders Ek, Bergman's longtime friend and the play's leading actor, caused its cancellation.

Without any 1978 film project on his agenda, he returned to Munich to prepare Molière's *Tartuffe*, which was poorly received at the Residenzteater in January 1979, followed by an acclaimed revival of his *Hedda Gabler* production. That July, with Bibi An-

dersson re-creating her original role, Bergman returned to Stockholm in triumph with *Twelfth Night*.

Despite his exile from Sweden, the filmmaker's enduring affection for Fårö and its populace moved him to devise a second television documentary on the island, *Fårö Document 1979*, on which cameraman Arne Carlsson and a sound technician worked for two years, amassing some twenty-eight hours of footage before it finally aired in a 103-minute print on Swedish TV on Christmas Eve, 1979. One local critic wrote that the documentary expressed "a tender, passionate love over land and sea, on forest and stone, and not least on the people who live there."

Bergman had passed the latter half of 1979 simply enjoying life on Fårö, where, during that summer, he had written the screenplay for a lengthy, nostalgic family saga he called *Fanny and Alexander*. However, its production would wait until after *From the Life of the Marionettes*, the film he returned to Germany to make in October. Beginning and ending with the color-filmed murder of a prostitute by a well-to-do young businessman, this chiefly black-and-white drama centers on an unhappily wed couple (Robert Atzorn and Bergman's Munich Hedda Gabler, Christine Bucheggeer) in an imaginative exploration of psychopathology that utterly failed to interest the public.

Between supervising the editing of *Marionettes* and directing the Residenzteater's spring production of a Polish play called *Yvonne, Princess of Burgundy*, Bergman expressed his inner thoughts to biographer Peter Cowie: "I want to stop now. I want to go to the island. I want to stay there and read the books I haven't written. To listen to music and talk to my neighbors. To live together with my wife a very calm, secure, very lazy life. It's a temptation to say: Now it's enough, it's done, I want to stop, to go away, to retire."

Those thoughts now seemed commensurate with the paucity of Bergman's professional activities. The year 1981 began with a whirl of creativity as he rehearsed a Scandinavian triptych for Munich that consisted of Strindberg's *Miss Julie*, Ibsen's *Doll's House*, and his own *Scenes from a Marriage*, adapted and abbreviated for the stage. Afterward, he retreated to Fårö until the following September, when *Fanny and Alexander* went into production as a miniseries for Swedish television — and, of course, a lengthy cinema feature elsewhere.

Set in 1910, *Fanny and Alexander* has some autobiographical base in the filmmaker's own childhood, with its twelve-year-old protagonist, Alexander, in certain ways representing Bergman. In part, its inspiration was an answer to those who associated the Bergman name with all that was gloomy and depressing in the arts. With what he began

to refer to as his "final" film, Bergman conceived the work on a grand scale, involving an enormous cast and with a costly production that required many elaborate sets and costumes. With the proviso that he make *Fanny and Alexander* in Sweden and in his native tongue, most of its $6 million funding was raised by the Swedish Film Institute in conjunction with West German TV and Gaumont in France. Its filming, which required a tiring six months, found Bergman affable and patient with the two youngsters (Pernilla Allwin and Bertil Guve) cast in the title roles. There were also parts for two of the director's offspring, Anna and Mats, while ex-wife Käbi Laretei (who had continued as musical consultant for most of his pictures) played a family aunt. Their son,

Fanny and Alexander (1982). Director Bergman and cinematographer Sven Nykvist. Sandrews.

Daniel, worked off camera as a grip, while Bergman's current wife, Ingrid, dedicated herself to pitching in wherever she was needed. And in a large ensemble cast there were important roles for many familiar actors from the director's past, including Harriet Andersson, Gunnar Björnstrand, Allan Edwall, Jarl Kulle, and Erland Josephson.

This episodic, Dickensian tale of a year in the life of an Uppsala family and its various branches was Bergman's TV Christmas present to his countrymen in 1982 and was warmly received. Its eventual feature presentation in the West also met with glowing notices and pleased many a surprised moviegoer who hadn't much cared for Ingmar Bergman pictures up to that point. *Fanny and Alexander* set a record for Oscars won by a foreign film on April 9, 1984, when it took home no less than four statuettes for Best Foreign-Language Film, Sven Nykvist's Cinematography, Art Direction, and Costuming. Bergman's excuse for not attending the ceremonies (he was also nominated once again as Best Director) were his stage rehearsals in Munich. Accepting the Foreign Film Award for him were his wife, Ingrid, and Jörn Donner, the film's executive producer.

In 1983, Ingmar Bergman prepared a brief film tribute to his late mother, entitled *Karin's Face*, which utilized archival photos to celebrate her life. Käbi Laretei provided the eloquent piano soundtrack. Onstage, Bergman directed a production of Molière's *Don Juan* for the Salzburg Festival.

The Last Film?

There were many who refused to believe this creative giant's announcements about retirement from feature filmmaking. And yet Bergman remained true to his word, limiting his artistic commitments to the theater and television. *After the Rehearsal* (1984), a Bergman-directed feature released to movie theaters, was made for TV and looks it, with its singleset and small-scale subject matter. It's about the backstage relationship between a director (Erland Josephson) and his present and past leading ladies (Lena Olin and Ingrid Thulin). Actually, it's little more than one long dialogue between Josephson and Olin, and probably of most interest to those of the theater.

Also in 1984, Bergman's innovative production of *King Lear* did away with all stage furniture (actors formed any necessary seating with unusual use of their bodies) and kept the entire cast in view (if sometimes in the shadows) at all times. His visual concept attired some of the men in black leather, while other cast members wore varying shades of pink and purple — against a scarlet drop curtain. Jarl Kulle played Lear.

In 1985, Bergman staged productions of Ibsen's *John Gabriel Borkman* for Munich and Strindberg's *Miss Julie* at Dramaten. The following year, he returned to television, directing Ulla Isaksson's *Blessed Ones*, a drama about middle-aged marital problems, with Harriet Andersson and Per Myrberg. But the former trend of showing his TV work in cinemas appeared to have stopped, following negative audience reactions to *After the Rehearsal*. Since then, Swedish television has aired the director's taped or photographed editions of works he created for the stage, including *Madame de Sade* (1992), *The Bacchae* (1993), and *The Last Gasp* (1995), about little-remembered Swedish silent-screen director Georg af Klercker.

Bergman's bold 1986 staging of *Hamlet* went on tour and made such a strong impression at New York's Brooklyn Academy of Music that the same venue later played, with great success, his subsequent productions of *Miss Julie*, *Long Day's Journey into Night*, *A Doll's House*, *Peer Gynt* and *Madame de Sade*.

In 1987, Bergman published *The Magic Lantern*, an acclaimed autobiography that was translated into many languages abroad. Although the book dwelt more on personalities and private memories than on filmmaking, this was compensated for in his subsequent volume, *Images*, which dwelt on all the director's great films, as well as many of the lesser ones.

Reflecting on his childhood and beyond, Bergman turned out two screenplays that were directed, with his blessing, by younger men: *The Best Intentions*— based on Bergman's novel about his mismatched parents, and shown as both a TV miniseries and a feature film — which went to *Pelle the Conqueror's* Bille August; and *Sunday's Children*, which was surprisingly well-handled by Bergman's youngest boy, Daniel. And, in the autumn of 1995, Liv Ullmann (already established as the capable director of two features) shot *Private Confessions*, from a screenplay that Bergman expressly wrote for her to direct. Interviewed on the eve of its production by *Newsday's* Jerry Tallmer, Ullmann revealed: "It's about a woman and her husband and her lover and how she can and cannot cope with love. And also about Ingmar Bergman finding God again. It's a long time since Ingmar played chess and since he stopped to believe. He didn't even want to christen his children." Then, with reference to the passing of Bergman's wife, Ingrid, of stomach cancer that past May, Ullmann added: "Ingmar just lost his wife, which is a terrible tragedy. No, she was not an actress. That's why it went so well. She went from being his secretary to being his lover to being his wife, and she took care of everything."

Although essentially a shy man who chooses to avoid most interviews, tributes and public appearances, Ingmar Bergman has been the subject of numerous TV documentaries and laudatory press assessments. Woody Allen, a Bergman champion whose adulation has sometimes been reflected in his own movies (*Interiors, September),* has called Scandinavia's most revered moviemaker, "probably the greatest film artist, all things considered, since the invention of the motion-picture camera."

Late in 1995, Bergman quietly announced, in what he told *Expressen* would be his final interview, that he would cease all theatrical activity before the end of 1996, with his final directorial chores slated to be two productions for the Royal Dramatic Theater — Witold Gombrowicz's *Ivona,*

Princess of Burgundia and *The Bacchae* of Euripedes — and a TV play. With regard to his retirement from filmmaking some twelve years earlier, he explained: "Film is so much more cruel and physically a lot more trying. After seven months of *Fanny and Alexander,* I was completely exhausted."

His future creativity, Bergman allowed, would be confined to writing ... "and I don't give a damn if I am published or not. I can afford not to care about that." Anticipating a quieter existence on Fårö, he concluded: "My schedule is strict, but it also includes reading a good book or taking a walk. It is a comfortable hell."

But in the autumn of 1996, Bergman proved unpredictable once again, and directed his own teleplay entitled *In the Presence of a Clown,* based on incidents in the life of his uncle Carl, portrayed in the TV film by the actor who had already brought this character to life on two previous occasions, Börje Ahlstedt. Set in 1925, and centering partly on a psychiatric clinic, the movie made few concessions to popular appeal, with its strange characters and blending of illusion with reality. Although not released commercially to cinemas, *In the Presence of a Clown* enjoyed public Festival screenings in 1998 in New York and Chicago. That year offered Scandinavian TV viewers an insightful 58-minute documentary on the feature entitled *The Making of In the Presence of a Clown.*

In late August of 1997, the Venice Film Festival hosted a well received feature-length documentary on the director, *The Voice of Bergman,* produced for the Swedish Film Institute by Gunnar Bergdahl and Bengt Toll. Solely intended for the world's film-festival circuit, this film is unavailable for sales to TV or any other medium, due to Bergman's contractual agreement.

The following February found Bergman back at Stockholm's Royal Dramatic Theater (after a two-year hiatus), directing a cast of four in Per Olov Enquist's play, *The*

Picture Makers, about legendary Swedish filmmaker/actor Victor Sjöström.

Bergman continued to exercise his creative muscles: early in 1999, he returned to the Dramaten to restage Strindberg's challenging *Ghost Sonata*, and he scripted yet another semi-autobiographical screenplay for Liv Ullmann to direct, this one entitled *Faithless*. Its subject: the love triangle between a woman, her husband and her lover. Reviewing the movie from the 2000 Cannes Film Festival, *Variety* called it, "a personal and revelatory film about the destructive forces unleashed by thoughtless sexual misbehavior." Ullmann was much lauded for extracting "every nuance from the tantalizing material."

Bergman was among those interviewed for the documentary feature *Light Keeps Me Company*, about cinematographer Sven Nykvist, with whom the director had collaborated more than twenty times. It was well-received at Sweden's Gothenburg Film Festival in February 2000, just a month before the death of 54-year-old Jan Bergman, the director's third son, of leukemia.

Once again faced with loss, Ingmar Bergman reflected: "I'm an old man. I am close to the great mystery. I am not afraid of it. I am fascinated, not afraid."

II
The Films

Kris
(Crisis)
Svensk Filmindustri: 1946
(No U.S. release)

CREDITS

Director: Ingmar Bergman; *producers:* Harald Molander and Victor Sjöström (artistic consultant); *screenwriter:* Ingmar Bergman; based on the radio play *Moderhjertet* (The Mother Creature) by Leck Fischer; *cinematographer:* Gösta Roosling; *editor:* Oscar Rosander; *art director:* Arne Åkermark; *music:* Erland von Koch; *sound:* Lennart Svensson; *assistant director:* Lars-Eric Kjellgren; *running time:* 93 minutes.

CAST

Dagny Lind (*Ingeborg Johnson*); Inga Landgré (Nelly); Marianne Löfgren (*Jenny*); Stig Olin (*Jack*); Alla Bohlin (*Ulf*); Ernst Eklund (*Ingeborg's Uncle Edvard*); Signe Wirff (*Ingeborg's Aunt Jessie*); Svea Holst (*Malin*); Arne Lindblad (*Mayor*); Julia Ceasar (*Mayor's Wife*); Dagmar Olsson (*Singer at Ball*); Siv Thulin (*Assistant in Beauty Salon*); Anna-Lisa Baude and M. Carelick (*Customers in Beauty Salon*); Karl Erik Flens (*Nelly's Friend at Ball*); Margit Andelius (*Treasurer's Wife*).

After the success of Alf Sjöberg's *Torment*, which Bergman had written and whose brief final sequence he had directed, Carl Anders Dymling, the head of Svensk Filmindustri, offered the ambitious young screenwriter a chance to direct an entire film. Bergman had no say in the choice of vehicle; Dymling assigned him to adapt a recently acquired Danish radio play by Leck Fisher called *Moderhjertet* (variously translated as *The Mother Animal*, *A Mother's Heart*, *The Mother Creature*, and *The Maternal Instinct*). The novice film director held no admiration for the material, but here was a major opportunity to expand from the staging of theatrical plays into motion pictures, and at age twenty-six, Bergman jumped at the offer.

Introduced as "only an ordinary sort of play — almost a comedy," *Crisis* centers on a

Crisis (1946). Marianne Löfgren and Stig Olin. Svensk Filmindustri.

teenager named Nelly (Inga Landgré), who shares quarters with her foster mother, Ingeborg (Dagny Lind), whose boarder Ulf (Alla Bohlin) attempts to court the disinterested girl. Interrupting their ordinary but peaceful small-town existence is Nelly's birth mother, Jenny (Marianne Löfgren), the flashy proprietor of a successful beauty parlor in Stockholm, who arrives accompanied by her lover, Jack (Stig Olin). Now that she has the means to take care of Nelly, Jenny intends to reclaim her from Ingeborg, regardless of anyone's feelings. Jenny's initial lure is an expensive party dress, which Nelly chooses to wear to the local dance in place of Ingeborg's more modest offering. Adding to the girl's excitement is the flashy Jack, who manages to charm her when they leave the festivities to take a solitary stroll.

When her real mother offers her a job in the big city, Nelly has few qualms about leaving life with Ingeborg for a more challenging future.

One evening, Jack takes advantages of Jenny's absence to seduce the impressionable young Nelly in the beauty salon, but they are discovered by the proprietress, who returns unexpectedly. After the ensuing emotional fireworks, Jack goes off and shoots himself in the street outside. The experience is sufficient to send Nelly back to Ingeborg and the prospect of marriage to Ulf.

A few of his critics found promise in Ingmar Bergman's official film debut as a director, while pointing out stylistic similarities to the Gallic master, Marcel Carné. But *Crisis* was not a success with moviegoers.

Bergman on Bergman

"The film's lousy through and through. It was an out-and-out bit of whoredom for the public — and no one could have called it anything else."

Critics' Circle

"Perhaps one of the top Swedish pictures for 1946, this is headed for strong returns here. Ably directed by Ingmar Bergman, cast includes two newcomers in Inga Landgré and Stig Olin who reveal potentialities. While few Swedish films mean much in the world market, Kris looks to have a chance for usual modest returns obtained by strongest product from Sweden in the American market."

— *Variety*

"Crisis is an appealing debut work, behind which the forces of misfortune and disharmony brood. There are many Swedish films from about the same period which are considerably better. A poll taken by the trade paper Biograf bladet, *covering the season 1945-46, gave* Crisis, *fourth place after* Blod och eld *(Blood and Fire),* Vandring med månen *(Journey with the Moon) and* Asa-Hanna. *In explaining his choice, one critic (Bengt Idestam-Almquist) wrote about* Crisis *that it was 'a daring shot by an eager hunter — in the right direction but shy of the mark.' Still, only* Crisis *has survived these other films. This is not just because it is Bergman's film. His production is a totality, in which his knowledge of the parts enriches our vision."*

— Jörn Donner in
The Personal Vision of Ingmar Bergman

Det Regnar på Vår Kärlek
(It Rains on Our Love/
Man with an Umbrella)

Nordisk Tonefilm release of a Severiges Folksbiografer Production: 1946
(No U.S. release)

CREDITS

Director: Ingmar Bergman; *producer:* Lorens Marmstedt; *screenwriters:* Ingmar Bergman and Herbert Grevenius; based on the play *Bra Mennesker* (Good People) by Oskar Braaten; *cinematographers:* Hilding Bladh and Göran Strindberg; *editor:* Tage Holmberg; *art director:* P.A. Lundgren; *music:* Erland von Koch, with extracts from Richard Wagner and Bernhard Flies; *running time:* 95 minutes.

CAST

Barbro Kollberg (*Maggi*); Birger Malmsten (*David Lindell*); Gösta Cederlund (*Man with Umbrella*); Ludde Gentzel (*Håkansson*); Douglas Håge (*Andersson*); Hjördis Pettersson (*Mrs. Andersson*); Julia Caesar (*Hanna Ledin*); Gunnar Björnstrand (*Purman*); Magnus Kesster (*Folke Törnberg, Bicycle Repairman*); Sif Ruud (*Gerti Törnberg*); Åke Fridell

(*Assistant Vicar*); Torsten Hillberg (*Vicar*); Benkt-Åke Benktsson (*Prosecutor*); Erik Rosén (*Judge*); Edvard Danielsson (*Hotel Porter*); Sture Ericson (*Kängsnöret*); Ulf Johansson (*Stalvispen*); Erland Josephson (*Clerk in Vicar's Office*).

Ingmar Bergman's second film as a writer-director began shooting in the late spring of 1946, nearly nine months after the completion of his first effort, *Crisis*. This time, he and collaborator Herbert Grevenius produced an adaptation of Oskar Braaten's Norwegian play *Bra Mennesker* (Good People). Despite the credit as coauthor, Bergman attributes the script almost entirely to Grevenius, admitting only to writing the trial scene, which marks the movie's climax. He also admits to having been heavily influenced by American film noir in his direction of the film. And he did make script revisions.

It Rains on Our Love returns its director to the troubled-youth atmosphere of his first filmed script, *Torment*. Its protagonists are star-crossed lovers, Maggi (Barbro Kollberg) and David (Birger Malmsten, who had been featured in a couple of striking close-ups as a bit-player student in *Torment*). Significantly, they meet in the rain at Stockholm's Central Station. He's fresh out of jail; she's pregnant and dejected. Neither harbors any optimism about the future — until they determine to chance facing life together. In a suburban community, they find temporary refuge from the weather, first in a seedy hotel room, then in a small, seemingly abandoned cottage (which they will later attempt to purchase). David finds work in a nursery but doesn't have an easy time of it there. When he discovers the truth of Maggi's pregnancy, he first gets drunk, then offers to marry her. Local bureaucracy prevents their union, which is delayed by clerical red tape, and Maggi suffers a miscarriage. A community civil servant attempts to evict them from their modest home, and David fights back, with the result that they're brought into court, but acquitted, thanks to the intervention of an enigmatic but kindly old man who carries an umbrella — and happens to be a lawyer. Free once more, they are last glimpsed out in the rain again, this time following a signpost which points to the city. And yet Bergman and his two young actors mine optimism from this downbeat tale, playing up moments of shared humor that balance amusing aspects of some of the film's peripheral characters.

Alert viewers will note Bergman's early use of two actors who would play important leads in many of his later, greater works: Erland Josephson and Gunnar Björnstrand. Along with Birger Malmsten, they would form the nucleus of the unofficial Bergman stock company.

Perhaps *It Rains on Our Love* appeared too depressing to interest Scandinavian audiences. Whatever the reason, they failed to patronize this movie's showings, and, despite some critical enthusiasm, it proved a failure. Of little help was its winning a "Charlie," the Swedish Academy Award.

Bergman on Bergman

"I read Herbert's screenplay and found it rather tedious. [Producer] Lorens Marmstedt agreed and asked me how much time it would take me to rewrite it. I promised to do it over the weekend if I was provided with a secretary. During the next thirty-six hours, I was sitting with a rather spunky beauty, dictating a new screenplay. Perhaps it wasn't any better, but at least the everyday pepper-and-salt tone was broken, which might have been an advantage."

It Rains on Our Love (1946). Birger Malmsten and Barbro Kollberg. Nordisk Tonefilm.

Critics' Circle

"It Rains on Our Love *is more strongly influenced by the French than* Crisis. *This is evident in the night pictures, in the poetic mood the narrator has tried to evoke. Aside from this, however, the film is weighted by a deterministic view of life. Neither the clergy nor the profane world can offer any help. But the two main characters do still go toward a happier future. They are not doomed, like Carné's actors. This is perhaps due to an optimism, an in-spite-of-all atti-tude which is present even in the most somber of Bergman's works."*

— Jörn Donner in
The Personal Vision of Ingmar Bergman

"Perhaps one of the best films any Swedish producer ever made, story's theme based on the premise that a man isn't a criminal just because he erred once, develops into excellent entertainment, chiefly due to fine scripting of Ingmar Bergman and Herbert Grevenius. Acting, lensing and direction are in keeping with other high production values."

— *Variety*

Skepp till Indialand
(Frustration/The Land of Desire/
A Ship Bound for India/A Ship to India)
Nordisk Tonefilm release of a Sveriges Filmbiografer
Production: 1947
(U.S. release by Film Classics: 1949)

CREDITS

Director: Ingmar Bergman; *producer:* Lorens Marmstedt; *screenwriters:* Ingmar Bergman and Herbert Grevenius; based on the play by Martin Söderhjelm; *cinematographer:* Göran Strindberg; *editor:* Tag Holmberg; *art director:* P. A. Lundgren; *music:* Erland von Koch; *sound:* Lars Nordberg and Sven Josephson; *running time:* 102 minutes.

CAST

Holger Löwenadler (*Capt. Alexander Blom*); Birger Malmsten (*Johannes Blom*); Gertrud Fridh (*Sally*); Anna Lindahl (*Alice Blom*); Lasse Krantz (*Hans*); Jan Molander (*Bertil*); Erik Hell (*Pekka*); Naemi Briese (*Selma*); Hjördis Pettersson (*Sofie*); Åke Fridell (*Cabaret Manager*); Peter Lindgren (*Foreign Sailor*); Gustaf Hiort af Ornäs and Torsten Bergström (*Blom's Companions*); Ingrid Borthen (*Girl in Street*); Gunnar Nielsen (*Young Man*); Amy Aaröe (*Young Girl*); Ingmar Bergman (*Man in Amusement Park*).

Bergman had yet to be given the opportunity to direct one of his own screenplays. Early in 1947 a strong script he had written under the title *Woman Without a Face* was assigned to the veteran Swedish director Gustaf Molander, while Bergman was offered another project by producer Lorens Marmstedt: an adaptation by Martin Söderhjelm of his stage play, *A Ship Bound for India*. In his autobiographical book *Images*, Bergman terms the original manuscript "unusable" and describes how he and Marmstedt flew to Cannes so that Bergman could attempt a rewrite while his producer played roulette. In a small room atop the Hotel Majestic, the director claims to have worked "like one obsessed, "turning out a draft in which "there were not many words left of Martin Söderhjelm's play."

Its plot, stylistically, owes not a little to Eugene O'Neill and a lot to Marcel Carné. It details the lack of rapport among a cruel, alcoholic seaman (Holger Löwanadler), his downtrodden wife (Anna Lindahl), and his despised son (Birger Malmsten), a withdrawn youth with a slightly hunched back. Their home is a Stockholm barge, to which, one day, the captain brings a cabaret girl (Gertrud Fridh). But the son and the girl soon form a romantic attachment, and a bitter rivalry develops between the generations, culminating in the father's attempting to cut off the boy's air supply and kill him during a salvage dive. Sought by the police, the captain is tracked down in his private hideaway, from which he makes a disastrous effort to commit suicide through a window.

Told in flashback form, through the son's recollections, the story ends on a positive note as he and the girl are reunited. She will accompany him aboard the handsome vessel which he now commands.

A Ship Bound for India reflects resourceful filmmaking on a very modest budget, and when it opened in Sweden that September, it was well received by the press. In

Frustration (1947). Holger Löwenadler and Gertrud Fridh. Nordisk Tonefilm.

France, critic André Bazin credited Bergman with "creating a world of blinding cinematic purity." But the filmgoing public seemed apathetic. Two years later, when it became the first Bergman-directed movie to play American cinemas—albeit in exploitation houses and under the more lurid title *Frustration*—it opened and closed very quietly.

Bergman on Bergman

"*A Ship Bound for India* was a major disaster."

Critics' Circle

"Translation of the Matin Söderhjelm play into celluloid has made a good film. Ingmar Bergman's crisp direction and scripting plus fine camerawork of Göran Strindberg are principally responsible for making this picture a crack tale of a salvage boat and four persons whose lives are tied up in the ship's destiny. Holger Löwenadler's portrayal of the captain is neat thesping, and others in cast measure up to his standard. Okay for the U. S. mart."

— *Variety*

"There is nothing on the screen of the Rialto theatre to warrant the cheap sensationalism of the poster display outside the house advertising Frustration, a Swedish importation. Frustration is simply a bad motion picture, photographed for considerable of its length in such murky tones that even a good many of the English subtitles are difficult to read when they are not actually indistinguishable. Just for the record, Frustration is a dark tale of enmity between a hunchbacked son and his cruel father, a salvage captain, who desires a tawdry singer."

— Thomas M. Pryor in
The New York Times

Musik i Mörker
(Night Is My Future/Music in Darkness)
Terrafilm release of a Terraproduktion: 1948
(U.S. release by Embassy Pictures: 1963)

CREDITS

Director: Ingmar Bergman; *producer:* Lorens Marmstedt; *screenwriter:* Dagmar Edqvist, based on her novel; *cinematographer:* Göran Strindberg; *editor:* Lennart Wallén; *art director:* P. A. Lundgren; *music:* Erland von Koch, with excerpts form Chopin, Beethoven, Badarczewska-Baranowska, Schumann, Handel, Wagner, and "Tom Andy" (Thomas Andersen); *running time:* 87 minutes.

CAST

Mai Zetterling (*Ingrid Olofsson*); Birger Malmsten (*Bengt Vyldeke*); Bibi Skoglund (*Agneta Vyldeke*); Olof Winnerstrand (*Kerrman, the Vicar*); Naima Wifstrand (*Beatrice Schröder*); Åke Claesson (*Augustin Schröder*); Hilda Borgström (*Lovisa*); Douglas Håge (Kruge, the Restaurant Owner); Gunnar Björnstrand (*Klasson, the Violinist*); Bengt Eklund (*Ebbe Larsson*); Segol Mann (*Anton Nord*); Bengt Logardt (*Einar Born*); Marianne Gyllenhammer (*Blanche*); John Elfstrom (*Otto Klemens*); Rune Andreasson (*Evert*); Barbro Flodquist (*Hjördis*); Ulla Andreasson (*Sylvia*); Sven Lindberg (*Hedström*); Svea Holst (*Postal Worker*); Georg Skarstedt (*Jönsson*); Arne Lindblad (*Chef*); Ingmar Bergman (*Passenger on Train*).

Despite the failure of their two previous pictures together, *It Rains on Our Love* and *A Ship Bound for India*, producer Lorens Marmstedt was not unwilling to experience a third collaboration — but on his terms. Proffering Dagmar Edqvist's script of *Night Is My Future*, he is reported to have told the director: "Ingmar, you are a flop. Here's a very sentimental story that will appeal to the public. You need a box-office success now."

Bergman and Marmstedt battled throughout the film's production (November–December 1947), sometimes over matters seemingly trivial, such as whether or not their star actress, Mai Zetterling, was being properly lighted. Obviously, Marmstedt had already learned something from Hollywood filmmaking that his fledgling director had yet to heed, for the resulting movie is often strikingly lit and photographed by Göran Strindberg, and both Zetterling and her costar, Birger Malmsten, positively glow with the beauty of well-formed youth.

In the Edqvist adaptation of her own novel, Malmsten portrays an unfortunate youth named Bengt, who is blinded in an accident during army training maneuvers. A gifted pianist, he recovers physically but is left to adjust to making his professional way in a darkened world. At first, he continues to live at home with his rural family, where he's looked after by Ingrid (Zetterling), a local girl who becomes a servant in their home and gradually falls in love with him. But they are soon separated, first by class differences (she's from a poor background; he's middle-class), then by his leaving to face life in the city, where he finds employment playing the piano in a café-restaurant. There, his violinist-colleague (Gunnar Björnstrand) cynically bad-mouths their boss (Douglas Håge), and Bengt is cruelly taken advantage of by others. It's one of a series of jobs that occupy him as he refuses to give in to loneliness or misplaced self-pity.

Eventually, Bengt is reunited with a

Night Is My Future **(1948). Birger Malmsten, Mai Zetterling and Bengt Eklund. Terrafilm.**

now-grown-up Ingrid, whose envious boyfriend (Bengt Eklund) hopes to cause a rift between their old friendship, but whose belligerent behavior ultimately drives Ingrid into Bengt's arms. Ultimately, they decide to marry, despite the objections of the local vicar (Olof Winnerstrand), and face an optimistic future together.

In *All Those Tomorrows*, her autobiography, Mai Zetterling describes the experience of working with *director* Bergman for the first and last time: "He is a formidable, intimidating person who can put on the charm at one moment and leave you out in the cold the next, who draws out both good and bad in people and can make them very dependent on him. I had a certain reserve with Ingmar, a reserve that I never got over, however closely we worked together. But he

managed to get amazing results from his actors and his staff, who idolized him and stayed with him picture after picture, however badly they were treated sometimes.... And he could be fun, too, in his very special personal way that made you forget the blows."

Oddly enough, it is *Night Is My Future*'s use of original music — supplementing the various excerpts from classical masters — that seems to date it today. At times, its silences are made to appear awkward, as in one sequence when, following a dramatic moment involving Birger Malmsten, suddenly melodramatic chords crash onto the soundtrack as the actor visibly collapses in a moment of defeat. In effect, this allies *Night Is My Future* with certain American films of the early thirties.

Bergman helps his leading actors avoid any excesses of sentiment here, sometimes playing against the more obvious turns in the story. Nevertheless, it is a sentimental tale, and it's undoubtedly that very factor that accounts for the picture's initial success. Proving that producer Marmstedt's instincts were in the right place, *Night Is My Future* drew enthusiastic audiences in Scandinavia and became Ingmar Bergman's first hit movie. Made for the independent Terrafilm organization, its box-office record impressed the more powerful Svensk Filmindustri, paving the way for Bergman's return there for *Port of Call.*

Bergman on Bergman

"Don't let's talk about it. It was a silly little film, but it was my first popular success."

Critics' Circle

"Night Is My Future *seems to be an almost completely commercial film. It still has some very strong scenes and a suggestive effect in details, although the direction seems awkward, uninterested and amateurish. There is not much of Bergman's personality in this film.*"

— Jörn Donner in
The Personal Vision of Ingmar Bergman

"Night Is My Future *is a movie Ingmar Bergman made in 1947— in parts the most puerile, as a whole the most heartwarming picture so far sent to the U.S. by the saturnine Swede. The Bergman who made this movie still had akvavit in his veins. Intellect, that glittering and treacherous Snow Queen, had not yet struck her icy sliver into his heart.*

— *Time*

"*Ingmar Bergman has become a directorial name to be reckoned with among film buffs in most Western countries.... This is an early one with melodramatic aspects but already interesting to his individual outlook and talents. It is well acted and incisively directed by Bergman. But its insistence on some sentimentality makes this somewhat chancey for offshore placement except for arty spots on his name alone.*"

— "Mosk" in *Variety*

"*The Bergman of 1947 conveniently shows plenty of signs of becoming a somber maestro, even when interpreting a screenplay written by someone else. For the allegorists this clearly anticipates later Bergmanisms; the pianist can be regarded as a fugitive in the dark coldness of agnosticism who finds his religion of sorts in that favorite Bergman sanctuary, womanhood. Music in this case provides an incidental panache equivalent to that of the subsequent* Wild Strawberries, *while such scenes as those with the awkward vicar and the family gatherings (with Naima Wifstrand presiding at the table, dominating her husband, and turning out remarks like 'Pain and suffering are part of God's design') are irresistible reminders of their own various repetitions in nearly every film that followed.*"

— Philip Strick in
Films and Filming

"*It is a soapy little picture whose showing now is only justified as demonstration for movie-lovers on how much Ingmar Bergman has improved. Dramatically, the story is loaded with heart-throbbed clichés and its few hints of social injustice toward the blind are dated by forty or fifty years. To be sure, there are hints and intimations of Bergman's later pictorial power in some of the scenes in this picture. But, for the most part,* Night Is My Future *is cinematic juvenilia of a painful sort.*"

— Bosley Crowther in
The New York Times

"*Yet another early Bergman is resurrected, but one that perhaps only the student of his artistic development would wish to see taken from the vaults. The highly individual style, though less finished than today,*

is as apparent as ever. But the allegory of spiritual and physical blindness, of darkness giving 'access to the garden of knowledge,' of all suffering as 'part of God's design,' wears *thin in a situation as trite as that of the blind pianist nursing his self-pity."*
— "T. K." in
Monthly Film Bulletin

Hamnstad
(Port of Call)
Svensk Filmindustri: 1948
(U. S. release by Janus Films: 1959)

CREDITS

Director: Ingmar Bergman; *producer:* Harald Molander; *screenwriters:* Ingmar Bergman and Olle Länsberg, based on Länsberg's story "Guldet Och murarna" (The Gold and the Walls); *cinematographer:* Gunnar Fischer; *editor:* Oscar Rosander; *art director:* Nils Svenwall; *music:* Erland von Koch, Adolphe Adam and Sven Sjöholm; *assistant directors:* Lars-Eric Kjellgren and Stig Ossian Ericson; *sound:* Sven Hanson; *running time:* 100 minutes.

CAST

Nine-Christine Jönsson (*Berit Holm*); Bengt Eklund (*Gösta Andersson*); Erik Hell (*Berit's Father*); Berta Hall (*Berit's Mother*); Mimi Nelson (*Gertrud*); Sture Ericsson (*Her Father*); Birgitta Valberg (*Agnes Vilander, the Social Worker*); Hans Straat (*Engineer Vilander*); Harry Ahlin (*Man from Skåne*); Nils Hallberg (*Gustav*); Sven-Eric Gamble (*"Eken," the Stockholm Kid*); Sif Ruud (*Mrs. Krona*); Kolbjörn Knudsen (*Seaman*); Yngve Nordwall (*Factory Foreman*); Torsten Lilliecrona and Hans Sundberg (*His Friends*); Bengt Blomgren (*Gunnar*); Helge Karlsson (*His Father*); Hanny Schedin (*His Mother*); Stig Olin (*Thomas*); Britta Billsten (*Street Girl*); Nils Dahlgren (*Police Commissioner*); Bill Houston (*Joe*).

Ingmar Bergman admits to having been heavily influenced by the postwar Italian films of Roberto Rossellini and Vittorio De Sica, and in *Port of Call* he takes a sort of neorealistic approach to the screenplay he and Olle Länsberg adapted from Länsberg's story "The Gold and the Walls." They filmed it on location in the dockside city of Gothenburg in the summer of 1948, and Bergman managed to cast aside the sentiment of his earlier waterfront film, *A Ship Bound for India*, as he wove the often-harsh working-class story of two lonely people adrift in an uncaring world. Berit (Nine-Christine Jönsson) is a disconsolate factory worker from a broken home who lives unhappily with her grim-faced mother (Berta Hall). As the story opens, Berit attempts suicide by jumping into the harbor. When she's rescued and taken to the hospital, her path unsuspectingly crosses with that of Gosta (Bengt Eklund), an equally disillusioned seaman, who finds employment on the docks. They later meet in a dance hall, and Gösta spends the night with Berit while her mother is away. When the girl's immoral past comes to light, Gösta is repelled and casts aside all thoughts of becoming more

Port of Call (1948). Sture Ericsson, Nine-Christine Jönsson, Bengt Eklund and Mimi Nelson. Svensk Filmindustri.

serious about her. He goes off on a drinking spree, while Berit accompanies her pregnant friend Gertrud (Mimi Nelson) to an abortionist. Afterward, as Gertrud's condition worsens, Berit frantically seeks Gösta's help, and in the wake of her friend's shabby demise, they are reunited to face an uncertain future together.

Reinforcing his later reputation with actresses, Bergman obtains an extraordinary performance from the plain-faced Nine-Christine Jönsson here. Unfortunately, she fails to surface again in any of his subsequent pictures; indeed, whatever other work she did in Swedish films appears to be unknown in the West. But her downtrodden, somewhat sullen young delinquent in *Port of Call*, with her occasional bursts of anti–Establishment anger and frustration, suggest a talent that might have transcended the ordinary in later opportunities. It is rare for so gifted a young Bergman actress not to find a repetitive place in his pantheon of players.

Bergman on Bergman

"*Port of Call* was not a remarkable story. To me, it was a question of piecing together a suitable movie out of Olle Länsberg's voluminous material. I tried to include as many exteriors as possible. What went wrong was that, in spite of my good intentions, too much of the film was shot in the studio for people to say that I had made a clean break with the Swedish film tradition of shooting films in the studio."

Critics' Circle

"Port of Call *belongs to Bergman's short 'realist' period; it contains no symbolism, and has only one short lyrical sequence, the slow unfolding of dawn in the docks.*

"*The film is largely and effectively shot on location, and its chief weakness is the failure to relate convincingly the melodramatic, often hysterical, course of the relationship to this coherent background—this, despite some fine acting, particularly by Nine-Christine Jönsson—a failure which again suggests that Bergman is probably at this best in handling characters set in a more bourgeois milieu.*"
— Max Neufeld in *Films and Filming*

"*The approach is sharply realistic, at times verging on documentary, and it is this anti-romantic, unsophisticated hardness of background, problems and faces which lends the picture its powerfully expressive flavor. Bergman discovers his own poetry in the harsh world that here obsesses him, balancing it with the emotional content of the characters and situations. The harbor with its depressing beauty makes a perfect background to the bitter, well-observed love story, and a rich soundtrack brings out all the coldly mechanical life of the city. The acting is brilliant, from the heroine, Nine-Christine Jönsson, down to the small-part players, and confirms* Hamnstad *as a grim but uplifting, almost transcendental experience, rich in imagination and humanity.*"
— "R. V." in *Monthly Film Bulletin*

"*The most dangerous thing that can happen to a director is to be discovered. Since the Swedish Ingmar Bergman was deservedly acclaimed for* The Seventh Seal *and* Wild Strawberries, *relics from his past keep turning up on the screen.*

"*This is one of them. A gloomy but affecting tale of a girl driven to delinquency by a broken home and now hopelessly trying to bury a past that haunts her. Her love affair with an embittered young sailor is touchingly handled. Stark and occasionally gruesome, the film is chiefly remarkable for Nine-Christine Jönsson, a chubby Swede with an amazing acting talent.*"
— *Continental Film Guide*

Fängelse
(The Devil's Wanton/Prison)
Terrafilm release of a Terraproduktion: 1949
(U.S. release by Embassy Pictures: 1962)

CREDITS

Director: Ingmar Bergman; *producer:* Lorens Marmstedt; *screenwriter:* Ingmar Bergman; *cinematographer:* Göran Strindberg; *editor:* Lennart Wallén; *art director:* P. A. Lundgren; *music:* Erland von Koch, Alice Tegnér and Oscar Ahnfelt; *sound:* Olle Jakobsson; *running time:* 80 minutes.

CAST

Doris Svedlund (*Birgitta-Carolina Söderberg*); Birger Malmsten (*Thomas*); Eva Henning (*Sofi, his Wife*); Hasse Ekman (*Martin Grandé*); Stig Olin (*Peter*); Irma Christenson (*Linnéa*); Anders Henrikson (*Paul, Professor of Mathematics*); Marianne Löfgren (*Signe Bohlin*); Curt Masreliez (*Alf, the Pimp*); Birgit "Bibi" Lindqvist (*Anna Bohlin*); Arne Ragneborn

(Postman); Carl-Henrik Fant *(Arne, an Actor)*; Inger Juel *(Greta, an Actress)*; Torsten Lil-liecrona *(Cinematographer)*; Segol Mann *(Lighting Technician)*; Åke Fridell *(Magnus)*; Börje Mellvig *(Commissioner)*; Åke Engfeld *(Policeman)*; Lasse Sari *(Lasse)*; Britta Brunius *(His Mother)*, Gunilla Klosterberg *(Dark Lady)*; Ulf Palme *(Man in Dream)*.

In *The Devil's Wanton*— to use the exploitative title given *Prison* in the United States — Bergman breaks new ground, for the first time directing a screenplay of which he was the sole author and guiding the project exactly as he wished. As such, it is perhaps the first of his films to anticipate some of the themes and complexities that would either charm or confound his critics in years to come.

The film was never intended as a commercial project, and Bergman had some trouble getting it made — until once again finding an ally in Terrafilm's Lorens Marmstedt. But there were conditions that had to be met, including a basement-level budget of some $30,000 and the necessity of his actors working at half their customary salaries. Shot in the winter of 1948-49, *The Devil's Wanton* is said to have been filmed in a brief eighteen days, which seems difficult to believe, considering the script's convoluted development.

A successful movie director named Martin (Hasse Ekman) is visited by his old professor, Paul (Anders Henrikson), who offers him an idea for a movie with the theme of hell being on earth and ruled by Satan. Bemused by the suggestion. Martin subsequently recounts this incident to his married friends, the alcoholic writer Thomas (Birger Malmsten) and his wife, Sofi (Eva Henning), who are beset by their own problems. Thomas is inspired to improve on the script idea by centering it on a prostitute, Birgitta-Carolina (Doris Svedlund), whom he had previously interviewed and who shares quarters with Peter (Stig Olin), her pimp, and his sister, Linnéa (Irma Christenson). Having given birth to a child, Birgitta allows her housemates to kill it, a turn of events that contributes to her somewhat un-hinged mental state. Birgitta, as it happens, also encounters Thomas at a time when he and his wife are considering suicide. For a time, she and he are romantically involved, but then Peter summons her back to him, and Thomas reunites with Sofi. After Birgitta is burned by the cigarette of a sadistic client, she takes refuge in the basement, where she slits her wrists. The movie ends very much as it began, back in the studio, where it's decided that no film could be made of the professor's story, since it would raise more questions than it could hope to answer.

In his book, *Ingmar Bergman: Film and Stage*, Robert Emmet Long calls *The Devil's Wanton* "the gem of Bergman's filmmaking in the 1940s," while admitting, "It is also seriously flawed." Indeed, existing subtitled prints are so inferior that it's not only almost impossible to read the often-white-on-white titles, but a difficult narrative becomes almost incomprehensible to the average viewer. Ambitious in the extreme, *The Devil's Wanton* seems light-years away from Bergman's previous *Port of Call*, and could only have struck the Swedish filmgoers who saw it in 1949 as the artiest of noncommercial motion-picture ventures — avant-garde in the extreme.

Bergman on Bergman

"It was the first time I was ever allowed to make my own script from an idea of my own. The whole thing was my own from beginning to end. For me, hell has always been a most suggestive sort of place; but I've never regarded it as being located anywhere else than on earth. Hell is created by human beings — on earth!"

The Devil's Wanton (1949). Birger Malmsten and Doris Svedlund. Terrafilm.

Critics' Circle

"The Devil's Wanton *is worth seeing as an example of the truth that many serious artists have only a few themes which they reuse all their lives. This is a kind of rough-* *draft film dealing with those questions of the purpose and loneliness of existence that are still Bergman's subjects. The picture is a bit tedious, except for the character of the pimp played by Stig Olin, but it is smoothly made and shows both fluency with the medium*

and an understanding of actors. It also fore-
casts the power of introspection that Bergman later developed so beautifully."
—Stanley Kauffamnn in
The New Republic

"Although there is a an abundance of
good, sharp movie-making here, the film
neither technically nor in its philosophical
implications comes near the stature of Bergman's later Wild Strawberries or The Virgin Spring. Still, the point is that such early
films do have a considerable interest for
Bergman fans in offering an opportunity to
learn more about the director's development
both technically and philosophically."
— Paul V. Beckley in
The New York Herald Tribune

'Fängelse finds Bergman in bleak mood
and at his least convincing. The agony is ap-

plied with a thick brush: in style, the film
looks back to German expressionism; in content, it employs all the paraphernalia associated with Scandinavian angst. Consequently, Bergman's pimps, prostitutes and
unhappily married couples parade their neuroses with little more conviction than pup-
pets, and not even a growing technical expertise can make their plight interesting or
revealing."
—"J. G."
in Monthly Film Bulletin

"Mr. Bergman cannot be censured for his
preoccupation with man's basic bafflement,
but his approach to the subject, which has
flashes of scintillating poetic allusions, is
merely a point of view that is heavily thought-
ful but often verbose, disjointed and fuzzy."
—A. H. Weiler in
The New York Times

Törst
(Three Strange Loves/Thirst)
Svensk Filmindustri: 1949
(U.S. release by Janus Films: 1961)

CREDITS

Director: Ingmar Bergman; *producer:* Helge Hagerman; *screenwriter:* Herbert Grevenius;
based on *Törst*, a collection of short stories by Birgit Tengroth; *cinematographer:* Gunnar Fischer; *editor:* Oscar Rosander; *art director:* Nils Svenwall; *music:* Erik Nordgren;
sound: Lennart Unnerstad; *choreographer:* Ellen Bergman; *costumes:* Gösta Ström; *running time:* 84 minutes.

CAST

Eva Henning (*Rut*); Birger Malmsten (*Bertil, her Husband*); Birgit Tengroth (*Viola*);
Mimi Nelson (*Valborg*); Hasse Ekman (*Dr. Rosengren*); Bengt Eklund (*Raoul*); Gaby
Stenberg (*Astrid, his Wife*); Naima Wifstrand (*Miss Henriksson, the Ballet Teacher*);
Sven-Eric Gamble (*Glass Worker*); Gunnar Nielsen (*Rosengren's Assistant*); Estrid Hesse
(*Patient*); Helge Hagerman (*Swedish Priest*); Calle Flygare (*Danish Priest*); Monica Wein-
zierl (*Little Girl on Train*); Verner Arpe (*German Conductor*); Else-Merete Heiberg (*Nor-
wegian Woman on Train*); Sif Ruud (*Garrulous Widow*); Ingmar Bergman (*Passenger on
Train*).

After the experimentation of *Prison/The Devil's Wanton*, Bergman returned to directing the work of someone else with *Three Strange Loves/Thirst*, which was adapted for the screen by Herbert Grevenius. His screenplay derived from a collection of short stories by the actress-writer Birgit Tengroth.

The film's structure is complex, employing a "framing" story in which Rut and Bertil (Eva Henning and Birger Malmsten), a restless, unhappy couple, travel by train through war-torn Europe. Prior to their marriage, the wife had had an affair with an army officer, Raoul (Bengt Eklund), that ended with an abortion, making her sterile. She has become difficult to live with, and her husband, taking refuge in introspection, daydreams of Viola (Birgit Tengroth), a past love of his own. All of this is depicted by flashbacks, dream scenes, and parallel sequences involving other characters, all of whom conveniently tie together by the end, at which point the miserable couple determine that "hell together is better than hell alone."

A modest box-office success, this picture attracted more Scandinavian filmgoers than had any previous Ingmar Bergman effort.

Bergman on Bergman

"*Thirst* is a collection of short stories by Birgit Tengroth that caused a sensation when it was first published. Herbert Grevenius wrote a good screenplay in which he tied the different stories together into one coherent script with parallel plots and flashbacks.

"Birgit Tengroth also made a directorial contribution that I will not forget; it taught me something new and decisive. The two women are sitting together in the summer twilight, sharing a bottle of wine. Birgit is rather drunk and gets a cigarette from Mimi, who also lights it for her. Then Mimi slowly brings the burning match toward her own face and holds it for a moment by her right eye before it goes out. This was Birgit Tengroth's idea.

I remember it clearly, since I had never done anything like that. To build the plot with small, almost imperceptible, suggestive details became a special component in my future filmmaking.

Critics' Circle

"Three Strange Loves *is staged with a cold, professional clarity. It deals with people who never have time for love — they are too busy suffering, as Siclier says in his book about Bergman. The possibility of death is always present. The characters in the film lack understanding of their own possibilities. They are, in a transferred meaning, too adult. This state of being grownup, in contrast to a child's openness and sensuality, is the central element in Bergman's artistic world.*"

—Jorn Dönner in
The Personal Vision of Ingmar Bergman

"*A Swedish dramatic film that is very well done, built around actress Birgit Tengroth's sensational novel. This film may be limited to Scandinavian markets, because of the way it deals with some erotic problems. Performances, especially by Eva Henning and Birger Malmsten, are outstanding.*"

—"Wing" in *Variety*

"*Interesting early Bergman drama which foreshadows much of his future work. This one explores the dynamics of a three-cornered love relationship, from a distinctly female perspective, and examines the possibility of two women having the same personality.*"

— *Leonard Maltin's Movie and Video Guide*

"*The two stories are unfolded in parallel time, together with a lot of flashback. This approach leads to a measure of confusion, while some of the connections made between the protagonists are tenuous and the arm of coincidence occasionally stretches too far. That said, this ambitious but uneven work brilliantly reflects the inner desolation of the married couple in powerful exterior images.*"

—Ronald Bergan and Robyn Karney in
The Holt Foreign Film Guide

Three Strange Loves (1949). Birger Malmsten and Eva Henning. Svensk Filmindustri.

"The most memorable moments of Thirst *occur during the train journey. Bertil, waiting for Rut to emerge from the toilet, sees his own reflection in the window of the corridor. It shakes as though he was being jolted in Hell. Then, as Rut comes out and tries to jump from the train, Bertil catches her and they cling together, terrified of the black void that lies beyond their infernal existence. It is unnerving— a moment when profound emotions are registered in terms of pure cinema."*

—Peter Cowie in *Swedish Cinema*

"Three Strange Loves *is pure Bergman in this exploration of men and women and their psychoneuroses. It also is primitive in comparison to Bergman's later, more polished works ('I just grabbed helplessly at any form that might save me, because I hadn't any of*

my own,' the director once wrote of his early efforts). But struggling, searching 1949 Bergman is still better than most directors in top 1988 form."

—V. A. Musetto in
The New York Post

"Already evident in Three Strange Loves *is the master's self-assured, steely, stripped-down directorial style, which is even more remarkable considering the awkward structure of Herbert Grevenius's screenplay.*

"The excitement of the film comes from the mounting viciousness with which Bergman portrays the no-exit marriage of Rut and Bertil. There is astonishing, virtuoso economy in the way in which he works in these scenes."

—Vincent Canby in
The New York Times

Till Glädje
(To Joy)
Svensk Filmindustri: 1950
(No U.S. release)

CREDITS

Director: Ingmar Bergman; *producer:* Allan Ekelund; *screenwriter:* Ingmar Bergman; *cinematographer:* Gunnar Fischer; *editor:* Oscar Rosander; *art director:* Nils Svenwall; *music:* Beethoven ("Egmont Overture," First and Ninth Symphonies), Mozart, Mendelssohn, Smetana, Sam Samson, and Erik Johnsson; *orchestrator:* Eskil Eckert-Lundin; *running time:* 98 minutes.

CAST

Maj-Britt Nilsson (*Marta*); Stig Olin (*Stig Eriksson*); Victor Sjöström (*Sönderby*); Birger Malmsten (*Marcel*); John Ekman (*Mikael Bro*); Margit Carlqvist (*Nelly Bro*); Sif Ruud (*Stina*); Erland Josephson (*Bertil*); Ernst Brunman (*Janitor at Concert House*); Allan Ekelund (*Vicar at Wedding*); Rune Stylander (*Persson*); Georg Skarstedt (*Anker*); Berit Holmström (*Young Lisa*); Björn Montin (*Lasse*); Svea Holst (*Nurse*); Maud Hyttenberg (*Saleswoman in Toy Store*); Ingmar Bergman (*Man Waiting in Hospital*); Carin Swensson (Anna); Dagny Lind (*Granny*).

With *To Joy*, Bergman returned to directing screenplays of his own, in this case one he developed during a two month Riviera vacation. Bergman biographers have traced this story's roots to his reflections on his own failed marriage to Ellen Lundström, his second wife. It centers on the problembeset union of a neurotic concert violinist (Stig Olin) and his alienated wife (Maj-Britt Nilsson), who eventually come to terms with their various obstacles. These encompass not only the usual marital ones but also those of the creative artist, especially that of self-doubt. Reunited after a long separation, they come to a mature realization that they need one another. However, in their country home a kerosene stove explodes, killing the wife while her husband rehearses Beethoven's "Ode to Joy" with his orchestra. The film closes with the couple's young son auditing that orchestra's dress rehearsal as he and his father exchange fond glances.

Unlike most of Bergman's films of this period, *To Joy* never had a formal U.S. release.

But unlike the little-seen *This Doesn't Happen Here/High Tension*, his subsequent picture, *To Joy*, has at least been available on videocassette.

Bergman on Bergman

"*To Joy* is a hopelessly uneven film, but it has a few shining moments. A good scene is the confrontation at night between Stig Olin and Maj-Britt Nilsson. It is good because her adept acting enriches the scene. The clear and honest depiction of a complicated relationship echoes the conflicts in my own marriage."

Critics' Circle

"*There is much sentimentality in* To Joy, *but there is much genuineness, too. It is least good in the documentary transition sequences. In those, Bergman holds to a faded and lifeless photographic tradition. Neither does he quite master the relationships*

To Joy (1950). Maj-Britt Nilsson and Stig Olin. Svensk Filmindustri.

between full pictures and close-ups, or the film's rhythmic outline. It is in the intimate action that he is most skillful where the camera, from being a penetrating observer, becomes a listener."

—Jörn Donner in
The Personal Vision of Ingmar Bergman

"Bergman's direction of To Joy, *which received miserable reviews, seems half-hearted. But the problem lies partly in his script, which is clichéd at important points. The sudden death of Marta and one of their*

children in the stove explosion is unconscionably melodramatic; and the concert-hall scene, where Stig's little boy looks on bravely as the orchestra plays the stirring, 'Ode to Joy' movement of Beethoven's Ninth Symphony, is too obviously designed to provide an emotional, uplifting ending. Victor Sjöström as the orchestra conductor projects a rich humanity and has one of the great faces in Bergman's films. Maj-Britt Nilsson is also an asset."

—Robert Emmet Long in
Ingmar Bergman: Film and Stage

Sånt Händer Inte Här
(High Tension/This Doesn't Happen Here/This Can't Happen Here)
Svensk Filmindustri: 1950
(No U.S. release)

CREDITS

Director: Ingmar Bergman; *producer:* Helge Hagerman; *screenwriter:* Herbert Grevenius; based on the novel *I løpet av tölv timer* (During Twelve Hours) by Peter Valentin (Waldemar Brøgger); *cinematographer:* Gunnar Fischer; *editor:* Lennart Wallén; *art director:* Nils Svenwall; *music:* Erik Nordgren; *sound:* Sven Hansen; *running time:* 84 minutes.

CAST

Signe Hasso (*Vera*); Alf Kjellin (*Björn Almkvist*); Ulf Palme (*Atkä Natas*); Gösta Cederlund (*Doctor*); Yngve Nordwall (*Lindell*); Hannu Kompus (*Priest*); Els Vaarman (*Female Refugee*); Sylvia Tael (*Vanja*); Edmar Kuus (*Leino*); Rudolf Lipp (*"The Shadow"*); Lillie Wästfeldt (*Mrs. Rundblom*); Stig Olin (*Young Man*); Magnus Kesster (*House Owner*); Alexander von Baumgarten (*Ship's Captain*); Ragnar Klange (*Motorist*); Helena Kuus (*Woman at Wedding*); Eddy Andersson (*Ship's Engineer*); Hugo Bolander (*Hotel Manager*); Fritjof Hellberg (*First Mate*); Mona Astrand (*Young Girl*); Mona Geijer-Falkner (*Woman in Apartment Building*); Erik Forslund (*Concierge*); Georg Skarstedt (*Worker with Hangover*); Tor Borong (*Caretaker*); Maud Hyttenberg (*Graduate*); Helga Brofeldt (*Shocked Old Woman*); Sven Axel Carlsson (*Youngster*); Segol Mann, Willy Koblanck, Gregor Dahlmann, Gösta Holström, and Ivan Bousé (*Liquidatzia Agents*).

This is among the most obscure of Bergman's early films, partly because the writer-director harbors no fondness for it whatsoever, a factor which may account for its failure to turn up in such otherwise comprehensive American retrospectives as the one that New Yorkers enjoyed in May-June 1995.

Herbert Grevenius based his screenplay on Waldemar Brøgger's novel *During Twelve Hours,* a political melodrama centering on a foreign agent named Natas (Ulf Palme) who returns from another country to Stockholm and his wife, Vera (Signe Hasso). Determined to free herself of him and his espionage activities, she gives him what she presumes to be a lethal injection. But he's saved by his fellow conspirators, who hope to turn up the secret documents he had in his possession. Afraid of the consequences of being apprehended, the fugitive Natas kills himself, while Vera, who has discovered a friend in the detective Almkvist (Alf Kjellin), finds herself involved with her late husband's sinister colleagues, who hide out on a ship in the harbor. Eventually, justice triumphs, and Vera faces a somewhat less hectic future with Almkvist.

Made directly after *Summer Interlude, This Doesn't Happen Here* was released almost immediately, while the earlier film was held back until the following year, perhaps to avoid giving the Swedish public too heavy a dose of Bergmania all at once.

Bergman on Bergman

"I only had one enjoyable day in the whole shooting. Otherwise it was a nightmare! For one thing, I was dead tired. I had to go from *Summer Interlude* to *This*

High Tension (1950). Unidentified actors (at left) with Signe Hasso and Ulf Palme. Svensk Filmindustri.

Can't Happen Here virtually from one day to the next; so I'd been preparing *This Can't Happen Here* while making *Summer Interlude*.

"I was dead tired and ill, and only made it for the money. There's nothing in it I like at all. I think it's disgusting. The film got a horrible bawling out."

Critics' Circle

"This very confused production may be termed a Swedish contribution to the current 'anti–Red' cycle. The agents are the usual hard-faced thugs who resort to violence at every possible moment, and the story follows the familiar pattern of chases, secret plans and sudden deaths. One redeeming feature is Gunnar Fischer's excellent location photography.

— *Monthly Film Bulletin*

"This film has been characterized as a Swedish contribution to the anti–Red pictures now in vogue. It was made to order, completed in a few weeks.

"The interesting part is Bergman's direction. It underlines the unreal character of the story. The serious scenes are exaggerated, and become comical instead. Excitement is whipped up by farcical pursuits and ridiculous complications. Thereby, even death becomes a divertissement. Bergman drives the spy thriller ad absurdum."

— Jörn Donner in
The Personal Vision of Ingmar Bergman

"Bergman's direction is a skillful parody of Hitchcock's, but the film is without substance, as Bergman well knew. It helped him

to negotiate his survival, but embarrasses him today."

—Robert Emmet Long in
Ingmar Bergman: Film and Stage

Sommarlek
(Illicit Interlude/Summer Interlude)
Svensk Filmindustri: 1951
(U.S. release by Gaston Hakim Productions, Inc.: 1954)

CREDITS

Director: Ingmar Bergman; *producer:* Allan Ekelund; *screenwriters:* Ingmar Bergman and Herbert Grevenius; based on the unpublished Story "Mari" by Ingmar Bergman; *cinematographer:* Gunner Fischer; *editor:* Oscar Rosander; *art director:* Nils Svenwall; *music:* Erik Nordgren, Delibes, Chopin, and Tchaikovsky; *orchestrator:* Eskil Eckert-Lundin; *running time:* 96 minutes.

CAST

Maj-Britt Nilsson (*Marie*); Birger Malmsten (*Henrik*); Alf Kjellin (*David Nystrom*); Georg Funkquist (*Uncle Erland*); Renée Björling (*Aunt Elisabeth*); Mimi Pollak (*Henrik's Aunt*); Annalisa Ericson (*Kaj, a Ballerina*); Stig Olin (*Ballet Master*); Gunnar Olsson (*Pastor*); John Botvid (*Karl, a Janitor*); Carl Ström (*Sandell, the Stage Manger*); Torsten Lilliecrona (*Lighting Man*); Marianne Schuler (*Kerstin*); Douglas Håge (*Nisse, a Janitor*); Julia Caesar (*Maja*); Olav Riego (*Physician*); Ernst Brunman (*Boat's Captain*); Fylgia Zadig (*Nurse*); Sten Mattson (*Boat Hand*); Carl-Axel Elfving (*Man with Flowers*); Eskil Eckert-Lundin (*Orchestra Conductor*); Gun Skogberg (*Marie as Ballerina*); and Stockholm's Royal Opera Ballet.

Among its director's personal favorite films, *Summer Interlude* was shot mainly in the Stockholm archipelago during April–June 1950, a period when rain often interfered with Bergman's daily plans and forced him to switch to indoor sequences at the Råsunda Studios in suburban Stockholm. Centering on Marie (Maj-Britt Nilsson), a prima ballerina at Stockholm's Royal Opera, the story is told in flashbacks. Marie is reluctantly courted by David (Alf Kjellin), a personable journalist who fails to understand her generally detached manner. During rehearsals of *Swan Lake*, she receives back-

stage an old diary she had kept as a teenager and which records a long-ago love affair with a student named Henrik (Birger Malmsten). The diary had been sent her by her spiteful, embittered uncle Erland (Georg Funkquist), with whom she had once lived as a ballet student. An electrical failure at the theater threatens to delay the rehearsal indefinitely, and Marie takes advantage of the break to board a steamer and revisit the island sites described in her diary. The locale is chilly and windswept, and the presence of her uncle proves more sinister than encouraging.

Flashbacks fill in details of the young

lovers' summer, when Henrik lived with his ailing aunt (Mimi Pollak) and shared secret trysts with Marie in a lakeside cabin that she now finds desolate. Their idyll ended tragically when Henrik suffered a diving accident and died in hospital soon after. Marie retreated into the rarefied world of the ballet and held her emotions in check thereafter, with perhaps a dozen years passing between her youthful romance and the resurfacing of the diary. Marie's visit to her uncle's island home helps heal old wounds and resolve the conflicts within her. When she returns to the theater for the opening of *Swan Lake*, she's ready to accept the love of David (who has since read the diary himself and understands). The film ends with a triumphant performance of the ballet.

The use of a dancing double for Maj-Britt Nilsson was so skillfully accomplished that the average viewer would assume that the actress had done her own performing in the ballet scenes. When the film was finally released, more than a year after its completion, Scandinavian critics reacted favorably. *Summer Interlude* was also very popular with moviegoers.

Bergman on Bergman

"For me *Summer Interlude* is one of my most important films. Even though to an outsider it may seem terribly passé, for me it isn't. This was my first film in which I felt I was functioning independently, with a style of my own, making a film all my own, with a particular appearance of its own, which no one could ape. It was like no other film. It was all my own work. Suddenly I knew I was putting the camera on the right spot, getting the right results; that everything added up. For sentimental reasons, it was also fun making it. Far back in my past there had been a love story, a romantic experience. I was writing about something which had hurt. But there's an awful lot of myself in Marie, too. Marie, the ballet-master and the some-

what world-weary and scabby journalist — all three are projections of myself."

Critics' Circle

"Not since the Swedes exported Torment *and* Miss Julie *has that country given us such a good film as* Illicit Interlude. *In fact, this moody, romantic drama of a ballerina's life must stand very high on the list of any foreign imports this year.... The ballet stage and the outdoor world rarely have been translated so beautifully onto film."*
— *Film Daily*

"*The early scenes between Marie and Henrik have a freshness and feeling for the young lovers' situation which owes much to Bergman's response to the heady atmosphere of the Swedish summer and to Gunnar Fischer's rich but naturalistic photography.* Summer Interlude, *at its best, is an atmospheric, intermittently poetic film, with considerable pictorial beauty in the outdoor and ballet scenes, and admirable performances by Maj-Britt Nilsson and Birger Malmsten.*"
— "J. M." in *Monthly Film Bulletin*

"*For the most part, Director Ingmar Bergman simply traces in clean, poetic terms the dancer's vivid recollections of a wonderful summer she spent in the home of an aunt and uncle by a beautiful Swedish lake and of the passionate discovery and fulfillment of love with the youth, who later died. But the romantic recollections are beautifully visualized, with tremendous energy and compassion, and the scenes of ballet groups performing at the Stockholm Royal Opera have a black-and-white crispness that is superb.*"
— Bosley Crowther in *The New York Times*

"*It represents Swedish film-making at its best. Maj-Britt Nilsson again documents herself as one of the best actresses in Sweden. Gunnar Fischer's camerawork is of the highest standard. His shots of the ballet and its dancers are outstanding.*"
— "Wing" in *Variety*

Illicit Interlude (1951). Stig Olin and Maj-Britt Nilsson. Svensk Filmindustri.

"Having seen his later films first, we have come to know his tricks — the pretentious symbolism, the well-calculated shock; how refreshing, then, to see a film devoid of these traits. If only Bergman would allow some of this simplicity to return to his current work, he might yet fulfill the faith that has been put in his fundamental genius."
— Max Neufeld
in *Films and Filming*

"Sun, sea and blighted young love are as much a cliché of Swedish filmmaking as the Wild West is of Hollywood film-making. It takes a director like Ingmar Bergman to give it a freshness and poignancy. Bergman's films are always brilliant, often cold. But this one seems to have been made straight from the heart. Maj-Britt Nilsson and Birger Malmsten exquisitely play on the twisting moods of the young lovers."
— "T. H." in *Picturegoer*

"This early Bergman film is about the loss of love: a tired ballerina of twenty-eight, who has ceased to feel or care, is suddenly caught up by the memory of the summer when her life ended. We see her then as a fresh, eager fifteen-year-old, in love with a frightened, uncertain student (beautifully played by Birger Malmsten), and we watch the delicate shades of their "summerplay," interrupted by glances at adult relatives, as Bergman contrasts decadence and youth, corruption and beauty."
— Pauline Kael in
1001 Nights at the Movies

"Realistic as Summer Interlude *is, it continually suggests a sense of fable. Part of the film's richness and resonance flows from its shaping as a fairy tale, a dimension of Bergman's art that will affect even such apparently realistic films as* Wild Strawberries."
— Robert Emmet Long in
Ingmar Bergman: Film and Stage

Kvinnors Väntan
(Secrets of Women/Waiting Women)

Svensk Filmindustri: 1952
(U.S. release by Janus Films: 1961)

CREDITS

Director: Ingmar Bergman; *producer:* Allan Ekelund; *screenwriter:* Ingmar Bergman; *cinematographer:* Gunnar Fischer; *editor:* Oscar Rosander; *art director:* Nils Svenwall; *music:* Erik Nordgren; *sound:* Sven Hansen; *running time:* 107 minutes.

CAST

Anita Björk (*Rakel*); Jarl Kulle (*Kaj, Her Lover*); Karl-Arne Holmsten (*Eugen, Her Husband*); Maj-Britt Nilsson (*Märta Lobelius*); Birger Malmsten (*Martin Lobelius, her Husband*); Eva Dahlbeck (*Karin Lobelius*); Gunnar Björnstrand (*Fredrik, her Husband*); Gerd Andersson (*Maj, Märta's Younger Sister*); Björn Bjelvenstam (*Henrik Lobelius, her Boyfriend*); Aino Taube (*Annette*); Håkan Westergren (*Paul, Her Husband*); Märta Arbiin (*Nurse Rut*); Torsten Lilliecrona (*Maitre D' at Nightclub*); Naima Wifstrand (*Old Mrs. Lobelius*); Carl Ström (*Doctor*); Douglas Håge (*Porter*); Lena Brogren (*Hospital Worker*); Kjell Nordensköld (*American Pilot*); Lil Yunkers (*Emcee*); Wiktor Andersson (*Trash Collector*); Victor Violacci (*Patron*); Ingmar Bergman (*Bit*).

In the late forties and early fifties, movies reflected a vogue for multipart stories unified in one package with a common theme. This sort of Scandinavian *Letter to Three Wives* centers on four sisters-in-law gathered at a summer vacation home in the Stockholm archipelago, awaiting the arrival of their working husbands. Together in the kitchen, they pass the time recounting previously unrevealed incidents (told in flashbacks) from their marriages. Each remembers something that sheds light on her spouse: Rakel (Anita Björk) admits to an indiscretions with a former boyfriend that almost brought about her husband's suicide (until, Bergmanically, he decided that having a faithless wife is preferable to none at all); Märta (Maj-Britt Nilsson in her final Bergman film) describes her student-days romance with a Parisian artist (Birger Malmsten) that resulted in a child before they eventually wed; and Karin (Eva Dahlbeck) recalls a postparty incident in which she and her husband were stranded in an elevator, thus reinforcing their wan-

ing relationship. In the only segment of the film which is outright comedy — a first for Bergman — Dahlbeck and Gunnar Björnstrand evince a kind of Nordic Tracy-Hepburn comic rapport that moved their director to cast them in comparable roles a year later in *A Lesson in Love*.

Bergman on Bergman

"It went like hot cakes. It was one of the happiest experiences of my life, to hang about in the foyer of the Röda Kvarn Cinema and suddenly hear people inside howling with laughter. It was the first time in my life people had ever laughed at something I'd made — laughed like that."

Critics' Circle

"The film's three consecutive playlets, linked in a single family frame and with another

Secrets of Women (1952). Anita Björk, Gerd Andersson, Eva Dahlbeck and Aino Taube. Svensk Filmindustri.

story about two adolescents adumbrated, are frequently graced with dazzling technical virtuosity and some characteristic performances. Maj-Britt Nilsson's placidly passionate student is far more interesting and spontaneous than her ballerina in Sommarlek, and Eva Dahlbeck's and Gunnar Björnstrand's ironic rendering of an overlong scene played in a lift, and allowing a minimum of gesture, proves a triumph of timing and under-playing."

— Peter John Dyer in
Monthly Film Bulletin

"Pic is technically outstanding, with acting tops. Superior treatment makes sudsy material appear deep and dynamic."
—"Mosk" in *Variety*

"Secrets of Women *is concerned with what to Bergman is the never-ending combat between the sexes. Its tone is comic,*

which may come as a surprise to viewers who prefer to notice only the somber side of Bergman.

"Although it can be appreciated for its own merits, I think that in the perspective of Bergman's recent films it can best be seen as a kind of notebook whose 'entries' suggest and define some of the themes and images which will later receive major expression."
—Alfred Appel, Jr. in
Film Quarterly

"Secrets of Women, *made some years ago by Ingmar Bergman, is understandably delayed in arriving here. Telling several artificially related vignettes involving women, their lovers and husbands, it has a slow pace and humor is seldom more than pallid. Yet, for all this, the people seem quite real, there are flashes of genuine insight, and the acting is always competent. Particularly good are Eva Dahlbeck and Gunnar Björnstrand,*

and Miss Dahlbeck's, it can be said, is the most interesting secret."

— Hollis Alpert in *Saturday Review*

"In the second episode, Mr. Bergman has done the difficult and somewhat arty thing of combining flashbacks within a flashback. But it is highly effective because the flashbacks of [the woman's] original seduction and romance, intercut against the cold reality of her terror and pain in the delivery room, are rendered the more compelling and reflective of the ironies of love. The episode is not especially lucid, but it is a real cinematic tour de force, and it is beautifully played by Maj-Britt Nilsson and Birger Malmsten."

— Bosley Crowther in
The New York Times

"Bergman's constant effort to express the subjective, the introspective man (or woman) makes dream sequences frequent in his films, and they are always remarkable for their peculiar aptness. Technically interesting as it is, this episode is somewhat redundant, a trifle drawn out—in the total picture it occupies

too large a chunk of time in relation to its relative importance.

"Most economical, most amusing in its ironic, slightly acid and typically Bergman-esque manner, is the elevator episode. Here Bergman is at his satiric best, abetted by the delightful Eva Dahlbeck and the superbly baffled Gunnar Björnstrand."

— Paul V. Beckley in
The New York Herald Tribune

"The film is a kaleidoscope: three tales from the past, another one that is never told, and a fifth that is the result of the other three, a story in the present. All of the three stories have a comic element; the last is almost pure farce. Film comedy demands a perfect sense of rhythm and an awareness of the relative lengths of scenes and sequences. The director of a comedy must be able to surprise and disarm the spectator. Bergman masters this art in Secrets of Women *without, however, being far from the tragic element which, after all, is the foundation and strength of his art.*"

— Jörn Donner in
The Personal Vision of Ingmar Bergman

Sommaren med Monika
(Monika/Summer with Monika)

Svensk Filmindustri: 1953
(U.S. release by Janus Films/Gaston Hakim: 1956)

CREDITS

Director: Ingmar Bergman; *producer:* Allan Ekelund; *screenwriters:* Ingmar Bergman and Per Anders Fogelström, based on the latter's novel; *cinematographer:* Gunnar Fischer; *editors:* Tage Holmberg and Gösta Lewin; *art directors:* P. A. Lundgren and Nils Svenwall; *music:* Erik Nordgren and Filip Olsson (the waltz "Kärlekens Hamn"); *sound:* Sven Hansen; *running time:* 96 minutes.

CAST

Harriet Andersson (*Monika*); Lars Ekborg (*Harry*); John Harryson (*Lelle*); Georg Skarstedt (*Harry's Father*); Gösta Eriksson (*Forsberg*); Dagmar Ebbeson (*Harry's Aunt*); Åke

Fridell (*Monika's Father*); Naemi Briese (*Monika's Mother*); Åke Grönberg (*Harry's Construction Boss*); Gösta Gustafsson (*Forsberg's Accountant*); Sigge Fürst (*Foreman at Porcelain Warehouse*); Arthur Fischer (*Head of Vegetable Warehouse*); Bengt Eklund (*Foreman at Vegetable Warehouse*); Torsten Lilliecrona (*Driver at Vegetable Warehouse*); Ivar Wahlgren (*Owner of Summer House*); Renée Björling (*His Wife*); Catrin Westerlund (*His Daughter*); Hanny Schedin (*Mrs. Boman*); Nils Hultgren (*Vicar*); Anders Andelius and Gordon Löwenadler (*Monika's Suitors*); Bengt Brunskog (*Sicke*); Ernst Brunman (*Tobacco-Store Owner*).

Begun directly after the completion of *Secrets of Women*, this was the film that introduced Bergman to the talents and personal charms of nineteen-year-old Harriet Andersson, a young actress who had already appeared in nearly a dozen movies for other directors. Bergman's directorial guidance would soon make her known internationally, partially through the sensationalism that would adhere to *Monika*. Because of brief scenes of nudity, the picture encountered censorship problems in Sweden, and Bergman was forced to make cuts before its release there. Later, ironically, an enterprising American distributor acquired a bootleg print of the film, interpolated *additional* nude footage into the print, and subtitled it *The Story of a Bad Girl*. It's interesting to note that the videocassette print currently in U.S. circulation contains only the briefest of long-shot nudity as Andersson takes a swim. In light of more recent cinematic trends, one can only wonder what all the shouting was about.

In essence, *Monika* is a simple tale about the birth and death of youthful love. The hero is a nice boy named Harry (Lars Ekborg) who's picked up by willful young Monika (Andersson) in a cheap café they frequent. Her ploy: She needs a light for her cigarette, which begins conversation culminating in a movie date that night. Both work in menial jobs they hate; Harry's habitually late for his, and Monika has acquired a reputation at hers, where it's strongly implied that she's been intimate with more than one of her co-workers. When the two teens quickly become friendly, she rebels against life in the crowded home she shares with younger siblings and walks out, ap-

pealing to Harry for help. Motherless since he was eight, Harry has only his father, with whom he's not very close.

Among the plot's conveniences is that Harry's father owns a motorboat with a small cabin. Thus, the scene is set not only for the young couple's first night alone together but for their escape from uncomfortable city lives. Having just been fired from his job, Harry is more than receptive when Monika suggests they take the boat out of the city, which leads to a summer sojourn in the Stockholm archipelago, where they live by their wits and without much concern for the real world. Eventually, of course, they run out of food, tire of cooking local mushrooms, and turn to thievery — none too successfully. By this time, Monika is pregnant and cranky and wants to return to civilization. They do so, and Harry marries her in time for the birth of their daughter, a child whom Harry now spends more time attending to than does his bored young wife, who misses her former good times. For Harry, who by now has settled down to become a full-time engineering student, the turning point comes when he returns home unexpectedly and finds Monika with a fellow she had dated prior to Harry. Their future seems to promise imminent divorce, with Harry raising his daughter while Monika pursues her penchant for good times and few cares.

Most of *Monika* was shot with a very small cast and crew on the island of Ornö from July to October 1952. Because the budget was minuscule, much of the production was improvised, and as cinematographer Gunnar Fischer had only a silent Mitchell camera, location scenes were shot silent,

Monika (1953). Lars Ekborg and Harriet Andersson. Svensk Filmindustri.

with dialogue and sound effect dubbed in later.

Bergman on Bergman

"I had just seen Harriet Andersson in *Defiance*, and no girl it seemed to me could be more Monika-ish. She was devastating. I was no little infatuated with Harriet. We were all stuck on her. There's never been a girl in Swedish films who radiated more uninhibited erotic charm than Harriet.

"Making *Summer With Monika* was a lot of fun. When it was over we came home and worked in the studio a bit. The whole film went like a song. And then — the censors cut it."

Critics' Circle

"*Miss Andersson emerges as a sultry, dynamic find as she firmly outlines the character and instability of Monika, the creature of a summer. Ekborg is gentle and affirmative as the loving Harry.*"
—"Mosk" in *Variety*

"*Monika belongs to Bergman's middle period when he was mainly concerned with the problems and tribulations of adolescence: its tone is far removed from the sophisticated ironies and complexities of his more recent work. And yet, in its frank and tender portrait of young love, as well as its realistic, anti-romantic account of a disintegrating marriage, it is unmistakably a Bergman film.*

"*Bergman has been well served by his two leading players. Lars Ekborg's characterization deepens as it progresses and remains, as it must, innocent and perplexed to the end. Even more remarkable is Harriet Andersson's Monika, slovenly, sensual, rejoicing in the power of her body—a portrait as vivid as it is uncompromisingly real.*"
—"J. G." in *Monthly Film Bulletin*

"*Monika personified quite remarkably by Harriet Andersson, is a fascinating study of*

a slut in the making—animal, sensual, un-inhibited, lazy, promiscuous, highly-strung, chain-smoking, all lips and puppy fat and dank, straggling hair. Harry, the errand boy, is an interesting extension of the director's obsession with innocent, betrayable, tor-mented young men: more accessible and less idealized than the usual Bergman juvenile, and faultlessly played (notably in the clos-ing scenes of disillusion and fatherhood) by Lars Ekborg. With Bergman's strong sense of atmosphere to lend a discreet lyricism and grace to their performances, the film achieves a genuine individuality that is rare indeed for such a lightweight script."
— Peter John Dyer in *Films and Filming*

"When some of the tumult and the shout-ing subsides, it may well be noticed that Ing-mar Bergman's earlier films possessed a con-siderable warmth and insight into character. This one is an excellent tragedy of young lovers destroyed by the illusions of an im-pulsive summer romance. The city of Stock-holm is the villain, and Gunnar Fischer's camera handles this with all of the ominous imagery of the drawings of Edvard Munch. Harriet Andersson and Lars Ekborg give brilliant performances as the doomed hero and heroine, and the film is a masterwork of naturalism."
— *Film Quarterly*

"The trouble with Monika is not its sim-ilarity to Illicit Interlude, but its dissimi-larity. The characters are seen in one di-mension only. It is correct to compare this film with Port of Call. In both cases the influence of Italian neorealism is felt: in Port of Call, Rossellini's; in Monika, most sharply de Santis' almost commercial sensu-alism."
— Jörn Donner in *The Personal Vision of Ingmar Bergman*

Gycklarnas Afton
(The Naked Night/Sawdust and Tinsel)
A Sandrews-Bauman release of a Sandrewsproduktion: 1953
(U.S. release by Times Film Corp.: 1956)

CREDITS

Director: Ingmar Bergman; *producer:* Rune Waldekranz; *screenwriter:* Ingmar Bergman; *cinematographers:* Hilding Bladh, Göran Strindberg, and Sven Nykvist; *editor:* Carl-Olov Skeppstedt; *art director:* Bibi Lindstrom; *music:* Karl-Birger Blomdahl; *costumes:* Mago (Max Goldstein); *sound:* Olle Jakobsson; *running time:* 92 minutes.

CAST

Harriet Andersson (*Anne*); Åke Grönberg (*Albert Johansson*); Hasse Ekman (*Frans*); An-ders Ek (*Frost*); Gudrun Brost (*Alma*); Annika Tretow (*Agda, Albert's Wife*); Gunnar Björn-strand (*Sjuberg*); Erik Strandmark (*Jens*); Kiki (*Dwarf*); Åke Fridell (*Officer*); Curt Löw-gren (*Blom*); Majken Torkeli (*Mrs. Ekberg*); Vanjek Hedberg (*Ekberg's Son*); Conrad Gyllenhammar (*Fager*); Mona Sylwan (*Mrs. Fager*); Hanny Schedin (*Aunt Asta*); Michael Fant (*Pretty Anton*); Naemi Brises (*Mrs. Meijer*); Juli Bernby (*Tightrope Walker*); Göran Lundquist and Mats Hådell (*Agda's Boys*).

When Bergman failed to interest Svensk Filmindustri's Carl Anders Dymling in *Gycklarnas Afton*, he found a more receptive producer in Rune Waldekranz, head of production at Sandrews. The project was never seen as a surefire picture for Scandinavian audiences, but Waldekranz reasoned that a "prestige" film by Bergman might attract distributors in other countries. The movie was shot in southern Sweden during the spring and early summer of 1953 and released there that autumn — with little success.

The story, which bore more than a passing resemblance to the German films *Variety* and *The Blue Angel*, is set at the turn of the century as a bankrupt little circus travels from town to rural town. In the course of a twenty-four-hour period, the Circus Alberti pulls into a small community where its middle-aged owner, Albert Johansson (Åke Grönberg), once left a wife and child, to whom he pays an awkward "courtesy" visit. While he is served dinner by his wife, Albert's young mistress, Anne (Harriet Andersson), the troupe's bareback rider, allows herself to be seduced by a glamorous local actor named Frans (Hasse Ekman), who later humiliates both her and Albert during a circus performance. Albert nearly succeeds in committing suicide with his pistol before he's stopped by the clown Frost (Anders Ek). Albert later turns his gun on the circus' ailing bear and kills it. At fade-out, Albert and Anne effect a sorry sort of resignation, to the end that (like the traveling couple in *Three Strange Loves*) reuniting in misery is preferable to facing the future alone.

Little appreciated when it was released, *The Naked Night* (as it was originally retitled by sensation-seeking U.S. distributors) or *Sawdust and Tinsel* (as the more poetic British entrepreneurs named it) has grown in stature as an important milestone — and turning point — in Bergman's evolution from an observer of troubled youth to a chronicler of adult anguish. For many, this film is the beginning of Ingmar Bergman as he has come to be known and appreciated by motion-picture scholars and historians.

Bergman on Bergman

"I though I'd made a good, vital film. Naturally, I experienced both box-office fiasco and critical fiasco as catastrophes. Every time things went to hell, I knew my chances of making any more films had grown slimmer, that they became more and more uncertain and risky every time it happened. My sector narrowed. And that was a most unpleasant sensation."

Critics' Circle

"The extremely turgid and oppressive plot development includes scenes of hysteria, sadism, eroticism and self-pity (with a suggestion of nudity, for good measure), and it is very reminiscent of the German school of the 1920s. There is a total lack of humor, and if the story was intended as a study in human degradation set against a picaresque background, the director's attitude excludes any expression of genuine pity or sympathy. The playing is grimly intense and includes a powerful Jannings-esque performance by Åke Grönberg and a sulky, sensual one by Harriet Andersson."
— "J. G." in *Monthly Film Bulletin*

"Bergman was a scriptwriter before he became a director. It seems incredible, therefore, that this script appears to be a mere peg for some high-class technical tricks. A flashback at the opening of the film, for instance, has no relevance to the plot. This is not to deny that it is quite a dazzling little sequence, full of really imaginative touches. But the script makes it no more than a pointless diversion.
— Derek Hill in *Films and Filming*

"The Naked Night *is a strange, off-beat Swedish film. At times powerful and moving,*

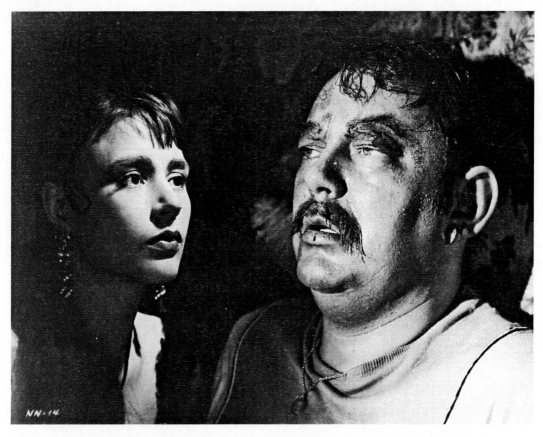

The Naked Night (1953). Harriet Andersson and Åke Grönberg. Sandres-Bauman.

at other moments filled with a virtuosic display of film technique, it is generally probably too heavy and exotic for other than moderate art house possibilities."

— *The Film Daily*

"Sex and morbidity are served up in this strange Swedish import. Directed and written by Ingmar Bergman, the film is a probing search of the tormented souls of a group of turn-of-the-century traveling circus performers.

"It is disturbing in its presentation of the utter degradation of helpless people, apparently caught up in a life from which they cannot escape.

"Miss Andersson and Grönberg provide excellent naturalistic performances. Bergman's direction adds to the overall weirdness of the film, and is especially effective in the close-ups. The photography ranges from interesting innovation to self-conscious arti-

ness. The flashback sequence is presented as if it were footage from early silent films."

— "Holl" in *Variety*

"Writer-director Ingmar Bergman has composed his scenes with a brilliant sense of irony. Above all, he has caught the irony of circus life that has fascinated so many artists. The tent is alive with artificial gayety — clowns, dancing bears, bareback riders and tinny music. But the man who generates all this gayety, the owner in his shiny top hat that is the badge of the carefree barker, is trapped in a life of deepest melancholy. Åke Grönberg gives a powerful performance in this role. He is a big, blustery man, too proud to admit his poverty, goaded first by rage and then by such shame that he tries to kill himself."

— William K. Zinsser in
The New York Herald Tribune

En Lektion i Kärlek
(A Lesson in Love)
Svensk Filmindustri: 1954
(U.S. release by Janus Films: 1960)

CREDITS

Director: Ingmar Bergman; *producer:* Allan Ekelund; *screenwriter:* Ingmar Bergman; *cine-matographer:* Martin Bodin; *editor:* Oscar Rosander; *art director:* P. A. Lundgren; *music:* Dag Wirén; *sound:* Sven Hansen; *assistant director:* Rolf Carlsten; *running time:* 95 minutes.

CAST

Eva Dahlbeck (*Marianne Erneman*); Gunnar Björnstrand (*Dr. David Erneman*); Yvonne Lombard (*Suzanne*); Harriet Andersson (*Nix*); Åke Grönberg (*Carl-Adam*); Olof Winnerstrand (*Prof. Henri Erneman*); Renée Björling (*Svea Erneman*); Birgitte Reimar (*Lise*); John Elfström (*Sam*); Dagmar Ebbesen (*Nurse*); Helge Hagerman (*Traveling Salesman*); Sigge Fürst (*Pastor*); Gösta Prüzelius (*Train Conductor*); Carl Ström (*Uncle Axel*); Arne Lindblad (*Hotel Manager*); Torsten Lilliecrona (*Hotel Porter*); George Adelly (*Bartender*); Yvonne Brosset (*Dancer*); Ingmar Bergman (*Man on the Train*).

A Lesson in Love, Bergman's first full-fledged venture into out-and-out comedy (at times, it's outright farce), came together very quickly. Having just divorced his third wife and on holiday with Harriet Andersson in a resort hotel in Arild, he was inspired to reflect on his marital experiences. Bergman reports that the screenplay was completed in two weeks and that fourteen days later filming got under way. Apparently, the motivation of alimony, children to support, and lack of money in the bank inspired him to the humorous, sometimes bittersweet rumina-tions that form the basis of this complex script about a middle-aged marriage in trouble, with both wife (Eva Dahlbeck) and her gynecologist-husband (Gunnar Björnstrand) straying with extramarital partners as their teenaged daughter (Harriet Andersson) experiences the growing pains of a tomboy who doesn't look forward to approaching womanhood.

Unless followed very closely, the movie's constant use of flashbacks can become terribly confusing, and even when the narrative turns more progressive, the viewer is hard put to know whether the next scene follows in time or is a jump back to yet another remembered incident. At times, Bergman evinces the sly, tongue-in-cheek comic inspiration of a Lubitsch; at others, his scenes of comedic bickering and arch game playing seem uncertain when and how to conclude. For Harriet Andersson, *A Lesson in Love*'s unhappy adolescent, Nix, displays as versatile a switch from the sultry Anne of Bergman's previous *Naked Night* as does that film's male star, Åke Grönberg, seen here as the humorously blustery "old flame" of Dahlbeck's who welcomes her back when Björnstrand finds temporary marital rejuvenation in an affair with a pretty and predatory young patient (Yvonne Lombard).

Not unexpectedly, Swedish audiences found much to amuse them in *A Lesson in Love*. Incidentally, Bergman does yet another Hitchcock-style cameo in the scene in which Gunnar Björnstrand passes him in the train corridor.

Bergman on Bergman

"*A Lesson in Love* grew out of my relationship with Gunnar Björnstrand and Eva Dahlbeck — and the lift sequence in *Waiting Women*. I began jotting down little scenes — marital scenes — which I found more and more amusing; and then I thought of Gunnar Björnstrand and Eva Dahlbeck, and they amused me even more. The whole job was entirely frivolous."

Critics' Circle

"*There are some good ideas, but the script wanders and is cluttered up with far too many second-rate-epigrams. The acting is uneven and sometimes grossly unsubtle. Björnstrand's astringent comic talent is swamped by orgies of plate-smashing slapstick; Harriet Andersson is faultless in the unrewarding part of a worried growing girl; Eva Dahlbeck alone manages to negotiate the film's ugly switches from low farce to high*

comedy with consummate ease and skill. But for these two actresses, I am afraid I would have found A Lesson in Love *absolutely intolerable.*"
— Peter John Dyer in
Films and Filming

"*Bergman keeps this moving with shrewd insight into character. However, there is a tendency to go in for too much talk and epigrams on the frailties of love and marriage. But cohesive acting, knowing direction and the right balance between character and complications make this an above average situation comedy.*"
— "Mosk" in *Variety*

"*This 1954 comedy finds Bergman doing a turn as Ernst Lubitsch, with a few epigrammatic flourishes à la René Clair. Except for some gifted clowning by Eva Dahlbeck, it is not very funny. It entertains by the number of elegant variations it makes on a favorite Bergman theme, the psychology of marriage, but its levity is severely qualified by intimations of anguish that challenge the spectator to deeper reflection than Bergman's tinselly resolution would seem to provoke.*"
— Arlene Croce in *Film Quarterly*

"*It is not the technical devices, such as his frequent flashbacks, that make his skill so impressive, but the way he can flit from high comedy to near slapstick to wry disillusionment to scenes of gentle pathos. His step is not only nimble, but sure. This is what gives* Lesson *its peculiar airiness while at the same time keeping it solid...*

"*No one interested in fine films should miss even a minor Bergman, for if it did nothing else it would give bright insights into the man's major works.*"
— Paul V. Beckley in
The New York Herald Tribune

"*The opening is a gem of indirection as Björnstrand disentangles himself from his mistress, then seemingly picks up an attractive matron on a train. Not until the picture leaps into flashback do we discover that she is in fact his wife. Piqued by his many infidelities, she is on her way to keep a tryst with a former lover. Past and present intermingle as husband and lover vie with each*

A Lesson in Love (1954). Harriet Andersson and Gunnar Björnstrand. Svensk Filmindustri.

other to win her back. Not much of a story perhaps; but Bergman, once again his own script writer, has threaded it with deliciously naughty dialogue, some wonderful farce comedy, and a good many telling jabs at the battle of the sexes."
— Arthur Knight in *Saturday Review*

"For those who have not seen Bergman pictures, A Lesson in Love *is a good one with which to begin. But for those who have become familiar with him, it will seem what it is—a precocious exercise."*
— Bosley Crowther in
The New York Times

Kvinnodröm
(Dreams/Journey into Autumn)
Sandrews-Bauman release of a Sandrewproduktion: 1955
(U.S. release by Janus Films: 1960)

CREDITS

Director: Ingmar Bergman; *producer:* Rune Waldekranz; *screenwriter:* Ingmar Bergman; *cinematographer:* Hilding Bladh; *editor:* Carl-Olov Skeppstedt; *art director:* Gittan Gutafsson; *music:* Stuart Görling; *sound:* Olle Jakobsson; *assistant director:* Hans Abramson; *running time:* 86 minutes.

CAST

Eva Dahlbeck (*Susanne*); Harriet Andersson (*Doris*); Gunnar Björnstrand (*Consul Sönderby*); Ulf Palme (*Henrik Lobelius*); Inga Landgré (*Mrs. Lobelius*); Sven Lindberg (*Palle*); Naima Wifstrand (*Mrs. Arén*); Benkt Åke Benktsson (*Magnus*); Git Gay (*Lady in studio*); Ludde Gentzel (*Sundström, the Photographer*); Kerstin Hedeby (*Marianne*); Gunhild Kjellqvist (*Dark-Haired Lady in Studio*); Renée Björling (*Mrs. Berger*); Jessie Flaws (*Makeup Artist*); Tord Ståhl (*Mr. Barse*); Marianne Nielsen (*Fanny*); Siv Ericks (*Katja*); Bengt Schütt (*Fashion Designer*); Axel Düberg (*Photographer in Stockholm*); Asta Beckman (*Waitress*); Carl Gustaf Lindstedt (Porter); Richard Mattson (*Månsson*); Inga Gill (*Shopgirl*); Per-Erik Åström (*Chauffeur*); Ingmar Bergman (*Man Walking Dog in Hotel Corridor*).

Dreams appears deceptively simple — at first. The focus here is on two women in the fashion business: Susanne (Eva Dahlbeck) is the beautiful, middle-aged manager of a Stockholm fashion-photography studio whose employees all seem to know that she is carrying the torch for a married man who lives in Gothenburg; Doris (Harriet Andersson) is apparently her favorite among the young models who work for her, but the girl is having problems with her boyfriend Palle (Sven Lindberg), who objects to Doris's business travels for locations shoots. When the two women board a train for Gothenburg, Palle breaks off with the unhappy Doris, and Susanne nervously anticipates contacting Henrik Lobelius (Ulf Palme), from whom she separated seven months earlier. In Gothenburg, Doris is an hour late for the fashion shoot after she allows herself to be picked up by a kindly older gentleman (Gunnar Björnstrand), who appears to take a fatherly interest in her, persuading her to let him buy her the evening dress she admires in a shop window, with shoes and necklace to match. Swept up in this Cinderella fairy tale, she persuades him to take her for an amusement-park ride that becomes an afternoon's outing and culminates in their going back to Lobelius's mansion, where she realizes that his interest in her stems from

her resemblance to a portrait of his mentally confined wife. A cruel confrontation with the man's avaricious daughter breaks the spell; Doris returns all the gifts to her momentary benefactor and flees from the house.

With the fashion shoot ruined for the day, Susanne turns her attentions to her former lover, spying on his house and family and even calling him at work. Finally, he agrees to meet her. It's a bittersweet, somewhat cool reunion that's interrupted by a surprise visitor — his wife (Inga Landgré), who quietly and calmly reveals that she knows all about their affair, but that Henrik, whose business is failing, will never leave her because not only does he need her wealth, but he's really too weak to leave their marriage. After she departs and the lovers say goodbye, Henrik returns, and Susanne's hopes soar, but only for a moment; he's forgotten his briefcase.

Back at their hotel, Doris and Susanne mend their differences, and the latter informs the younger woman that she'll help her win back Palle's affections. Back in Stockholm, a letter arrives from Henrik as Susanne is supervising a camera session; he writes that he wants them to meet again and resume their liaison. Wisely, Susanne tears up his message and throws it away. Finally, she seems to have outgrown her need for him.

Dreams (1955). Eva Dahlbeck, Ulf Palme and Inga Landgré. Sandrews-Bauman.

In the year that *Dreams* was released, many would probably have termed it "a woman's picture," for Bergman had by now determined that the fair sex was assuredly of more interest to him as a creative artist than was his own. As writer-director of *Dreams*, he was obviously well equipped at this stage of his artistic growth to probe the female psyche, especially with such expressive interpreters at his command as Eva Dahlbeck and Harriet Andersson. Gunnar Björnstrand, fine character actor that he is, makes Consul Sönderby's enigmatic behavior always interesting, but the role is sketchily developed, and there remain details of his odd behavior that leave the viewer dissatisfied.

Again, Bergman makes a brief appearance, this time passing Dahlbeck and Andersson in their hotel corridor, pulling a small dog on a leash and sporting his then-customary black beret.

For some reason, *Dreams* was not a local success, not even with Swedish shopgirls.

Bergman on Bergman

"It's a boring film. I must have been tired when I made it. That wasn't a good time."

Critics' Circle

"*Bergman shrewdly dovetails the adventures of an older and younger woman before they come of emotional age. Though seemingly slick and melodramatic on the surface, the keen notations, solid narrative and*

expert blending of direction and acting make this a deep tale of emotional upheavals."
— "Mosk" in *Variety*

"Within the framework of two overlapping episodes, in the past one of Bergman's most successful devices, are contrived scenes of austere anti-romanticism and painful irony. The very beginning, in Susanne's studio, is frankly terrible: tapping fingers, ticking clocks, enigmatic stares, a caricature of a 'queer' and heaps of theatrical menace. But this is directly followed by one of the best things in the film, the overnight train journey to Gothenburg. Bergman has always adored playing trains, and the visual excitement and evocative soundtrack of this sequence are remarkable: Susanne leaning suicidally from the corridor window, her face streaked with rain and smoke, then returning to the compartment and the cold stare of the intrigued girl.
— Peter John Dyer in
Films and Filming

"With bittersweet delicacy no longer present in Ingmar Bergman's films, this Swedish director is musing over the fragile nature of romantic hopes in Dreams, *a film from an earlier period of Bergman's development. One of his striking ideas at the time was his use of pantomime, particularly in the occasional moments of sly comedy. The film runs for nearly ten minutes before the dialogue begins."*
— Alton Cook in
The New York World-Telegram

"Eva Dahlbeck contributes a largely introspective portrayal of the disillusioned career woman. It is a finely shaded stint in which a viewer is delicately shown the capitulation of an intelligent woman, against her best intentions, to the dictates of her heart. Harriet Andersson's delineation of the model is a similarly sensitive job, one in which the petulance, ardor and abandon of youth are expertly projected. Ulf Palme is properly tender and weak as the lover who chooses the respectability of wife and home over the love he desperately seeks from his mistress."
— A. H. Weiler in
The New York Times

"Although hardly on a level with his works of more recent vintage, Dreams *reveals Bergman in full technical control of each element—actors, camera, lighting, sound. The photographer's neurasthenia is conveyed by exaggerating the sounds she hears in her studio. Flashing lights and criss-crossing rails suggest her emotions as she rushes by train to her lover. Mirrors, the reflectors of reality, abound in the love passages. And there are long dialogue sequences daringly played from a single camera position, the movement of the performers subtly shifting the emphasis of the scene from moment to moment. Because Bergman knows precisely what each shot must convey in the overall pattern of his picture, there is nothing wasted, no pauses for pretty scenery or repetitive action. He doesn't need them. It is his story; and obviously what animates him is his theme, not the effects he can introduce to put it across."*
— Arthur Knight
in *Saturday Review*

"A sophisticated serio-comic study of four women and three men, it is almost without the symbolist touches Bergman so often employs and, for all that it is a minor work, one might say now a work of portent rather than achievement, it is none the less an intriguing picture."
— Paul V. Beckley in
The New York Herald Tribune

Dreams *is the second installment of the shrewdly ironic, lewdly hilarious trilogy, beginning with* A Lesson in Love *(1953) and ending with* Smiles of a Summer Night *(1955), in which Bergman submits His frontline report on the war between the sexes. In* Lesson, *the war begins with crockery barrages. In* Smiles, *it ends in a saraband of sophisticated satire that the winners and the losers dance together. In* Dreams, *the battle rages in full fury, and Bergman zooms above the field like a happy gadfly, pranging everything in sight. He obviously relishes the idea of feminine superiority. His actors, as usual, are excellent."*
— *Time*

Sommarnattens Leende
(Smiles of a Summer Night)

Svensk Filmindustri: 1955
(U.S. release by Rank Film Distributors of America: 1957)

CREDITS

Director: Ingmar Bergman; *producer:* Allan Ekelund; *screenwriter:* Ingmar Bergman; *cinematographer:* Gunnar Fischer; *editor:* Oscar Rosander; *art director:* P. A. Lundgren; *costumes:* Mago (Max Goldstein); *music:* Erik Nordgren; *sound:* P. O. Pettersson; *assistant director:* Lennart Olsson; *running time:* 108 minutes.

CAST

Eva Dahlbeck (*Desirée Armfeldt*); Gunnar Björnstrand (*Fredrik Egerman*); Ulla Jacobsson (*Anne Egerman*); Björn Bjelvenstam (*Henrik Egerman*); Naima Wifstrand (*Old Mme. Armfeldt*); Harriet Andersson (*Petra*); Margit Carlquist (*Charlotte Malcolm*); Jarl Kulle (*Count Carl-Magnus Malcolm*); Åke Fridell (*Frid*); Jullan Kindahl (*Beata, the Cook*); Gull Natorp (*Malla, Desirée's Maid*); Birgitta Valberg and Bibi Andersson (*Actresses*); Anders Wulff (*Desirée's Son*); Gunnar Nielsen (*Niklas*); Göstas Prüzelius (*Footman*); Svea Holst (*Dresser*); Hans Straat (*Photographer Almgren*); Lisa Lundholm (*Mrs. Almgren*); Sigge Fürst (*Policeman*); Lena Söderblom and Mona Malm (*Chambermaids*); Josef Norrman (*Elderly Dinner Guest*); Arne Lindblad (*Actor*); Börje Mellvig (*Assessor*); Ulf Johansson (*Legal Assistant*); Yngve Nordwall (*Ferdinand*); Sten Gester and Mille Schmidt (*Servants*).

Ingmar Bergman's second costume piece announces itself as a "romantic comedy" on the film's title frame. As such, it marks a groundbreaking milestone in his filmography and a far cry from what his previous works might have let one to expect, despite the sexual humor of *A Lesson in Love*. But its sly and elegant wit impressed critics and audiences alike, making this *La Ronde* of period manners a success of international proportions.

In turn-of-the-century Sweden, a well-to-do, middle-aged lawyer (Gunnar Björnstrand) behaves like a doting father with his still-virginal second wife (Ulla Jacobsson), a girl the same age as his equally innocent but lovesick son (Björn Bjelvenstam), a theology student who's sexually tempted by their flirtatious maidservant (Harriet Andersson). When the lawyer takes his wife to the theater, she tearfully discovers that the play's glamorous leading lady (Eva Dahlbeck) is her husband's former mistress. When the lawyer pays his old flame a postperformance visit, he's caught in a compromising position by her current love, a jealous but married count (Jarl Kulle). The actress moves to straighten out some of these entanglements with the help of her elderly mother (Naima Wifstrand), whose country estate becomes the scene of a midsummer weekend house party, during which a few changes take place. Almost suicidal with despair, the student is unexpectedly thrown together with his stepmother, and they decide to run off together. A mock game of Russian roulette ends with the lawyer turning back to the actress, while the count is forgiven by his all-knowing wife (Margit Carlquist). And the maid, who has spent the night with the old lady's footman (Åke Fridell), appears headed for the altar.

Smiles of a Summer Night **(1955). Harriet Andersson and Ulla Jacobsson. Svensk Filmindustri.**

It's interesting to note the versatile role-changes achieved by the "Bergman stock company"; following their respective parts in *Dreams*, Gunnar Björnstrand goes from indulgent, elderly consul to Van Dyke–bearded lawyer and lover; Eva Dahlbeck switches from lovelorn businesswoman to great actress of affairs; and Harriet Andersson moves from sophisticated fashion model to bawdy maidservant, turning her brunet hair blonde in the process.

At the 1956 Cannes Film Festival, *Smiles of a Summer Night* won a Special Jury Prize for its "most poetic humor." Bergman's original screenplay would go on to provide the basis for Stephen Sondheim's sparkling 1973 stage musical *A Little Night Music*, as well as its curiously lackluster 1978 movie adaptation. And the Swedish original also inspired Woody Allen's 1982 film *A Midsummer Night's Sex Comedy.*

Bergman on Bergman

"As for *Smiles of a Summer Night*, the situation was simply that I needed another success. I'd promised Carl Anders Dymling that my next film wouldn't be a tragedy. He'd also intimated that if it was to be a serious piece, well then I hardly need bother my head about making a film that summer. I needed money, so I thought it wise to make a comedy."

Critics' Circle

"Turning from the contemporary scene to a period comedy of manners, Ingmar Bergman has evoked the spirits of Schnitzler,

Wilde and Strindberg in this decidedly Nordic morality play. Maneuvering his collection of fickle husbands and scheming wives and mistresses with cool detachment, Bergman delivers his sardonic comments on the vagaries of love mainly through epigrammatic dialogue closely reflecting 19th–century models. Consequently, one is lightly amused without being either emotionally involved or moved by this parade of infidelity. There are some lively performances by Eva Dahlbeck as the resourceful mistress and Gunnar Björnstrand and Jarl Kulle as the husbands. Delicately luminous photography and some stylish set decorations give the film an attractive visual gloss."
— "J. G." in *Monthly Film Bulletin*

"The bulk of this hothouse comedy concerns the weekend party. The intricate sexual relationships involved throughout its duration are as claustrophobic and compelling as a plot fabricated by Jean Cocteau.

"'Youth is unkind,' says the lonely, wicked old lady; but young Henrik finds his elders cruel and disgusting. Nevertheless, I can find no bitterness to spoil the taste of the film — nothing can take away its beauty. Bergman explores its moods of longing and regret with wonderful compassion and perception. The entire, vibrant wealth of this film is exquisite."
— Peter John Dyer in
Films and Filming

"In a style of writing more characteristic of the French or perhaps the pre-war Hungarians than the usually solemn Swedes, Mr. Bergman skips us gaily through a mix-up of youthful and adult love affairs, which, while timed around the turn of the century, are as spicy as any such today."
— Bosley Crowther in
The New York Times

"Smiles of a Summer Night *lies complete and closed within itself, to some extent impossible to reach. Of its kind, it is perfect. But the picture has a strange, perfumed, ingratiating atmosphere which scarcely harmonizes with the predominant line in Bergman's production. Still, the tragic element exists, based on the characters presented. The laughter is bitter.*"
— Jörn Donner in
The Personal Vision of Ingmar Bergman

"Ingmar Bergman achieves one of the few classics of carnal comedy: a tragicomic chase and roundelay that raises boudoir farce to elegance and lyric poetry. The film becomes an elegy to transient love; a gust of wind, and the whole vision may drift away."
— Pauline Kael in
5001 Nights at the Movies

"One of the finest romantic comedies ever made, a witty treatise on manners, mores and sex during a weekend at a country estate in the late 19th century."
— *Leonard Maltin's Movie and Video Guide*

Det Sjunde Inseglet (The Seventh Seal)

Svensk Filmindustri: 1957
(U.S. release by Janus Films: 1958)

CREDITS

Director: Ingmar Bergman; *producer:* Allan Ekelund; *screenwriter:* Ingmar Bergman, based on his play *Painting on Wood; cinematographer:* Gunnar Fischer; *editor:* Lennart Wallén;

art director: P. A. Lundgren; *costumes:* Manne Lindholm; *music:* Erik Nordgren; *sound:* Aaby Wedin; *special sound effects:* Evald Andersson; *choreographer:* Else Fisher; *assistant director:* Lennart Olsson; *running time:* 96 minutes.

CAST

Max von Sydow (*Antonius Block*); Gunnar Bjornstrand (*Squire Jöns*); Nil Poppe (*Jof*); Bibi Andersson (*Mia*); Bengt Ekerot (*Death*); Åke Fridell (*Plog, the Blacksmith*); Inga Gill (*Lisa, Plog's Wife*); Maud Hansson (*Witch*); Inga Landgré (*Knight's Wife*); Gunnel Lindblom (*Mute Girl*); Bertil Anderberg (*Raval*); Anders Ek (*Doomsday Monk*); Gunnar Olsson (*Church Painter*); Erik Standmark (*Skat*); Lars Lind (*Young Monk*); Benkt-Åke Benktsson (*Innkeeper*); Gudrun Brost (*Woman in Tavern*); Ulf Johansson (*Leader of the Soldiers*).

With *The Seventh Seal*, Bergman, taking a giant step beyond anything he'd previously accomplished, offered a bleak allegory on man's spiritual destiny. Its medieval setting, its sometimes enigmatic narrative, and its vivid images of sea and sky and human suffering take his audience to places Bergman had never led them before. In going against the grain of so-called populist cinema, he has created a classic for the ages and one of the motion-picture monuments for which he will be remembered. This was the first of several movies that would put Bergman high on the roster of international directors considered giants of the twentieth century.

Svensk Filmindustri's Carl Anders Dymling only agreed to produce this admittedly noncommercial project if Bergman could film it on a modest budget and bring it in within thirty-five days, which he proceeded to do in July–August 1956. *The Seventh Seal* had had its genesis in a one-act play Bergman called *Painting on Wood*. Its inspiration was the church paintings that had so intrigued the young Ingmar, with their depiction of the Black Plague, flagellants, the burning of witches, and Death leading a macabre dance.

The film's story line is relatively simple. During the plague-ridden Middle Ages, a disillusioned knight (Max von Sydow) returns from the Crusades with his squire (Gunner Björnstrand) after a ten-year absence. On the seashore, they encounter Death (Bengt Ekerot), for whom the knight isn't yet ready. Instead, he proposes a game of chess as a means of gaining time to allay his doubts about God. Death agrees, permitting the two men to journey into the land as their game progresses. Consequently, the knight gets a firsthand glimpse of the devastation waged by the Black Plague amid a populace rife with evil and corruption. They also encounter more encouraging examples of human goodness in the person of a little family of strolling players (Nils Poppe and Bibi Andersson, standing in for the biblical Mary and Joseph, with their little son). Eventually, the knight manages to distract Death by upsetting the chess pieces, thus allowing the family to escape safely before the Dark One leads the others over the crest of a hill to their final destination.

The Seventh Seal retains a number of the proverbial "Bergman stock company" players while discarding others. For the first time, he introduces Max von Sydow, who will continue to play major roles in most of the Bergman films to come. And making a near debut with Bergman is Bibi Andersson, who enjoys a major role here after first appearing in the bit part of a stage actress in the play-within-the-film sequence of *Smiles of a Summer Night*.

Among its various accolades, *The Seventh Seal* took home a Special Jury Prize as the Most Artistic Film at 1957's Cannes Film Festival and won a Grand Prix International du Film d'Avant Garde from the French Cinema Academy in 1958.

Bergman on Bergman

"As a film it just happened. I can't remember any complications. The complications began when Svensk Filmindustri celebrated some sort of mysterious half-centenary by showing it. As a first night the atmosphere was less festive than murderous.

"It was a triumph to have carried through that large and complicated shooting schedule in such a short time, and so cheaply. It was fun reconstructing a whole epoch with such incredibly simple means."

Critics' Circle

"As a piece of story-telling, the film is rich in detail, complex, ominous: while the bones of the fable stand out strong, compelling, almost over-simple. There are many superb performances, notably from Gunnar Björnstrand, terse and precise as the squire, and Bengt Ekerot's sardonic, impassive, macabre Death; the photography by Gunnar Fischer is quite outstandingly beautiful; and everywhere there is a faultless sense of period. The film, indeed, incorporates all the traditions of Scandinavian period cinema, with the spiritual doubt and savage battle personal to Bergman.

"In every way, then, this is a rare and moving masterpiece. The Swedish cinema must still be very, very much alive."

— Peter John Dyer in
Films and Filming

"Essentially, it is a morality play set against the Black Plague that raged through Europe in the middle of the fourteenth century. But the beauties of The Seventh Seal — both a physical beauty and a loftiness of conception — are accented by a terror that Bergman produces with the simplest of means. We are told of the Black Plague, and we see a great hawk hovering motionless in an empty sky. We are told of Death, and we see two horses standing alone, riderless on a rocky beach. A man sits huddled in a cowl, and for a moment the camera reveals his plague-ridden face. A band of flagellants make their way across a plain, and the cam-

era holds upon the desolation in the wake of their passing. As the Knight makes his confession in a lonely church, his confessor turns and it is Death. These are moments of psychological, not physical, horror. The Seventh Seal *is not a horror picture; but in the end, when the light returns, it produces the same sensation of having been purged and cleaned.*"

— Arthur Knight in *Saturday Review*

"This initially mystifying drama slowly turns out to be a piercing and powerful contemplation of the passage of man upon this earth. Essentially intellectual, yet emotionally stimulating, too, it is as tough — and rewarding — a screen challenge as the moviegoer has had to face this year.

"Mr. Bergman uses his camera and actors for sharp, realistic effects. And his actors are excellent, from Max von Sydow as the gaunt and towering knight, through Gunnar Björnstrand as his squire and Bengt Ekerot as Death to Maud Hansson as the piteous 'witch.' Nils Poppe as the strolling player and Bibi Andersson as his wife are warming and cheerful companions in an uncommon and fascinating film."

— Bosley Crowther in
The New York Times

"Bergman has an undeniable gift for expressing anguish, humiliation, and dread — a gift which found a much better vehicle in a much less ambitious film, Sawdust and Tinsel/The Naked Night. *In fact, the scene that rings most true in* The Seventh Seal *is one in which the strolling player is grotesquely humiliated in the tavern. Nevertheless, the film is full of beautiful images and powerful atmosphere. The acting of the leading players is stylish and strong, injecting more humanity into their allegorical characters than might have seemed possible.*"

— "J. M." in *Monthly Film Bulletin*

"The various internal dramas of the film are brilliantly controlled by Bergman. His skill in staging a scene, in composing it, in moving the camera, and in obtaining performances of stature from a varied cast is breathtaking. He owes much to his cameraman, Gunnar Fischer, who also photographed

The Seventh Seal (1957). Bengt Ekerot and Max von Sydow. Svensk Filmindustri.

Smiles of a Summer Night, *and it is only in minor places that Bergman might be thought to falter, although the choice of music (by Erik Nordgren) seems oddly theatrical. Perhaps his principal dramatic achievement, in the script as much as in the direction, is to leave us with a feeling always of character, never only of symbol. In a piece which is nonetheless rich in symbolic imagery, the characters emerge as people.*
— Colin Young in *Film Quarterly*

"It's a magically powerful film—the story seems to be playing itself out in a medieval present. The images and the omens are medieval, but the modern erotic and psychological insights add tension, and in some cases, as in the burning of the child-witch, excruciating. The actors' faces, the aura of magic, the ambiguities, and the riddle at the heart of the film all contribute to its stature."
— Pauline Kael in
5001 Nights at the Movies

Smultronstället
(Wild Strawberries)

Svensk Filmindustri: 1957
(U.S. release by Janus Films: 1959)

CREDITS

Director: Ingmar Bergman; *producer:* Allan Ekelund; *screenwriter:* Ingmar Bergman; *cinematographer:* Gunnar Fischer; *editor:* Oscar Rosander; *art director:* Gittan Gustafsson; *costumes:* Millie Ström; *music:* Erik Nordgren; *sound:* Aaby Wedin; *assistant director:* Gösta Ekman; *running time:* 90 minuets.

CAST

Victor Sjöström (*Prof. Isak Borg*); Bibi Andersson (*Sara*); Ingrid Thulin (*Marianne*); Gunnar Björnstrand (*Evald*); Folke Sundquist (*Anders*); Björn Bjelvenstam (*Viktor*); Naima Wifstrand (*Isak's Mother*); Jullan Kindahl (*Agda, the Housekeeper*); Gunnar Sjöberg (*Alman*); Gunnel Broström (*Mrs. Alman*); Gertrud Fridh (*Isak's Wife*); Åke Fridell (*Her Lover*); Max von Sydow (*Åkerman*); Sif Ruud (*Aunt*); Yngve Nordwall (*Uncle Aron*); Per Sjöstrand (*Sigfrid*); Gio Petré (*Sigbritt*); Gunnel Lindblom (*Charlotta*); Maud Hansson (Angelica); Anne-Mari Wiman (*Mrs. Åkerman*); Per Skogsberg (*Hagbart*); Göran Lindquist (*Benjamin*); Eva Norée (*Anna*); Monica Ehrling (*Birgitta*); Vendela Rudbäck (*Elisabeth*); Helge Wulff (*Rector, University of Lund*); Gunnar Olsson (*Bishop*); Josef Norman (*Professor Tiger*).

Although it never descends to sentimentality, *Wild Strawberries* evinces a sense of loss and what-might-have-been better than most films that have touched on this elusive subject. It is also one of the rare pictures to have dealt with the unpopular subject of old age, and managed it in such a way that audiences don't seem to have been turned off by it. In short, *Wild Strawberries* has become a motion-picture classic in spite of its themes. Surprisingly, it was released in the same year its auteur brought forth *The Seventh Seal*. That Ingmar Bergman could have created two such different, such widely admired works in succession marks 1957 as the early apex of his richest filmmaking period.

Characteristically, *Wild Strawberries* follows a deceptively simple story line: An elderly professor (Victor Sjöström) is driving to an awards ceremony with his coolly detached daughter-in-law (Ingrid Thulin). En route, certain locales where they pause inspire daydreams and a flood of memories as the professor reflects on his life, with its joys and its sorrows. Three young people, whom he offers a ride, elicit thoughts of his youth, especially since the girl (Bibi Andersson) closely resembles the youthful love who was taken away from him by a rival. Before they reach their destination, his daughter-in-law reveals that her marriage may be about to end, since she is pregnant with a child her husband (Gunnar Björnstrand) wants her to abort. The old man realizes that his son's lack of humanity derives from his own cold personality. A brief stop to pay his respects to his ninety-six-year-old mother (Naima Wifstrand) reminds him of the emotional independence he has inherited from her. Reflecting on what he has become, in light of the reactions of others, the professor realizes it isn't too late to respond to life and the living.

Although the professor, as so warmly played by the superb Victor Sjöström (one of the great directors in the annals of Swedish cinema), never quite convinces us that he is as cold and unfeeling as the screenplay asks us to believe, *Wild Strawberries* sometimes plays like a far subtler variation on Dickens's *Christmas Carol*, with its ghosts, its dream scenes, and its psychological rejuvenation of an elderly man whose self-absorption has left no room for friends or family. Bergman's own family voids and childhood memories undoubtedly brought much to the creation of this screenplay.

Wild Strawberries proved extremely popular in Sweden as well as elsewhere, and

***Wild Strawberries* (1957). Ingrid Thulin and Victor Sjöström. Svensk Filmindustri.**

it won prestigious awards at the film festivals in Berlin (Grand Prize), Mar del Plata (Grand Prize), and Venice (Critics' Prize). America's National Board of Review named it 1959's Best Foreign Film and Victor Sjöström that year's Best Actor. Hollywood awarded it only an Oscar *nomination*— for Best Screenplay.

Bergman on Bergman

"Nowadays I don't suffer much from nostalgia, but I used to. I think [Swedish poet] Maria Wine has said somewhere that one sleeps in one's childhood shoes. Well, that's exactly how it was. Then it struck me: supposing I make a film of someone coming along, perfectly realistically, and suddenly opening a door and walking into his childhood? And then opening another door and walking out into reality again? And than walking round the corner of the street and coming into some other period of his life, and everything still alive and going on as before? That was the real starting point of *Wild Strawberries.*"

Critics' Circle

"At a time when so much kindness, tolerance and security have gone out of life, when faith has been at its lowest ebb for centuries, it is not surprising that the stark and relentless quest of an uncommercial director like Ingmar Bergman should make such a unique impact on the cinema. There is nobody quite like him. He is cruelly unsentimental, yet shows deep human sentiment. He has the rapt wonder of a poet, yet is fully conscious of the bustling, bourgeois world around him. He hangs on to youth and life, yet remains preoccupied with old age and death. He is austere, yet accessible; lauded yet lonely; sophisticated yet wild ... and one

is reminded of these paradoxes more strongly than ever in Wild Strawberries. *"*

— Peter John Dyer
in *Films and Filming*

"The framework for Wild Strawberries *is deceptively simple: it is a tale of one day in the life of an elderly professor of medicine, who is being honored for fifty years of service. But within the frame are fascinating complexities, minglings of dream and reality, of past and present. The time shifts and back-flashes, although on occasion cumbersome, are achieved with lucidity. The professor is played by Victor Sjöström, once a famed director of silent films who returned to acting after a frustrating Hollywood career and who is now Sweden's most eminent actor. His performance is remarkably subtle and sensitive, as he lives through a dreamlike day and a past that is nostalgic and painful."*

— Hollis Alpert in *Saturday Review*

"Bergman's use of sound and silence is so strong it can shock more emphatically than his visual images. He has obviously made use of the fact that sound goes more swiftly to the nerve centers than things seen.

"This man has made a movie out of such a wealth of photographic images of unusual power that if such were cut into more conventional films, a few of them would be enough to haunt a whole movie. His Wild Strawberries, *if nothing else, is a visual adventure, and bits of it will cling in the memory a long time."*

— Paul V. Beckley in
The New York Herald Tribune

*"*Wild Strawberries *is Director Bergman's 18th film, and it has been widely acclaimed as his masterpiece. Like most of Bergman's pictures,* Wild Strawberries *is smashingly beautiful to see. He works in chiaroscuro—the light expresses the innocence of the doctor's youth, the dark describes the moral gloom of his old age. More important, Bergman employs the language of dream and symbol with an eerie, sleep-talking sureness; some of the old man's dreams are as believable and profound as any ever filmed."*

— *Time*

"If any of you thought you had trouble understanding what Ingmar Bergman was trying to convey in his beautifully poetic and allegorical Swedish film, The Seventh Seal, *wait until you see his* Wild Strawberries. *This one is so thoroughly mystifying that we wonder whether Mr. Bergman himself knew what he was trying to say.*

"Mr. Bergman, being a poet with a camera, gets some grand, open, sensitive images, but he has not conveyed full clarity in this film. And the English subtitles are not much help.

— Bosley Crowther in
The New York Times

"Man's inability to communicate with other men has always been an essential part of Bergman's philosophy, but he has never expressed this theme so strongly or indicated so passionately his belief in the necessity of making a positive attempt. Wild Strawberries *is a film about life, and life, to Bergman, can only be expressed through man's relationship to other men.*

"In every respect a great film, Wild Strawberries *is something more; a profoundly modern work of art. It is Ingmar Bergman's personal answer to the widespread theory that modern civilization is incapable of producing tragedy, and, to anyone who appreciates Bergman's significance in modern cinema, modern philosophy, and modern art, it is probable that his answer will seem decisive."*

— Eugene Archer
in *Film Quarterly*

"It's a very uneven film, an eminent physician looks back over his life, which is tricked up with gothic effects and contrasts and with peculiarly unconvincing flashbacks and over-explicit dialogue. It's a very lumpy odyssey, yet who can forget Sjöström's face, or the vicious, bickering couple who rasp at each other in the back seat of a car, or the large-scale mask of the beautiful Ingrid Thulin as the physician's unhappy daughter-in-law? Few movies give us such memorable, emotion-charged images."

— Pauline Kael in
5001 Nights at the Movies

"The great problem for the film is that the beneficence Victor Sjöström projects is at odds with Bergman's conception of Isak as a man who is cold and withdrawn. Yet in terms of emotive effect and richness of texture, Sjöström's performance is the most absorbing feature of the film. The humanity of his face is constantly fascinating, as Bergman himself notes in a diary he kept during the shooting of the movie. 'I never stop prying, shamelessly studying this powerful face,' he writes."

— Robert Emmet Long in
Ingmar Bergman: Film and Stage

Nära Livet
(Brink of Life/So Close to Life)

Nordisk Tonefilm: 1958
(U.S. release by Ajay Film Co.: 1959)

CREDITS

Director: Ingmar Bergman; *producer:* Gösta Hammerbäck; *screenwriters:* Ingmar Bergman and Ulla Isaksson; based on Isaksson's short stories *"The Friendly and Dignified"* and *"The Immovable"* in her book *Döndens Faster* (Death's Aunt); *cinematographer:* Max Wilén; *editor:* Carl-Olov Skeppstedt; *art director:* Bibi Lindström; *sound:* Lennart Svensson; *medical advisor:* Dr. Lars Engström; *running time:* 84 minutes.

CAST

Eva Dahlbeck (*Stina Andersson*); Ingrid Thulin (*Cecilia Ellius*); Bibi Andersson (*Hjördis Pettersson*); Barbro Hiort af Ornäs (*Sister Brita*); Erland Josephson (*Anders Ellius*); Inga Landgré (*Greta Ellius*); Max von Sydow (*Harry Andersson*); Gunnar Sjöberg (*Dr. Nordlander*); Anne-Marie Gyllenspetz (*Social Worker*); Sissi Kaiser (*Sister Marit*); Margareta Krook (*Dr. Larsson*); Lars Lind (*Dr. Thylenius*); Monica Ekberg (*Hjördis's Friend*); Gun Jönsson (*Night Nurse*); Inga Gill (*New Mother*); Kristina Adolphson (*Practical Nurse*); Gunnar Nielsen (*Doctor*); Maud Elfsiö (*Trainee Nurse*).

After the intense complexities of *The Seventh Seal* and *Wild Strawberries*, the simple, naturalistic human situations and emotions of *Brink of Life* seem like a throwback to an earlier chapter in the development of Bergman's art. Undoubtedly, the almost claustrophobic drama of a small hospital's maternity ward — mostly filmed within the confines of a room housing three pregnant women — must have come as a relief to the director. He and his old friend Ulla Isaksson developed the screenplay from a pair of her short stories, and the film was made for Nordisk Tonefilm, to whom Bergman owed a picture, since he had once promised them an adaptation of Strindberg's *Crown-Bride*, which his busy schedule had kept him from fulfilling. *Brink of Life* was made to compensate for that old obligation and was shot quickly under fairly primitive conditions.

Unquestionably, Isaksson's attitudes toward life and death awakened a response in Bergman. Her own words about this project seem eloquently worth repeating here: "There is a secret about life, about birth and

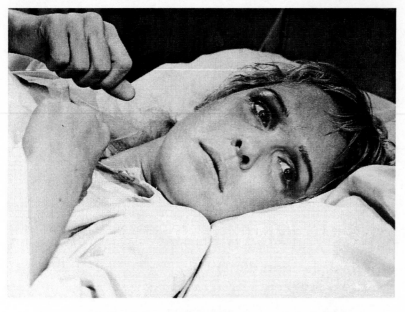

Brink of Life (1958). Eva Dahlbeck. Nordisk Tonefilm.

by actresses accustomed to knowing what their director required of them, that there doesn't appear to be a false move among them. Indeed, the judges at 1958's Cannes Film Festival accorded Bergman the Best Director Prize and, based on their fine ensemble playing, split that year's Best Actress award four ways, encompassing the performances of Ingrid Thulin, Bibi Andersson, Eva Dahlbeck and Barbro Hiort af Ornäs (who plays the comforting Sister Brita).

death, a secret about why some are called to live, and others are called to die. We can assail Heaven and science with questions — all answers will be half-truths, while life pursues its course, crowning the living with suffering or happiness.

"There is the one who yearns for tenderness, yet is forced to repress her longing and accept her childlessness — the healthy, vital one who is deprived of her long-desired child — then the little, immature creature, suddenly overwhelmed by life, and placed among the mothers. Life crowns them all but asks no questions, gives no answers, is ever on the march towards new births, new life... Humanity alone is left questioning."

Today *Brink of Life* would be called a "docudrama," so realistically does it reflect life in a maternity ward. In the hands of anyone less strong-minded — and more sentimental — than Ingmar Bergman, it would easily slip into bathos and be tagged "soap opera," simply because its focus is on women seen at a time of great vulnerability, when their emotions lie close to the surface. But so fine-tuned are the performances, all

Bergman on Bergman

"All together, the film isn't much. The actresses remain its biggest asset. Just as in other pressured situations, these women proved their professionalism, inventiveness, and unshakeable loyalty. They had the ability to laugh in the face of trouble. They had sisterhood. Consideration and caring for each other."

Critics' Circle

"Although it evolves as a basically somber, constricted, almost wholly distaff picture, Brink of Life is, nevertheless, a strikingly realistic, saccharine-free, clinical slice of life. Mr. Bergman and Ulla Isaksson use a lean script untainted by overly theatrical dialogue. And they have been given more than mere lip service by their principals. Ingrid Thulin does a masterly job as the woman whose miscarriage gives rise to her doubts about her marriage. Bibi Andersson contributes a touching portrait of a seemingly hard

youngster who finally confesses her fears, and Eva Dahlbeck, as the happily expectant mother, is outstanding in several stark, memorable scenes in a labor room."

       — A. H. Weiler in
       The New York Times

    "Brink of Life *is a deceptively simple and emotionally hard Ingmar Bergman picture which stays for its entire length in a Swedish maternity ward and never lets up its tension, which being distinctively Bergman is a blend of mysticism, philosophy and stinging drama.*

    "The acting is perfect. It is not taking anything away from the high professional level of the performers to say that here, too, it is Bergman's imagination and eye and camera that put their every facial nuance so inevitably in place that nothing, not one blink of an eye, is meaningless or superfluous, but all concurs and contributes to the flow of detail like the collecting of rivulets down a watershed to culminate in Bergman's conception of the river of life."

       — Paul V. Beckley in
       The New York Herald Tribune

    "In Brink of Life *we find Bergman working austerely on a small canvas after the more monumental and ambitious* Seventh Seal *and* Wild Strawberries, *which immediately preceded it. There are no flashback scenes and no dream sequences. The camera works quietly and the editing is unobtrusive. The material is equally stark. There is no attempt to make an anecdote out of each woman's experience—the action unfolds simply and with little elaboration, and in two of the three cases the resolutions are only sketched.*

    "Brink of Life *is Bergman's chamber music. It is not, however, of the quality that Bergman himself has led us to expect."*

       — R. H. Turner in *Film Quarterly*

    "The appearance of any new film by Ingmar Bergman is an event in the Cinema, even when it is an early, minor piece, tardily rescued from oblivion. So Close to Life is no early, minor piece, but mature and major Bergman; the product of a master-craftsman. Deceptive in its simplicity, often harrowing in its realism, but always unconsciously moving; with characters that are deeply and—considering this is a man's film about women—almost miraculously understood.

    "There is no mysticism, no symbolism. Ostensibly this is a plain, human story, easy to understand. But behind it one can, perhaps fancifully, discern a deeper note. The hospital is not only a microcosm but a confessional, a place where patients shuffle off the past and start again."

       — C. A. Lejeune in
       Films and Filming

Ansiktet
(The Magician/The Face)
Svensk Filmindustri: 1958
(U.S. release by Janus Films: 1959)

CREDITS

Director: Ingmar Bergman; *producer:* Allan Ekelund; *screenwriter:* Ingmar Bergman; *cinematographer:* Gunnar Fischer; *editor:* Oscar Rosander; *art director:* P. A. Lundgren; *costumes:* Manne Lindholm and Greta Johansson; music: Erik Nordgren; *sound:* Aaby Wedin; *assistant director:* Gosta Ekman; *running time:* 102 minutes.

CAST

Max von Sydow (*Albert Emanuel Vogler*); Ingrid Thulin (*Manda Vogler/Aman*); Åke Fridell (*Tubal*); Naima Wifstrand (*Vogler's Grandmother*); Gunnar Björnstrand (*Dr. Vergérus*); Bengt Ekerot (*Johan Spegel*); Bibi Andersson (*Sara Lindqvist*); Gertrud Fridh (*Ottilia Egerman*); Erland Josephson (*Consul Abraham Egerman*); Lars Ekborg (*Simson, the Coachman*); Toivo Pawlo (*Starbeck*); Ulla Sjöblom (*Henrietta*); Axel Duberg (*Rustan, the Butler*); Birgitta Pettersson (*Sanna, the Maid*); Oscar Ljung (*Antonsson*); Sif Ruud (*Sofia Garp*).

After the uncharacteristic filmmaking "respite" of *Brink of Life*, Bergman turned to the signs and symbols and costumed mysticism of *The Magician* (or, to directly translate its Swedish title, *The Face*). That "face" belongs to the "magician" portrayed, at first almost unrecognizably, by Max von Sydow, whose blond natural appearance is shrouded in black wig and facial hair. With his own intense eyes, this impersonation of mesmerist Albert Emanuel Vogler, initially as silent as he is enigmatic, brings an eerie Rasputin-like quality to the film's early scenes.

It's set in mid–nineteenth-century Sweden, where a troupe called the Magnetic Health Theatre is traveling by coach through a gloomy forest, led by Vogler and his wife, Manda (Ingrid Thulin), who's attired in male clothing, posing as his "boy" assistant, Aman. Also in their company is Vogler's witchlike grandmother (Naima Wifstrand), who dabbles in mysterious potions, and their manager, Tubal (Åke Fridell). The Voglers are in disguise because of a prior incident with the law which has motivated them to head for Stockholm under the cover of night, after which they hope to perform their trickery before the king.

In the city, they're detained by its police chief, Starbeck (Toivo Pawlo), and invited by Consul Egerman (Erland Josephson) to spend the night at his home, where they stage a special private performance for Dr. Vergérus (Gunnar Björnstrand), the court medical officer, who plans to expose Vogler as a fake. After a sleepless night of sexual tensions, the magic troupe is challenged in performance, and Vogler is humiliated. His ingenious path of retaliation involves his own apparent "murder" by their host's coachman, Antonsson (Oscar Ljung), after which Vogler substitutes for his own the body of Spegel (Bengt Ekerot), a dying actor the troupe had picked up before their arrival at Egerman's estate. The subsequent attic autopsy sequence not only turns the tables on Vergérus but enables director Bergman to stage a succession of bizarre tricks and shocks that suspend disbelief while nevertheless failing to explain logically just how it has all been accomplished. And yet, sinister as much of these proceedings are, relationships are conveniently sorted out and reversals of fortune nicely designated for some of the supporting cast prior to a finale which sees the Vogler troupe (or what remains of it) heading for the royal audience, after all.

Bergman apparently much enjoyed the making of this film, and his audiences have had fun attempting to sort out the main themes and tie together the puzzling digressions of character and plot. At 1958's Venice Film Festival the movie won a Special Jury Prize, designated for the "best directing, poetic originality and style."

Bergman on Bergman

"It caused a certain amount of confusion when it came out. It was regarded as odd, artificial, complicated and theatrical."

Critics' Circle

"Technically, this is an expert film, with its brilliant camerawork, its assured evocation of the Bergman world of sunshot glades and elegant interiors, and its three compelling

The Magician (1958). Ingrid Thulin and Max von Sydow. Svensk Filmindustri.

performances by Björnstrand as the desiccated medical officer, von Sydow as the mesmerist, all brooding magnificence, and Naima Wifstrand as an amiable witch. But Bergman's script is weak, with a confused and repetitive story and various rich themes never fully worked out. The Face is never much more than a series of dramatic tricks. All the cunning of Bergman and his able cast can't in the end save the film from seeming rather hollow."

—"E. H. R." in
Monthly Film Bulletin

"The Magician pleases the eye and agitates the mind. But drifting with its phan-

tasms is no easy matter, and many a moviegoer is likely instead to drift right out of the theatre.

"In illustrating this text, Bergman wobbles between drama and melodrama, alternates genuine horrors with sham tricks, comic sex with serious sex, and poetry with lampoon. The Magician manages to fascinate as it confuses, and demonstrates that even inferior Bergman is worth sampling."

—Time

"The astonishing Swedish director Ingmar Bergman is up to several more of his tricks in The Magician, a faintly dizzying mixture of the macabre, the comic, the mystical, and the supernatural. *Like others of his films, it is darkly, moodily, beautifully photographed; it compels and fascinates; and it is also strangely, unexpectedly charming, for such Gothic material as he has chosen.*

"It may be a sideshow he has given us this time, but what an absorbing one he has prepared for all who enter his magic tent. A remarkable movie indeed, from the most remarkable director extant."

— Hollis Alpert in *Saturday Review*

"Ingmar Bergman is having some of his comparatively lucid moments as writer and director of his latest Swedish picture, The Magician. *But he still has a stout reserve of obscurity for his eager and numerous disciples to ponder.*

"In The Magician, *he has taken a simpler story than usual, but he narrates it in his typical tortured, cloudy style. He also has stuck to his strikingly stark black-and-white photography, with a minimum of delicate shading. The clearest detail about the picture is the precedent that makes it seem reasonably certain to be a box-office success."*

—Alton Cook in
The New York World Telegram

"That the film works so well, sequence by sequence if not as a satisfying whole, is due as much to his actors as to Bergman's plausibility. Gunnar Björnstrand as the doctor, Max von Sydow as Vogler, Naima Wifstrand as the witch, Lars Ekborg and Bibi Andersson as the young lovers — the parts Are tailor-made and the performances impeccable. There

is also an extraordinary display of versatility from Bengt Ekerot, who played Death in The Seventh Seal *and who here, heavily disguised, plays the drunken, tattered old actor."*

—Peter John Dyer in
Films and Filming

"As in all his pictures, Mr. Bergman (who does everything) has achieved remarkable magic with his camera and with his cast. Max von Sydow, as the magician, is a haunting figure who floats between the realms of an agonized mystic and a vulgar charlatan. And he recalls the late Lon Chaney in his sad unmaking scene and in the one he plays with the surgeon, brilliantly performed by Gunnar Björnstrand."

—Bosley Crowther in
The New York Times

"This Ingmar Bergman film isn't a masterwork, or even a very good movie, but it is clearly a film made by a master. It has a fairy-tale atmosphere of expectation; then it becomes confused and argumentative. But the mysterious images of Max von Sydow as the 19th-century mesmerist, Vogler, and Ingrid Thulin as his assistant, Aman (Vogler's wife, Manda, in male disguise), carry so much latent charge of meaning that they dominate the loosely thrown-together material. Bergman labels the film a comedy, though audiences may not agree. It's a metaphysical gothic tale, with some low-comedy scenes and some grisly jokes involving an eyeball and a hand."

—Pauline Kael in
5001 Nights at the Movies

Jungfrukällan
(The Virgin Spring)
Svensk Filmindustri: 1960
(U.S. release by Janus Films: 1960)

CREDITS

Director: Ingmar Bergman; *screenwriter:* Ulla Isaksson; based on the fourteenth-century ballad "Töres Dotter i Vänge"; *cinematographer:* Sven Nykvist; *editor:* Oscar Rosander;

art director: P. A. Lundgren; *costumes:* Marik Vos; *music:* Erik Nordgren; *sound:* Aaby Wedin; *assistant director:* Lenn Hjortzberg; *running time:* 88 minutes.

CAST

Max von Sydow (*Töre*); Birgitta Valberg (*Märeta*); Gunnel Lindblom (*Ingeri*); Birgitta Pettersson (*Karin*); Axel Düberg (*Thin Herdsman*); Tor Isedal (*Mute Herdsman*); Allan Edwall (Beggar); Ove Porath (*Boy*); Axel Slangus (*Bridge Keeper*); Gudrun Brost (*Frida*); Oscar Ljung (*Simon*); Tor Borong and Leif Forstenberg (*Farmhands*).

The Virgin Spring came about, reports its screenwriter, Ulla Isaksson, after Bergman (with whom she had collaborated previously on *Brink of Life*) asked her to read a fourteenth-century ballad, "Töres Dotter i Vänge" (The Daughter of Töre of Vänge). The folk song, which existed in both prose and verse versions, dealt with a miracle that followed a rape, and Bergman thought it had filmic possibilities. In Isaksson's words: "The ballad censored nothing. It reported its tale harshly and ruthlessly, and when it reached its last stanza, a human and divine comedy had been completed."

The screenplay was written in the Swedish province of Dalarna, near the forest of the ballad's setting, where the filming took place from mid–May to late August 1959. And if one is reminded that *Rashomon*, Akira Kurosawa's 1950 Japanese classic, also shared a similar theme (a rape in a forest, as seen through various pairs of eyes), it's interesting to know that Bergman not only studied that film but also other works of Kurosawa prior to making *The Virgin Spring*.

Among the film's various awards, perhaps the most prestigious were its International Critics Prize at the 1960 Cannes Film Festival and that year's Academy Award for Best Foreign Film.

Bergman on Bergman

"I want to make it quite plain that *The Virgin Spring* must be regarded as an aberration. It's touristic, a lousy imitation of Kurosawa. At that time, my admiration for the Japanese cinema was at its height. I was almost a samurai myself!"

Critics' Circle

"Karin Toresdotter, a maiden on her way to church for confirmation, is raped and murdered by three men in a forest glade; a spring of water rises and flows beneath her dead body, and her father kills the offenders. No devices of characterization or suspense, no scenery, no psychological elaboration. On this stark basis, Bergman conceived a film nearly as simple in story line as its source. But he so enriched and intensified each detail that the whole becomes unbearably fraught with potency and terror, and with pity that opens one to the bone."
—Vernon Young *in Film Quarterly*

"Out of the somber story embodied in the legend, Bergman and his scriptwriter, Ulla Isaksson, have made a chillingly dramatic miracle play, clear and bold in its outlines, and acted with power and simplicity by a fine Swedish cast. Within the confines of what had been attempted, the realization is flawless. If Bergman has been richer and more evocative in others of his films, he has never made anything quite so crystalline as this one."
—Hollis Alpert in *Saturday Review*

"In this space age of wonders, the greatest miracle remains the thousand-fold nature of man. And the hallmark of an Ingmar Bergman film is its deep probing of the human condition. No other practicing director I know of dares what Bergman dares. Mr. Bergman may well be the only motion picture artist of today whose body of work bears the stamp of genius.

"Like the accompanying folk-ballad motif and the sharply edited sequences, the camerawork is at the same time straightforward, essential, yet wonderfully eloquent. From a

The Virgin Spring (1960). Birgitta Valberg and Max von Sydow. Svensk Filmindustri.

medieval folk-song, Ingmar Bergman has fashioned a magnificently poetic film."
      —John Beaufort in
      The Christian Science Monitor

   "The Bergman cult, which will flock to see this picture with the same enthusiasm it takes to all his films, will doubtless find an excess of hidden meanings. The Bergman obsession with dreams, the occult, religion, good and evil, and the like is as evident here as before to help them in their search for clues. What everyone should be able to agree on, however, is the brilliance with which Bergman has made this film. His control of milieu and moods is masterful; he handles the light-hearted scene of the daughter's departure on her journey with the same assurance and complete realization of effect that he brings to the sickening terror of the rape scene and the violent horror of the slaughter of the herdsmen."

      —Richard Gertner in
      Motion Picture Daily

   "The film is well-made in the conventional sense, both in the way the various sequences interdepend (the irony of the herdsmen coming back to the house after they have raped the daughter, for instance) and within the individual sequences themselves. The same sense of a well-thought-out construction operates on a religious as well as an artistic level. It may be that Bergman is at his best when he has a myth to draw on—particularly, it would seem from this and The Seventh Seal, *when it allows him the distance and richness of the Middle Ages, and a framework of Christian morality."*
      —"P. J. R." in *Monthly Film Bulletin*

   "The picture is filled with scenes that are simply unforgettable. There can be no question that this film is a work of art, but it is

one that will not provide pleasure. It is heart-rending, exhausting, breath-taking, but it is not something to be enjoyed. Like most of Bergman's works, it turns the camera so that the viewer sees into the people on the screen, and sees himself at one and the same time."
—Jacob Siskind in *The Montreal Star*

"He has created a rape scene explicit enough to shock sophisticated European audiences, perhaps leaving local censors too dumbfounded to cut it. He also keeps a fascinated camera eye on a boy subject to fits of violent vomiting. The story he tells does not seem to demand this sustained shock treatment. But Bergman apparently was determined to make his impact explosive—and Heaven help the queasy stomachs. Bergman found his story material in a medieval folk song, but his treatment is unflinching and modern realism."
—Alton Cook in
The New York World Telegram

"With The Virgin Spring, *Ingmar Bergman has arrived at the definitive point of his career. By recounting a fourteenth-century Swedish legend of rape and revenge, he is able to express with unaccustomed clarity the survival of faith, despite incomprehension, despite the inscrutability of God. To reach this affirmative conclusion, he has shown human nature at its most bestial, and Max von Sydow, as the father who kills his daughter's murderers, gives a masterly study of strength imbued with human frailty.*
—Gordon Gow in
Films and Filming

"The Virgin Spring *is at least one of Ingmar Berman's best. It is the simplest in the*

telling if likewise the hardest on the nerves. One can understand why it roused some tremors of dispute in Europe, for the rape sequence which is at the dramatic center of its story is the most uncompromising thing of its kind on film. But it could not have been otherwise or Bergman's remarkable reactivating of a medieval Scandinavian legend and folk song would fail to reach the religious power it does.
"This is unquestionably one of the film events of the year."
—Paul V. Beckley in
The New York Tribune

"Using fewer of his misleading clues than usual, Bergman probably allows some to creep into The Virgin Spring *to indicate that no one knows all the answers to man's behavior—or to man's search for answers. There won't always be a miracle to prove the existence of God; some things must be taken on faith. I doubt if* The Virgin Spring *will be as popular as the other Bergman films; it lacks the humor, warmth and fanciful flights of some of his other pictures. But it is another positive step forward in the Bergman repertory, which is one long autobiography. And its viewers will be rewarded by it rich black-and-white tapestry."*
— *The Commonweal*

"This is an extremely powerful film, possibly Bergman's strongest. However, it lacks the human warmth of Wild Strawberries *and the majesty of* The Seventh Seal. *Audiences will likely leave the theatre torn and shattered by an unpleasant experience. This is a technical masterpiece and will be loved by the technically minded."*
—"Flei" in *Variety*

Djävulens Öga
(The Devil's Eye)
Svensk Filmindustri: 1960
(U.S. release by Janus Films: 1961)

CREDITS

Director: Ingmar Bergman; *producer:* Allan Ekelund; *screenwriter:* Ingmar Bergman; based on the radio play *Don Juan vender tilbage* (Don Juan Returns) by Oluf Bang; *cinematographer:* Gunnar Fischer; *editor:* Oscar Rosander; *art director:* P. A. Lundgren; *costumes:* Mago (Max Goldstein); *music:* Erik Nordgren, with excerpts from Domenico Scarlatti, Played by Käbi Laretei; *Sound:* Stig Flodin; *assistant director:* Lenn Hjortzberg; *running time:* 90 minutes.

CAST

Jarl Kulle (*Don Juan*); Bibi Andersson (*Britt-Marie*); Stig Järrel (*Satan*); Nils Poppe (*Pastor*); Gertrud Fridh (*Renata, the Pastor's wife*); Sture Lagerwall (*Pablo, Don Juan's Servant*); Georg Funkquist (*Count Armand de Rochefoucauld*); Gunnar Sjöberg (*Marquis Giuseppe Maria de Maccopazza*); Torsten Winge (*Old Man*); Kristina Adolphson (*Veiled Woman*); Axel Düberg (*Jonas*); Allan Edwall (*Ear Devil*); Ragnar Arvedson (*Guard Demon*); John Melin (*Beauty Doctor*); Sten-Torsten Thuul (*Tailor*); Arne Lindblad (*Tailor's Assistant*); Svend Bunch (*Quick-Change Expert*); Börje Lundh (*Hairdresser*); Lenn Hjortzberg (*Enema Doctor*); Tom Olsson (*Black Masseur*); Inga Gill (*Housemaid*); Gunnar Björnstrand (*Actor and Narrator*).

Bergman introduces this (for him) unusual comedy-fantasy of sexual manners by reiterating an old Irish (actually Bergmanian) proverb that he claims inspired it: "A woman's chastity is a sty in the Devil's eye." This movie, in fact, was part of a deal Bergman made with Svensk Filmindustri's Carl Anders Dymling; if he followed it with a comedy, then Bergman would win backing for *The Virgin Spring*. As a result, he was working on this script even as Ulla Isaksson was preparing her medieval morality story. Bergman's actual source for *The Devil's Eye* was a Danish radio play by Oluf Bang that Svensk Filmindustri owned, and as was often his way, Bergman made it directly on the heels of the Isaksson script as part of the annual two films he chose to complete before the onset of Sweden's long, cold winter.

The film's structure is more theatrical than anything Bergman had yet offered up for the screen; it opens and closes with Gunnar Björnstrand as a narrator who addresses the camera and who appears, as in a stage play, to speak between what he refers to as the story's "three acts." Despite its cinematic camera work and multiplicity of settings, *The Devil's Eye* often has the look of a stage play as it weaves a fanciful story of Don Juan

(suave Jarl Kulle) sent to Earth by Satan (Stig Järrel, barely recognizable from the sadistic schoolmaster of Bergman's first screenplay, *Torment*). His destination: the home of a naïve country vicar (Nils Poppe), where the man's virgin daughter (Bibi Andersson), about to wed, becomes the lustful target of the world's legendary lover; at the same time, the cleric's frustrated wife (Gertrud Fridh) appears a pushover for the attentions of Don Juan's servant Pablo (Sture Lagerwall). But the events of one night, during which the two strangers from Hell are given shelter by the vicar, are not what one might have expected; Don Juan returns to the fiery place in embarrassing defeat — in love, yet unfulfilled!

Bergman on Bergman

"In Svensk Filmindustri's archive there was a wretched old play called, I think, *The Return of Don Juan* or something of that sort — by a Danish author. I thought it might be rather fun to make a comedy out of it. First I wrote a script. Then Ulla Isaksson and I wrote *The Virgin Spring* ... I thought it admirable. Then I made *The Virgin Spring*, in May and June I took a

The Devil's Eye (1960). Bibi Andersson and Jarl Kulle. Svensk Filmindustri.

month or so off, and then got busy with *The Devil's Eye*.... It's not that I'm ashamed of having made it; it's simply that it turned into a series of mistakes and misunderstandings. Otherwise, I think it does have a few good qualities."

Critics' Circle

"*Inevitably a minor film and obviously for Bergman no more than an elegant diversion (he subtitles it 'A Rondo Capriccioso'),* The Devil's Eye *gives much the same impression as* The Face. *Both are comedies first and foremost, but both give tantalizing hints of the* kammerspiel *and stern morality that underline Bergman's more characteristic works.*"

—Peter Cowie in
Films and Filming

"*Mr. Bergman is far from his best form in this tediously talkative exercise, which ap-*

pears an intellectual imitation of G. B. Shaw's one-act discourse Don Juan in Hell. *The action is slow and unexciting, the ideas are not clarified and the psychology of the people is quite as elusive as their morals.*"

—Bosley Crowther in
The New York Times

"*What happens between Don Juan and the girl, between the servant and the girl's mother, and between the demon and the girl's father is the substance of Mr. Bergman's elaborate prank. He brings it off with ease—there are three or four very funny scenes and a couple of very touching ones—and I'm only sorry that in the course of doing so he felt obliged to hector us with ironic epigrams, most of which gives off the oddest ghostly echo of Oscar Wilde.*"

—Pauline Kael in
The New Yorker

"*Bergman wrote the screenplay as well as directed the film, so the dialogue has a cynical* but curiously wistful quality, just as the photography retains that luminous delicacy characteristic of Bergman films. I got a little tired of the narrator's constant intrusions and the formal breaking of the film into three acts, which seems a trifle arch, though I must admit that this probably serves well enough to break up any tendency to take this comic parable too naturalistically."

—Paul V. Beckley in
The New York Herald Tribune

"*Eye may not be one of Ingmar Bergman's masterpieces, but it is a well-made film with a fair amount of racy dialog that can be humorous if not hilarious. It should be a box-office tantalizer. Some of the arty audiences may be disappointed, but should find material to dissect.*"

— "Fred" in *Variety*

The Devil's Eye *is a curious mixture, fragments of it almost vintage Bergman, but on the whole showing every sign of having* been hastily slapped together without much care. The trouble is that Bergman's attempts at self-parody (The Face, for example) come dangerously close to being indistinguishable from his more serious work; and his inability to resist being serious within the parody unbalances it all."

—Tom Milne in
Monthly Film Bulletin

"*One of Bergman's least important pictures. Still, the comedy is staged with sureness and a great sense of style. Some of the figures become really interesting, such as, for instance, the simple-minded and credulous minister, who awakens to reality when his wife is seduced by Don Juan's servant. As a whole, though,* The Devil's Eye *is an uninteresting film, a commissioned job, done with skilled craftsmanship, nothing more.*

—Jörn Donner in
*The Personal Vision
of Ingmar Bergman*

Såsom i en Spegel
(Through a Glass Darkly)

Svensk Filmindustri: 1961
(U.S. release by Janus Films: 1962)

CREDITS

Director: Ingmar Bergman; *producer:* Allan Ekelund; *screenwriter:* Ingmar Bergman; *cinematographer:* Sven Nykvist; *editor:* Ulla Ryghe; *art director:* P. A. Lundgren; *costumes:* Mago (Max Goldstein); *music:* Erik Nordgren, with excerpts from Bach's Suite No. 2 in D Minor for Cello, played by Erling Bengtsson; *sound:* Stig Flodin; *assistant director:* Lenn Hjortzberg; *running time:* 91 minuets.

CAST

Harriet Andersson (*Karin*); Max von Sydow (*Martin, Karin's Husband*); Gunnar Björnstrand (*David, Karin's Father*); Lars Passgård (*Fredrik, David's Son, known as "Minus"*).

This chamber drama — the first in what Bergman would term his "faith trilogy," which would include the subsequent *Winter Light* and *The Silence*— focuses on four members of a family summering on an isolated Baltic island. It was filmed mostly on

Fårö, a location with which Bergman was so enamored that he later made it his home. And with this picture, the director began his consistent collaboration with cinematographer Sven Nykvist, who had first worked with him eight years earlier, when he had stepped in to help photograph *The Naked Night*. Initially, the two men intended making *Through a Glass Darkly* as their first color film together, but experimental footage dissuaded them, and two years would pass before they would depart from the monochromatic photography that now seems the hallmark of Bergman's great middle years as a filmmaker.

Through a Glass Darkly, simple in its story but highly complex in its emotions, centers on one woman and three men. The focus is on Karin (Harriet Andersson), newly come home from a mental hospital, where she has been treated for schizophrenia. Karin is enjoying the relative peace and calm of the island home she shares with her doctor-husband, Martin (Max von Sydow); her self-absorbed writer-father, David (Gunnar Björnstrand); and her younger brother, Minus (Lars Passgård), a teenager just coming of sexual age. Karin is inclined to imagine that she hears voices from behind the wallpaper in her room, advising her that God will soon appear to offer her salvation. Discovering that her illness is apparently incurable, Karin suffers a lapse and seduces her brother. It's an experience that traumatizes him into silence.

A recurrence of her voices inform Karin that God's appearance is imminent, although all that passes through the doorway is a large black spider. The insect terrorizes her ("I have seen the face of God"), and she suffers a complete breakdown, requiring the restraint of both her father and husband until the arrival of an ambulance. After Karin has been returned to the institution and the three men are left alone, the confused Minus appeals to his father for an explanation. He is told that love is man's sole salvation, and he reacts with a surprised comment: "Father *talked* to me!"

Not unexpectedly, the acting here is superb, especially in the demanding role played by Harriet Andersson, who gives what may be her finest performance under Bergman's direction. In April 1962 she put in an appearance at the Academy Awards to accept the Oscar won by Bergman for *Through a Glass Darkly* when it was named 1961's Best Foreign film.

Bergman on Bergman

"I don't remember very much about *Through a Glass Darkly*. I'm a bit shy of it. But while I was preparing the film, I became interested in the human drama surrounding another human being who really was in process of slipping away — that is, in the whole syndrome of her sickness and the human groupings around such a syndrome. I felt I had to drop all artistic tricks and simply concentrate on the human drama. And that was how this play came into being — for a play it is. The cinematic aspects of *Through a Glass Darkly* are rather secondary."

Critics' Circle

"Ingmar Bergman, in Through a Glass Darkly, *tells a story that is in many ways reminiscent of* Long Day's Journey into Night. *Pic deals with four members of a family who are estranged from one another through their inability to express feelings for each other. The action is limited to twenty-four hours in the lives of the four. The time is the nightless Scandinavian summer and the setting is an isolated island in the Baltic. Not a pleasant film, it is a great one."*
—"Wing" in *Variety*

"Here, in this tightly constructed and starkly realistic little film, which concentrates upon the experiences of four people on an isolated island, Mr. Bergman is tensely

Through a Glass Darkly **(1961). Harriet Andersson and Lars Passgård. Svensk Filmindustri.**

exposing some aspects of shock and tragedy that evolve from the painful paroxysms of a young woman going mad.

"Harriet Andersson is beautifully expressive of the haunting awareness, the agony of madness, that move the girl. In one scene, where she takes leave of her senses, she does a masterpiece of marbling her face. Through her, one sees the mysteries that move within the dark glass of the soul.

— Bosley Crowther in
The New York Times

"Like all Bergman films, Through a Glass Darkly *is an intensely personal work. Yet none of his previous films have been so profoundly Scandinavian in their composition or outlook on life. The isolation, the hostile duologues, the psychological malady are all reminiscent of Ibsen and Strindberg.*

"I am puzzled by those who call this film depressing. On the contrary, it is among the most mature of Bergman's works and ends on a note of conviction. But the characters can

only reach this state of calmness if they have endured the most intense experiences and scrutiny. If one is prepared to enter Bergman's world, to accept his sudden variations of mood, and to accept in their context his conclusions, one will find this film a somber but stimulating work of art."

—Peter Cowie in *Films and Filming*

"A study in insanity that is at once touching, horrifying and inspiring. I can think of no previous Bergman work so direct, so simple, so precise in its effects, and so unequivocal in its meaning. He seems deliberately to have eschewed the symbolism, the convoluted flashbacks, and the lush imagery of his most popular films to create a new style with its own rewards — all sinew and bone, stripped down to the essentials. Its story takes no sudden tangents; its conclusion is stated with unabashed baldness. This does not mean, however, that Bergman has given us an easy entertainment. Quite the contrary. He develops his theme with agonizing deliberateness,

drawing his audience slowly into the private hell of each of his four protagonists.

—Arthur Knight in *Saturday Review*

"Once again Bergman poses the agonized question, 'Where is God?' and in synopsis form, Through a Glass Darkly *probably sounds like a choice sample of Swedish angst and self-torture. In fact, it is a warm and highly controlled work which revolves round the father's failure as a human being.*

"As usual, Bergman has coaxed brilliant, three-dimensional performances from his cast of four, Harriet Andersson in particular; and it is the living, breathing vulnerability of the characters which turns the film from a metaphysical exercise into an image of three people rent apart by the inability of the fourth to respond to their needs.

—Tom Milne in
Monthly Film Bulletin

Nattvardsgästerna
(Winter Light/The Communicants)
Svensk Filmindustri: 1962
(U.S. release by Janus Films: 1963)

CREDITS

Director: Ingmar Bergman; *producer:* Allan Ekelund; *screenwriter:* Ingmar Bergman; *cinematographer:* Sven Nykvist; *editor:* Ulla Ryghe; *art director:* P. A. Lundgren; *costumes:* Mago (Max Goldstein); *music:* excerpts from Swedish psalms; *sound:* Stig Flodin; *assistant directors:* Lenn Hjortzberg and Vilgot Sjöman; *running time:* 80 minutes.

CAST

Ingrid Thulin (*Märta Lundberg*); Gunnar Björnstrand (*Tomas Ericsson*); Gunnel Lindblom (*Karin Persson*); Max von Sydow (*Jonas Perrson*); Allan Edwall (*Algot Frövik*); Kolbjörn Knudsen (*Knut Aronsson*); Olof Thunberg (*Fredrik Blom, the Organist*); Elsa Ebbeson-Thornblad (*Magdelena Ledfors*); Tor Borong (*Johan Åkerblom*); Bertha Sånnell (*Hanna Appelblad*); Helena Palmgren (*Doris*); Eddie Axberg (*Johan Strand*); Lars-Owe Carlberg (*Police Superintendent*); Ingmari Hjort (*Persson's Daughter*); Stefan Larsson (*Persson's Son*); Johan Olafs (*Man*); Lars-Olof Andersson and Christer Öhman (*Boys*).

Again working with a small cast of characters in an austere setting (in this one the action is almost entirely confined to the interior of a small rural church), Bergman creates a second chamber work in his "faith" trilogy. Better known in some locales as *The Communicants* (a more faithful translation of the Swedish original), *Winter Light* focuses on Tomas Ericsson (Gunnar Björnstrand), the troubled pastor of a church whose congregation has become pitifully small; diminished at the same time, his own faith in God has begun to leave him as well. Among the most faithful, however, is Märta Lundberg (Ingrid Thulin), a village schoolteacher who has been his mistress since the death of his wife five years earlier. Although she continues to love him, the pastor's dispassionately cruel treatment of her has apparently become Märta's cross to bear, for no amount of humiliation will cause her to forsake him in what she feels is his hour of need. At the same time, one of his parishioners, the fisherman Jonas Persson (Max von Sydow) is sorely troubled by his fears of China's possession of the atom bomb and that country's lack of concern for human life. When Persson needs his consolation most, Ericsson finds his own words inadequate, and Persson's subsequent suicide causes him to reflect as he visits the fisherman's pregnant widow, Karin (Gunnel Lindblom). At that evening's service, the faithful Märta is the pastor's only congregant.

Bergman's inspiration for *Winter Light* came from a conversation with a clergyman, who had told him of a fisherman who had once come to him for spiritual counsel and who had later taken his own life. Adding to the pastor's character's fabricated issues of faith, ill health and emotional problems relating to a woman who wasn't his wife gave *Winter Light* a story line of workable dimensions. And yet this remains essentially a difficult work, of interest most to those who are already followers of Bergman. Certainly it isn't for seekers of "entertainment."

Bergman on Bergman

"I have always tried to make my films appealing in some way to my audience. But I was not so stupid as to believe that *Winter Light* would be a public favorite. Unfortunate, perhaps, but inevitable. Even Gunnar Björnstrand had great difficulties with his part. We had worked together on a long line of comedies, but the role of Tomas Ericsson made harsh demands on him. Gunnar found it painful to portray a person who was unsympathetic to such a degree. His inner turmoil became so acute that he had trouble remembering his lines, a problem that had never happened before.

"It is satisfying to see *Winter Light* after a quarter of a century. I believe that nothing in it has eroded or broken down."

Critics' Circle

The film deals more with religious doubting and searching than any of Bergman's earlier works. The foundation is solid. There is nothing flashy, showy or unnecessary. He uses no tricks to awaken the attention of those who are not interested. The result is an extremely moving and fascinating film for the religiously aware, and a somewhat boring one for the religiously indifferent."

—"Fred" in *Variety*

"In Bergman's absorbing, deeply moving and provocative drama of ideas—set in a drab, wintry countryside—the pastor finds himself unable to console a would-be suicide fleeing the world in fear of atomic destruction and God's abandonment. He cannot love the homely woman who would die for him; he cannot console; he cannot counsel; he cannot share others' love or pain. And in this spiritual void, cannot find himself, either. The spare, taut, darkly lit drama has been superbly photographed and beautifully played—almost as though a one-act drama—with simplicity, directness and dramatic integrity. The film, however, comes to an abrupt conclusion that leaves the ultimate Question unanswered, as perhaps it may always be."

—Jesse Zunser in *Cue*

"Sven Nykvist's photography performs its usual miracles, as when the pastor and the teacher are driving across a darkening snowy landscape, and their faces are shot behind a passing parade of wintry trees reflected in the car window through which we look in. But more important than any tricks, the photography faithfully yet economically conveys the bleakness of the weather, the atmosphere and the condition humane.

"Winter Light is inferior Bergman. But it is Bergman, and, despite its limitations, deserves to be seen."

—John Simon in *The New Leader*

"Technically, of course, there is much to admire in the film, the acting is brilliant (Ingrid Thulin in particular), the photography impeccable. All through, however, effects seem to be too coldly and precisely calculated. For example, a series of shots—a

Winter Light **(1962). Ingrid Thulin and Gunnar Björnstrand. Svensk Filmindustri.**

man putting his glasses away in their case while chanting 'Amen,' the organist discreetly yawning — establish the hollow ritual of the service, then one final shot sums it all up; a hand empties the collection-bag on the vestry table, another places a thermos flask and cup beside it. Clever, certainly; irreproachable, in a way; and yet, because the film is empty, the effect is sterile, even mannered."

—Tom Milne in
Monthly Film Bulletin

"Surely Mr. Bergman would not make such a film without meaning it to be symbolic. And it is on the inevitable score of its shattering symbolism that he must have known it would be challenged and criticized. But the vividness with which he has presented this cold and relentless display of spiritual poverty and pathos cannot be criticized — at least, not for its expression in brilliant poetic images. Mr. Bergman's actors, as always, are as sensitive as actors can

be, and his camera still frames compositions that fairly pierce one with a nameless poetry."

—Bosley Crowther in
The New York Times

"Winter Light casts a gloom-tinged glare upon the human condition with chilling clarity. It is a study of despair, the despair that engulfs the hopeless, the unloving and the unloved, told largely in terms of religious faith, which Bergman equates with human love.

"Ingrid Thulin draws a remarkable portrait of the schoolmistress, a woman no longer able to cloak her anguish in ironies. Gunnar Björnstrand succeeds in lending dignity to a soul in agony, in bringing true pathos to the fall of pride.

"It is a taut film, bleak and cold in its abstract ideas, deeply passionate in its concern for the human torment."

—Judith Crist in
The New York Herald Tribune

"Ingmar Bergman has been fortunate in having a company in Svensk Filmindustri that has allowed him more artistic freedom than any European director. Certainly no other company would have let his latest film, Winter Light, *pass as a commercial proposition. For* Winter Light *is Bergman's barest film, even more spartan in presentation than* Through a Glass Darkly. *Technically, it is*

uninteresting, except of course for Bergman's customary skill at composition and for Sven Nykvist's crystalline lighting and photography. Here, then, stripped of all decoration and sub-plots, is the essential Bergman thesis. Everything is in the dialogue, as dense as ever in Bergman's concentrated, often brutal style."

— Peter Cowie in *Films and Filming*

Tystnaden
(The Silence)

Svensk Filmindustri: 1963
(U.S. release by Janus Films: 1964)

CREDITS

Director: Ingmar Bergman; *producer:* Allan Ekelund; *screenwriter:* Ingmar Bergman; *cinematographer:* Sven Nykvist; *editor:* Ulla Ryghe; *art director:* P. A. Lundgren; *costumes:* Marik Vos-Lundh and Bertha Sånnell; *music:* Ivan Renliden, with excerpts from Johann Sebastian Bach's "Goldberg Variations" And R. Mersey's "Mayfair Waltz"; *sound:* Stig Flodin; *assistant directors:* Lars-Erik Liedholm and Lenn Hjortzberg; *running time:* 105 minutes.

CAST

Ingrid Thulin (*Ester*); Gunnel Lindblom (*Anna*); Jörgen Lindström (*Johan, Her Son*); Håkan Jahnberg (*Room-Service Waiter*); Birger Malmsten (*Bar Waiter*); The Eduardinis (*Seven Dwarfs*); Eduardo Gutierrez (*Their Impresario*); Lissi Alandh (*Woman in Cabaret*); Leif Forstenberg (*Man in Cabaret*); Nils Waldt (*Cashier*); Birger Lensander (*Cinema Doorman*); Eskil Kalling (*Man in Bar*); Karl-Arne Bergman (*Newspaper Vendor*); Olof Widgren (*Old Man in Hotel Corridor*).

In this conclusion to his "faith" trilogy, Bergman forsakes cinematic realism to offer a strange and dreamlike account of the sojourn of three visitors, who arrive by rail to stay in a city so foreign that communication with the populace appears impossible. Ester (Ingrid Thulin) and Anna (Gunnel Lindblom) are sisters, but completely unalike. Sensual Anna maintains a close relationship with her young son Johan (Jörgen Lindström) and a more distant one to her un-

married sibling, an ailing translator who harbors an unrealized lesbian interest in Anna. Apart from a troupe of seven performing dwarfs, they appear to be the only guests at the large old hotel where they arrange to stop over and where the elderly room-service waiter (Håkan Jahnberg) evinces a subtle but unhealthy interest in the child. Anna leaves the hotel to find escape in a local cinema, where she witnesses a couple making love, a sight that awakens her own sensuality sufficiently to move her to seek sexual solace with an attractive bar waiter (Birger Malmsten), whom she brings back to her hotel room. As Ester's condition deteriorates, the sisters quarrel violently, and Anna leaves the hotel with Johan, abandoning the dying Ester to the care of the old waiter. As their train takes them away, Johan tries to decipher a note form Ester, written in the strange language of the country they have just left.

Swedish filmgoers may not have been prepared for this mysterious change in the creative imagination of their most celebrated moviemaker, but the more sensational aspects of his latest work attracted them in considerable crowds. With reference to its several erotic scenes, Werner Wiskari reported from Stockholm in *The New York Times*: "The film has disturbed some of its viewers enough to impel them to walk out in the middle of its screenings. Others have muttered angrily through much of the picture. But, in general, it has frozen its audiences, and embarrassed smiles have been a widespread reaction as the lights went up."

Questioned as to possible censorship cuts, Svensk Filmindustri said that there would be no specially edited export version of the movie. However, the version eventually released in the U.S. by Janus Films was shorter by ten minutes than the 105-minute version originally released in Sweden.

Bergman on Bergman

"When you see *The Silence* today, you have to admit that it suffers from a severe literary list (as a ship with an unbalanced load) in two or three sequences. First and foremost, that is true in the confrontations between the two sisters. The tentative dialogue between Anna and Ester with which the film ends is also unnecessary. Other than that, I have no objections. I can see details we could have improved upon if we had had more time and more money; a few street scenes, the scene in the

variety theatre, and so on. But we did what we could to make the scenes comprehensible. Sometimes it's actually an advantage not to have too much money."

Critics' Circle

"*In* Tystnaden *Bergman is delving still deeper into his own private world, so deep that he has lost contact with the outside almost completely. In spite of masterly performances from the whole cast and some impressive sequences — the opening as the train edges in to the town past a moonscape mountain range; the last blaring brazen trump as Ester struggles for breath after her sister has left her — the audience is never involved. It is as though the film were being viewed through a glass screen.*"
—"N. M. H." in *Monthly Film Bulletin*

"*Just what Ingmar Bergman set out to say in* The Silence *is anybody's guess. Obscurity has always been the dominant note of the pictures made by the Swedish writer-director, and it's even more so in his new one...*

"*That's not to deny his skill with the camera. Bergman has a keen sense of dramatic design, lighting and mood, and, furthermore, is able to draw strong portrayals from his actors. Ingrid Thulin, a veteran of the Bergman stock, agonizes through her role as the elder sister, and the highly decorative Gunnel Lindblom makes vivid her interpretation of the younger. But there's never any indication of what it's all supposed to mean, if anything. Even the identity of the town and its people remains a mystery. It's all very pretentiously arty, very deliberately downbeat.*"
—Rose Pelswick in
The New York Journal-American

"*Ingmar Bergman's* The Silence *is, I am sorry to say, a disappointing film. We are in what might be called Bergman's Antonioni period. Like Antonioni, Bergman chose to make a trilogy about the emptiness, boredom, and lack of transcendental values in life; like Antonioni's, Bergman's third installment stringently divests itself of narrative content and shifts the burden of communication*

The Silence (1963). Gunnel Lindblom, Jörgen Lindström and Ingrid Thulin. Svensk Filmindustri.

from incident to implication, from statement to symbol.

—John Simon in *The New Leader*

"The Silence *is a symphony of despair, a harrowing harmony of the unspoken anguish and the unheard lament of the loveless. And it is, perhaps, the most psychologically complex and symbol-laden of Ingmar Bergman's movies and one of his most demanding. The* Silence *is not for the prudish. It demands maturity and sophistication from the viewer. The drama is of character; the plot is barely incidental. But every action, every verbalization carries a variety of implications. To each his own inference. This is the burden Bergman places upon his audience, and it must be borne with intellectual patience while he fascinates the eye and touches upon the emotions.*"

—Judith Crist in
The New York Herald Tribune

"The grapplings of Ingmar Bergman with loneliness, lust and loss of faith, so weirdly displayed in his last two pictures, have plunged him at last into a tangle of brooding confusions and despairs in his latest film. What Mr. Bergman is trying to tell us is something each individual viewer must fathom and discover for himself. They say when it was shown in Sweden, its several erotic scenes were so detailed and explicit that they literally shocked audiences. Perhaps these scenes were essential to a superheated mood required for the psychological context. But obviously these scenes have been cut or trimmed for this market. Here the whole thing is rather tame, mystifying and morbid. The* Silence *is almost like death.*"

—Bosley Crowther in
The New York Times

"His new film represents Bergman neither at his best nor his worst. It can be seen as a phase in his continuing artistic progression, and it can also be judged out of that context. Standing on its own, The Silence *conveys its meanings at best obliquely, and mainly*

through antithesis. If the two sisters are comprehensible in their anguish, they are not
tragic, because they have not been made so,
and one is more chilled than moved by the
delineation of their condition.
—Hollis Alpert in *Saturday Review*

"*The film closes the ring of the trilogy that
began with* Through a Glass Darkly *and
continued with* Winter Light. *In those films
Bergman sought to illuminate the ills of men
by poking through the ashes of religious faith.
His concluding statement is a bold, unpredictable work, touched with genius, but at
the same time murky, exasperating and occasionally dull. Those expecting a magnum
opus will be disappointed; so will those looking solely for sensation. For the blunt dia-

logue and the erotic scenes seem justified as
part of the film's theme and development.
The visible story is slow and simple. The
silence is the silence between and within
human beings when faith has failed. Dialogue is sparse, but Bergman's close-ups pry
secrets from a human face with uncommon
skill. Actress Lindblom writes a whole chapter in promiscuity in one perfervid glance.*"
— *Time*

"*Unlike previous pictures in which he is
investigating the human mind and looking
for God, Ingmar Bergman is turning his attention in* The Silence *exclusively to the
body and its passions; this is a film without
God. Rather say, full of the devil.*"
—"Denk" in *Variety*

För att Inte Tala om Alla Dessa Kvinnor (All These Women/Now About These Women)

Svensk Filmindustri: 1964
(U.S. release by Janus Films: 1964)

CREDITS

Director: Ingmar Bergman; *producer:* Allan Ekelund; *screenwriters:* "Buntel Eriksson"
(Ingmar Bergman and Erland Josephson); *Eastmancolor cinematographer:* Sven Nykvist;
editor: Ulla Ryghe; *art director:* P. A. Lundgren; *costumes:* Mago (Max Goldstein); *music:*
Erik Nordgren, with excerpts from Johan Sebastian Bach's Suite No. 1 in C Major and
Suite No. 3 in D Major; *sound:* P. O. Pettersson; *assistant directors:* Lenn Hjortzberg and
Lars-Erik Liedholm; *running time:* 80 minutes.

CAST

Jarl Kulle (*Cornelius*); Bibi Andersson (*Bumble Bee, Felix's Mistress*); Harriet Andersson
(*Isolde, Felix's Chambermaid*); Eva Dahlbeck (*Adelaide, Felix's Wife*); Karin Kavli (*Madame
Tussaud*); Gertrud Fridh (*Traviata*); Mona Malm (*Cecilia*); Barbro Hiort af Ornäs (*Beatrice, Felix's Accompanist*); Allan Edwall (*Jillker, Felix's Impresario*); Georg Funkquist (*Tris-
tan*); Carl Billquist (*Young Man*); Jan Blomberg (*English Radio Announcer*); Göran Graff-
man (*French Radio Announcer*); Jan-Olof Strandberg (*German Radio Announcer*); Gösta
Prüzelius (*Swedish Radio Announcer*); Ulf Johansson, Axel Duberg and Lars-Erik Liedholm (*Men in Black*); Lars-Owe Carlberg (*Chauffeur*); Doris Funcke (*First Waitress*);
Yvonne Igell (*Second Waitress*).

All These Women **(1964). Bibi Andersson and Jarl Kulle. Svensk Filmindustri.**

After the somber inner probings of his chamber trilogy, Bergman could not have chosen anything further afield in mood, content and style than *All These Women*, his first color film. In fact, the movie is nearly all style and artifice as it weaves a farcical tale — complete with periodic intertitles — centering on a famed, womanizing cellist (seen only from the rear or at an unrecognizable distance) who lives in a lavish country villa with his wife and assorted mistresses and hangers-on. To this estate comes Cornelius (Jarl Kulle), an effete music critic who's writing a biography of the Great One, and who proceeds to sneak about the place in the course of a weekend, mixing with the women, writing down his observances with an absurdly long quill pen, and having absolutely no success in meeting with his host for an interview.

The movie begins with the funeral of the deceased cellist, then proceeds to fill in the events of the days prior to his death, as he prepares for a private concert for his retinue of women. With a frequent refrain of the song "Yes, We Have No Bananas," Bergman settles into a Ken Russellish mood as he adds dashes of silent-film farce, a wild fireworks sequence, and a great deal of superficial artifice, all photographed in pastel colors by Sven Nykvist. Writing with actor Erland Josephson under the joint pseudonym of "Buntel Eriksson." Bergman reasoned that a comedy would offer his public a welcome change of pace after the erotic enigmas of *The Silence*. But he miscalculated; not only was the earlier film a surprise hit, but *All These Women* became a dismal failure.

Bergman on Bergman

"When farce is good, there's nothing better. But it's practically the hardest thing of all. Very few people could swallow that film. The whole of this question of the artist and his critics is totally uninteresting...

People made up their minds to loathe the film, and deliberately did so. Yet it was funny. I had two fiascos in one week! Harry Martinson's play *Three Knives from Wei*, which had its first night at the Dramaten, and which I'd been working on all winter. Then, three days later, came *Now About These Women*! No one had the least intimation it would turn out an all-time fiasco."

Critics' Circle

"*Coming from the hand of Bergman, master of spiritual torment and elegant comedy, it was calculated to disappoint: silent film comedy techniques; stretches of crude, almost custard-pie slapstick; stylishly flimsy settings, shot in delicious pastel colors and looking like some exquisite Ruritanian brothel; Edwardian costumes for the men, Twenties flapper dresses for the women. Bergman, of course, is having fun in this film, revenging himself with amiable malice on the critics at whose hands he has so often suffered.*"

— Tom Milne in *Monthly Film Bulletin*

"*Bergman is, of course, no stranger to comedy, but his treatment of it has been in the relatively conventional forms of such films as* Smiles of a Summer Night *or* Secrets of Women. *Now he has gone* nouvelle vague *on us with the 'in' movie jokes, the Mack Sennettisms, the visual and written asides to the audience and the pseudosurrealism that lesser movie-makers have belabored to a fare-thee-well.*

"*The pace is slow, the jokes and special effects all too obviously premeditated and executed with a heavy hand. Pie-throwing, pratfalls and madcap chases cannot survive such treatment. There is no underlying joy — nor is there an overlay of sophisticated irony or satire to compensate.*"

— Judith Crist in
The New York Herald Tribune

"*Bergman, with his first color film, proves as masterful as with black and white. A mischievously amusing free-style frolic, playfully*

throwing darts at critics, fame, censors and female admirers.*"

— Jesse Zunser in *Cue*

"*This is a much-awaited production, since it's the color debut by Ingmar Bergman and a comedy after all the dark, dramatic stories this Swedish director has done in recent years. The result is confusing. After each new Bergman picture, the question always appears: What does he mean? The same question appears here, too, but maybe with a little change: What does he mean, and why?*

"*The film is slow-moving most of the time. The fact that Bergman can get every actor or actress to do his best in any role can't save the audience from the tedious pace. There might be a world market for this film, thanks to the name of Ingmar Bergman, but it is doubtful of any great success.*"

— "Wing" in *Variety*

"*Ingmar Bergman's foray into high satiric comedy doesn't come off as well as might have been expected from the creator of some of the most arresting films of the past decade. The film's most intriguing quality is the manner in which Bergman has used color to suggest fantasy. He has put his performers through their paces against a white, pink and pale gray background, giving an out-of-this-world atmosphere to the action. He has, too, stylized the action to accommodate the unrealistic background.*

"*Bergman seems to be having a private joke on his contemporary movie-makers, but he has over-reached himself, as not too many people in the audience will appreciate his little joke, which is a bad one to begin with.*"

— Kate Cameron in
The New York Daily News

"*The gothic, brooding introspection that have been the hallmarks of his black-and-white Swedish dramas have been supplanted by pastel shades, slapstick and satire to little effect in* All These Women. *His latest work energetically takes pot shots at artists, their critics and women that are largely obvious and unfunny. The director, who also collaborated on the script, is labyrinthine in his approach to his story and his initial use of color.*

"Jarl Kulle plays the critic as broadly as Buster Keaton would, but with little flair for the timing and nuances that made some silent slapstick art.... As the widow, the stately, blonde Eva Dahlbeck appears to be the least quixotic in her characterization of a woman bearing her love and humiliation. Bibi Andersson makes a pretty and vacuous flirt; Harriet Andersson is pixyish and wise as an all-knowing maid, and Gertrud Fridh

and Barbro Hiort af Ornäs are momentarily seductive as the other charmers of the seraglio. Allan Edwall and Georg Funkquist add cynical vignettes as the manager and butler.

"'Genius,' Mr. Bergman has his critic say, 'is making a critic change his mind.' It is pretty difficult to do in the case of All These Women.*"*

—A. H. Weiler in
The New York Times

Persona
Svensk Filmindustri: 1966
(U.S. release by Lopert Pictures: 1967)

CREDITS

Director: Ingmar Bergman; *producer:* Lars-Owe Carlberg; *screenwriter:* Ingmar Bergman; *cinematographer:* Sven Nykvist; *editor:* Ulla Ryghe; *art director:* Bibi Lindstrom; *costumes:* Mago (Max Goldstein); *music:* Lars Johan Werle, with excerpts from Johann Sebastian Bach's Violin Concerto in E Major; *sound:* P. O. Pettersson; *assistant director:* Lenn Hjortzberg; *running time:* 84 minutes.

CAST

Bibi Andersson (*Sister Alma*); Liv Ullmann (*Elisabet Vogler*); Margaretha Krook *(Doctor)*; Gunnar Björnstrand (*Mr. Vogler*); Jörgen Lindström (*Elisabet's Son*).

Following his breakthrough into color film and the frivolous period comedics of *All These Women*, Bergman verged farther afield than ever before with the highly experimental and enigmatic chamber drama *Persona*. The director has termed this film "a poem of images" and explained that its genesis derived from a photograph taken of actresses Gunnel Lindblom and Bibi Andersson sunning together against a wall.

Using very little dialogue, *Persona*'s dreamlike—sometimes nightmarish—continuity involves a noted actress named Elisabet Vogler (Liv Ullmann*)* who's stricken with a nervous breakdown that renders her mute amid a performance of *Electra*. Her condition relegates her to the care of Sister

Alma (Bibi Andersson), a compassionate and admiring young nurse who cares for the woman at her remote beach house. Although physically fit, the actress chooses to remain silent, a condition that first challenges and then irritates Alma, whose bid for friendship is coolly rejected, even when she reveals secrets of her own past. Eventually, the two women's personalities appear to fuse, then separate, leaving the film open to wildly varying interpretations. Some have suggested that it's apparently a fourth entry in Bergman's "Silence of God" series, returning to the stark black-and-white austerity of earlier chamber pieces.

Persona was much written about and has become highly revered in the thirty-odd years since its premiere. America's National Society of Film Critics awarded it their Best Picture prize for 1967, with *Bonnie and Clyde* and *Closely Watched Trains* its nearest competition. At the same time, that group also named Ingmar Bergman the year's Best Director and Bibi Andersson Best Actress for her highly emotional work in *Persona*. Swedish critics considered *Persona* among Bergman's "simplest, freest and most powerful" motion pictures.

Bergman on Bergman

"At some time or other, I said that *Persona* saved my life — that is no exaggeration. If I had not found the strength to make that film, I would probably have been all washed up. One significant point: for the first time I did not care in the least whether the result would be a commercial success…

"Today I feel that in *Persona* — and later in *Cries and Whispers* — I had gone as far as I could go. And that in these two instances, when working in total freedom, I touched wordless secrets that only the cinema can discover."

Critics' Circle

"*Sven Nykvist's cinematography — I think black-and-white photography can achieve no greater heights — manages to abolish the boundaries between dream and waking. Liv Ullmann's actress and, even more so, Bibi Andersson's nurse, are overwhelming characterizations, the one making silence, the other chitchat, supremely eloquent. Bergman's dialogue, rhythms and mise en scène — the hospital, all vacuous white austerity; the seaside, beautiful yet also harsh; only the women, with their jolly dayclothes, frilly nightwear, or dreamily mingling blondness generating ephemeral warmth — are masterly every step of the arduous way.*"
— John Simon in *The New Leader*

"*In effect, the rule of the cinematic day seems to be the less palatable, the more in-*

volved — the less comprehensible, that is — the greater the creator. Thus, Persona, because it is in part perplexing (as well as intellectually complex), in part simpleminded (as well as sophisticated), in part exquisitely clear (as well as obscure) and in part sparkling with truth (as well as befogged by pretension), must be hailed as perhaps one of Bergman's best films."
— Judith Crist in
The New York World Journal Tribune

"*Liv Ullmann could have played the actress's role as 'just another pretty face,' but her face implies every nuance of feeling that her silence stifles; as for Bibi Andersson, her performance as the nurse is perhaps the best Bergman has ever coaxed from an actress.*"
— Richard Corliss in *Film Quarterly*

"*Most movies give so little that it seems almost barbarous to object to Bergman's not giving us more in* Persona, *but it is just because of the expressiveness and fascination of what we are given that the movie is so frustrating. There is, however, great intensity in many of the images, and there's one great passage: the nurse talks about a day and night of sex on a beach, and as she goes on talking, with memories of summer and nakedness and pleasure in her voice and the emptiness of her present life in her face, viewers may begin to hold their breath in fear that the director won't be able to sustain this almost intolerably difficult sequence. But he does, and it builds and builds and is completed. It's one of the rare truly erotic sequences in move history.*"
— Pauline Kael in
5001 Nights at the Movies

"*Reactions to* Persona *have mostly ranged from incomprehension to irritation with what is dismissed as a characteristic piece of self-indulgence on Bergman's part — Bergman talking to himself again. Certainly* Persona *is Bergman's most concentrated work, in a sense a summation of the themes dominant in most of his previous films; and it is undeniably a difficult film, if only because it leaves itself open to so many interpretations. But then so does* Hamlet; *and one suspects that negative reactions to* Persona *are*

Persona (1966). Bibi Andersson as Nurse Alma. Svensk Filmindustri.

afflicted with what medieval theologians called accidie—*a total indifference to life. Her doctor sends her packing to a villa on the Baltic in the company of a nurse. Slowly and subtly, a transference begins; the actress cannot, or will not, speak about her husband and son; the nurse cannot stop speaking—about herself. Without realizing it, the babbling nurse becomes the patient and the silently listening patient the nurse.*

— *Time*

"*The two actresses are handled with the usual Bergman insight into women, and are extraordinarily effective. Bibi Andersson's distraught, knowing, naïve, helpful and then resentful performance of the nurse is a tour-de-force, and Liv Ullmann's patient has the right luminous, questioning and sometimes impenetrable face and projection for the part of the beauteous but mute actress. The two women do look alike and this duality works visually and on a narrative plane. A scene of the nurse telling of an orgy is one of the most explicit scenes of this kind ever heard. But it is never scabrous, since it rings true, as the nurse tells all that happened* sans *moral restrictions.*"

—"Mosk" in *Variety*

more a response to Bergman than to the film itself."

— David Wilson in
Monthly Film Bulletin

"*Ingmar Bergman, during his last few films, has seemed to be in a decline; his work has gotten heavy and lackluster. Not that he is in a sparkling mood in* Persona, *by any means, be he has regained his vividness, his ability to surprise, while being as knotty and, in a way, as difficult as ever. In* Persona *he has chosen to tell the story of two women obliquely, and has introduced some of his favorite symbols, which might confuse unless one is already an indoctrinated Bergmanite. But even without a few necessary and clarifying keys, the film constantly absorbs.*"

—Hollis Alpert in *Saturday Review*

"*Director Ingmar Bergman is modern cinema's most persistent observer of the human condition.* Persona *fuses two of Bergman's familiar obsessions: personal loneliness and the particular anguish of contemporary woman. It is the story of a great stage actress*

"*The performances by Andersson and Ullmann are perfect. Any lesser word would be footling. Andersson, carrying almost all the dialogue, never fluctuates from a complete grip on the truth of the moment and the means of conveying it truly. Ullmann, silent almost throughout, nevertheless creates a complex human being in herself and by the use of things that are said to her—an extraordinary debut, silent but eloquent.*"

—Stanley Kauffmann in *Horizon*

Stimulantia
(Episode: *"Daniel"*)
Svensk Filmindustri: 1967
(No U.S. release)

CREDITS

Director/screenwriter/Eastmancolor cinematographer/narrator: Ingmar Bergman; *editor:* Ulla Ryghe*: music:* Käbi Laretei plays Mozart's "Ah, vous dis-je, Madame"; *running time:* 16 minutes.

CAST

Daniel Sabastian Bergman (*Himself*); Käbi Laretei (*Herself*)

Released in Sweden in the spring of 1967, *Stimulantia* consists of eight separate episodes, each shot by a different director, among them Hans Abramson, Jörn Donner, Lars Gorling, Arne Arnbom, Gustaf Molander, Vilgot Sjöman, Tage Danielsson and Hans Alfredson (the latter two in collaboration of one episode). Bergman's episode, entitled *Daniel*, is a sixteen-minute segment constructed form home-movie footage (shot in both color and black-and-white), focusing on the director's son, Daniel Bergman, in the first two years of his life. Also seen is the child's mother, Bergman's then-wife, Käbi Laretei, along with Ingmar's mother, Karin, all photographed between 1963 and 1965. Bergman himself introduces *Daniel*.

Despite the presence of actors as internationally known as Ingrid Bergman and Gunnar Björnstrand in other segments. *Stimulantia* appears not to have been shown in the English-speaking world. However, the *Daniel* segment was included in a 1995 Bergman retrospective in New York.

Vargtimmen
(Hour of the Wolf)
Svensk Filmindustri: 1968
(U.S. release by Lopert Pictures: 1968)

CREDITS

Director: Ingmar Bergman; *producer:* Lars-Owe Carlberg; *screenwriter:* Ingmar Bergman; *cinematographer:* Sven Nykvist; *editor:* Ulla Ryghe; *art director:* Marik Vos-Lundh; *costumes:* Mago (Max Goldstein); *music:* Lars Johan Werle, with excerpts from Johann Sebastian Bach's Sarabande in Partita No. 3 in A Minor and Mozart's opera "Die Zauberflöte" (The Magic Flute); *sound:* P. O. Pettersson; *assistant director:* Lenn Hjortzberg; *running time:* 89 minutes.

CAST

Liv Ullmann (*Alma Borg*); Max von Sydow (*Johan Borg*); Erland Josephson (*Baron von Merkens*); Gertrud Fridh (*Corinne von Merkens*); Gudrun Brost (*Old Mrs. von Merkens*); Ingrid Thulin (*Veronica Vogler*); Bertil Anderberg (*Ernst von Merkens*); Georg Rydeberg (*Archivist Lindhorst*); Ulf Johanson (*Curator Heerbrand*); Naima Wifstrand (*Old Woman with Hat*); Lenn Hjortzberg (*Kapellmeister Kreisler*); Agda Helin (*Maid*); Folke Sundquist (*Tamino*); Mikael Rundquist (*Boy in Dream Sequence*); Mona Seilitz (*Corpse in Morgue*).

Once again Bergman uses the setting of a desolate island to tell an enigmatic, narrow-focused tale of a tormented couple (Liv Ullmann and Max von Sydow), affording us a series of events and images which may or may not be real or which may or may not be nightmares. The story is introduced, directly to the camera, by Alma, the pregnant wife of Johan Borg, an artist beset increasingly by his own personal demons. Did Johan actually kill a strange and predatory little boy and toss his body into a tidal pool? Has a seductive mistress from his scandalous past returned to tempt him anew? Are the residents of that sinister old castle actually vampires? Characteristically, Bergman creates fascinating, mystifying images and events that confound the viewer and invite interpretation. But this time his vehicle is a dark and downbeat tale more likely to elicit a hopeless shrug and a dismissive gesture.

The film's forbidding title is explained in an on-screen quotation, to the effect that: "The hour of the wolf is the hour between night and dawn. It is the hour when most people die, when sleep is deepest, when nightmares are most real. It is the hour when the sleepless are haunted by their greatest dread, when ghosts and demons are most powerful. The hour of the wolf is also the hour when most children are born." Not that this makes lucid the events that follow. For many it's a phantasmagoria of dark and dreamlike images, most memorable of which may be the plaintive and recurring countenance of Liv Ullmann, her marvelous cheekbones and unvarnished beauty captured by the carefully lit camera work of Sven Nykvist.

Bergman on Bergman

"*Hour of the Wolf* is seen by some as a regression after *Persona*. It isn't that simple. *Persona* was a breakthrough, a success that gave me the courage to keep on searching along unknown paths. For several reasons that film has become a more open affair than others, more tangible: a woman who is mute, another who speaks; therefore, a conflict. *Hour of the Wolf*, on the other hand, is more vague. There is within that film a consciously formal and thematic disintegration. When I see *Hour of the Wolf* today, I understand that it is about a deep-seated division within me, both hidden and carefully monitored, visible in both my earlier and later work: Aman in *The Magician*; Ester in *The Silence*; Tomas in *Face to Face*; Elisabet in *Persona*; Ismael in *Fanny and Alexander*. To me, *Hour of the Wolf* is important, since it is an attempt to encircle a hard-to-locate set of problems and get inside them."

Critics' Circle

"*This is a brilliant Gothic fantasy in which Bergman keeps his hero's obsession under perfect control as it grows like a cancer from the menacing calm of the opening, through the whispered fears of the night, to the full-blooded terrors of the end: nowhere else has he so displayed and dominated his taste for the flamboyant techniques of expressionism, surrealism and Gothic horror. At the same time, the film is much more: seen in relation to* Persona, *it is the submerged half of the iceberg, an attempt to portray the state of mind which made Elisabet Vogler (in* Persona*) retreat into despairing silence.*
— Tom Milne in *Monthly Film Bulletin*

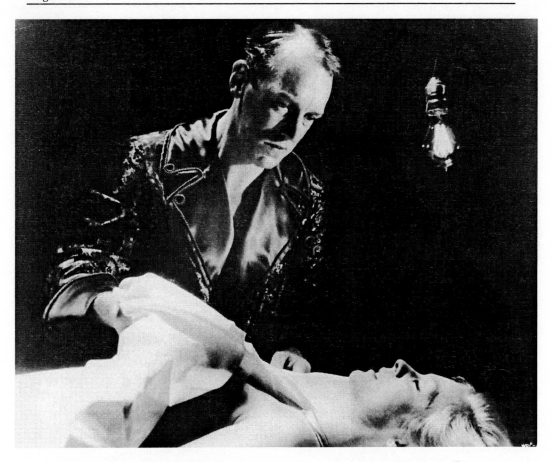

Hour of the Wolf **(1968). Max von Sydow and Ingrid Thulin. Svensk Filmindustri.**

"Coming after Persona, *Ingmar Bergman's* Hour of the Wolf *is something of a letdown, because, while continuing the Swedish director's more recent preoccupations, the film is far less evocative, narrower in scope, and, consequently, less intriguing. In* Persona, *the actress-struck-dumb could be taken as representative of the artist sensibility (although not all commentators on the film agreed to this interpretation); in* Hour of the Wolf, *it is an actual artist—a painter, to be precise— who teeters on the verge of insanity, and finally goes over. That much can be said, with some certainty, about the film. Beyond this, Bergman offers only speculation and mystification...*

"Nothing Bergman does is, for me, without interest, but I am not particularly fond of enigmas, and with this one he tries the patience."

— Hollis Alpert in *Saturday Review*

"Though he has glaring faults as a scenarist, director Bergman is supreme in handling his troupe; the actors, like Sven Nykvist's phosphorescent photography, can render reality and surreality without missing a heartbeat. Von Sydow is gothically brilliant as the madman; Ullmann's tragedienne reinforces her position—already secured by Persona *—as one of Scandinavia's major actresses. If, in the end,* Hour of the Wolf *suffers from simplistic psychiatry and some less-than-fresh observations of man's fate, it remains worthwhile simply because Ingmar Bergman can turn homilies into revelations"*

— *Time*

*"*Hour of the Wolf *feels like two films. The first half focuses on Alma, the pregnant wife, and on the problems of human communication and love; the second half is a chamber of horrors in which the artist struggles for*

survival. *Even though a disappointment, Hour of the Wolf is still the work of an extraordinary craftsman, but it is hardly a film to attract large audiences outside of those seriously interested in films.*"

—"Fred" in *Variety*

"*True, this exploration of madness, half-observed, half-shared by the wife of the painter who is obsessed thereby, is filled with the stark intellectualizing and the lush fantasizing that are the distinctions of Berg-*

man's world and work; but it seems a minor effort on his part and does not extend our realization of his art or his mind beyond what his other films show.*"

— Judith Crist in *New York*

"*Rather like the gloomy side of Smiles of a Summer Night, this very typical Bergman melodrama doesn't quite flow as intended, and whatever its meaning may be, its surface is less entertaining than usual.*"

—*Halliwell's Film Guide*

Skammen (Shame/The Shame)

Svensk Filmindustri: 1968
(U.S. release by Lopert Pictures: 1968)

CREDITS

Director: Ingmar Bergman; *producer:* Lars-Owe Carlberg; *screenwriter:* Ingmar Bergman; *cinematographer:* Sven Nykvist; *editor:* Ulla Ryghe; *art director:* P. A. Lundgren; *costumes:* Mago (Max Goldstein) and Eivor Kullberg; *music:* Lars Johan Werle, with excerpts from Bach and Mozart; *sound:* Lennart Engholm; *military advisers:* Lennart Bergqvist and Stig Lindberg; *assistant director:* Raymond Lundberg; *running time:* 103 minutes.

CAST

Liv Ullmann (*Eva Rosenberg*); Max von Sydow (*Jan Rosenberg*); Gunnar Björnstrand (*Jacobi*); Birgitta Valberg (*Mrs. Jacobi*); Sigge Fürst (*Filip*); Hans Alfredson (*Lobelius*); Ingvar Kjellson (*Oswald*); Frank Sundström (*Interrogator*); Ulf Johansson (*Doctor*); Frej Lindqvist (*Stooped Man*); Rune Lindström (*Fat Man*); Willy Peters (*Elderly Officer*); Bengt Eklund (*Guard*); Åke Jörnfalk (*Condemned Man*); Vilgot Sjöman (*Interviewer*); Lars Amble (*Officer*); Björn Thambert (*Johan*); Karl-Axel Forsberg (*Secretary*); Gösta Prüzelius (*Pastor*); Brita Öberg (*Lady in Interrogation Room*); Agda Helin (*Woman in Shop*); Ellika Mann (*Prison Warden*); Jan Bergman (*Jacobi's Chauffeur*); Stig Lindberg (*Doctor's Assistant*).

Shame is like nothing Bergman had attempted heretofore. Lacking the customary searches for God and meaning amid symbols, abstract images and ambiguities, this is another kind of nightmare story. Unable, because of an ear infection, to attend the film's premiere at the International Cinema

Incontri in Sorrento, Italy, the writer-director sent the following message: "As an artist, I am horror-stricken by what is happening in the world, and I cannot side with any political system. I hope that in *The Shame* I have been able to convey the intense fear I experience." And he added that this movie was

Shame (1968). Max von Sydow, Liv Ullmann and Björn Thambert. Svensk Filmindustri.

designed "to show unpretentiously how humiliation and the rape of human pride can lead to the loss of humanity in the victim himself."

This somewhat futuristic tale takes place in 1971 on an island of an unnamed country where a terrible civil war is raging on the mainland. Classical musicians Eva and Jan Rosenberg (Liv Ullmann and Max von Sydow) took refuge here when their symphony orchestra was disbanded. They now appear to subsist modestly on produce grown on their property and sold in town. The war has been remote for them, for they harbor no political affiliations, but there are increasing signs of its approach as menacing planes fly over and church bells ring inexplicably. When an aircraft is shot down near their farm, soldiers from both armies swarm over the island. The Rosenbergs are unintentionally caught up, politically, when they're arrested on suspicion of collaboration and are subjected to a filmed TV interview that is later tampered with, dubbing outrageous rhetoric into their mouths. Their release is effected through the intervention of Colonel Jacobi (Gunner Björnstrand), an old friend who's in charge of the army defending the island. But Jacobi's help costs them dearly; resulting in a sexual episode with Eva while Jan dozes drunkenly. By the film's end, the pacifistic Jan has been forced to shoot Jacobi and has even gone so far as to kill an innocent young soldier for his boots. As their terrible ordeal comes to a close, the now homeless Rosenbergs share a crowded boat, with equally desperate strangers, as it drifts by a tide swell of dead soldiers in the waters off their island.

Shame, as it was called in America, won awards from the National Society of Film Critics for Best Film, Best Director, and Best Actress (Ullmann).

Bergman on Bergman

"When I see *Shame* today, I find that it can be divided into two parts. The first half, which is about the events of the war, is bad. The second half, which is about the effects of the war, is good. The first half is much worse than I had imagined; the second much better than I had remembered. There are bits and pieces of the first half that are all right. The movie begins well. The couple's situation and background are effectively established. The good part of the film starts with the moment the war is over and the pain of the aftermath sets in. It begins in a potato field, where Liv Ullmann and Max von Sydow move in oppressing silence."

Critics' Circle

"*By contrast with* Persona *and* Hour of the Wolf, *Bergman's new film is starkly pruned to absolute necessity — no flashbacks, no fantasies, and barely a touch of the eccentric — but thematically it forms a compendium of all the points raised by its predecessors...*

"*Most of all,* The Shame *is a film about betrayal, a sickness which spreads out almost tangibly from the fisherman, Filip, until he slips despairingly into the sea: the Rosenbergs betray each other, they are betrayed by their television 'interviewers,' they betray the savior-betrayer Jacobi, and they kill the exhausted young soldier who trusts them. Finally, of course, they have betrayed themselves.*"

—Philip Strick in
Monthly Film Bulletin

"*One of the noteworthy films of the year. It can easily be said that any Ingmar Bergman film is noteworthy outside the context of his own creations. Within the framework*

of his films, however, Shame *stands as perhaps the most unrelenting in its theme, going beyond the chilling exploration of a loveless humanity in* Winter Light *and* The Silence *to cry shame upon the God who has reduced man to bestiality and his civilization to nihilism. It is late in the creative day to be antiwar in specific terms, but Bergman's genius translates the specifics into universals: his is a nameless and continuing civil war in which only the animal instinct for survival motivates human relations.... Shame is Bergman's definitive apocalyptic vision, painful and powerful. Strangely, it is more statement than revelation to Bergman devotees, who will have the strength to take this film; those whom it may inform and enlighten, who need the warning of holocaust most, will, as always and perhaps understandably, avoid it as they have other Bergmanian truths.*"

—Judith Crist in *New York*

"*Shame could be a film about the tenacity of civilians, but it is more like a document just before extinction. There is no strength in it. It is at Bergman's wit's end. Even the idea that a childless couple would go to such limits of energy simply not to die is not self-evident or even convincing any more.*"

—Renata Adler in
The New York Times

"*After a series of films with small casts and a concentration on personal, private problems, Ingmar Bergman had made a film with a large cast that deals with the more impersonal relationship between war and man, about the destructive impact of war that can drive people to most shameful acts. Bergman has said that he was inspired by the Vietnam War and World War II.*

—"Fred" in *Variety*

"*Ingmar Bergman's simple, masterly vision of normal war and what it does to survivors.*

"*Shame is a masterpiece, and it is so thoroughly accessible that I'm afraid some members of the audience may consider it too obvious.*

"*It is the chaos of life in wartime seen*

through an ordering intelligence. One of Bergman's greatest films, this is one of the least known."

—Pauline Kael in *The New Yorker*

"For the last several years, it has been unfair to judge Bergman on an individual film. What matters is the body of his work — comprising twenty-nine films — which now amounts to a great literature of heroic despair. Nor is it legitimate to speak of Berg-

man's players merely as actors. People like Von Sydow and Björnstrand have been with him for over a decade. What the Moscow Art Theatre was to Stanislavsky, these performers are to Bergman — ensemble members who function like fingers on a hand. Liv Ullmann, newest member of the troupe, is, astonishingly, the best, portraying a whole range of feminine response, from molten eroticism to glacial hate."

— *Time*

Riten
(The Ritual/The Rite)

Svensk Filmindustri/Sveriges TV/Cinematograph: 1969
(U.S. release by Janus Films: 1969)

CREDITS

Director: Ingmar Bergman; *producer:* Lars-Owe Carlberg; *screenwriter:* Ingmar Bergman; *cinematographer:* Sven Nykvist; *editor:* Siv Kanälv; *art director:* Lennart Blomkvist; *costumes:* Mago (Max Goldstein); *sound:* Lennart Engholm and Berndt Frithiof; *special effects:* Nils Skippstedt; *assistant director:* Christer Dahl; *running time:* 74 minutes.

CAST

Ingrid Thulin (*Thea Winklemann*); Anders Ek (*Albert Emmanuel Sebastian Fischer*); Gunnar Björnstrand (*Hans Winkelmann*); Erik Hell (*Judge Ernst Abrahamsson*); Ingmar Bergman (*Priest in Confessional*).

With this relatively short film (seventy-five minutes), Bergman ventured into television with yet another chamber drama. In rehearsal for a month, it was filmed in a mere nine days in May and June 1968, utilizing a tiny cast of four actors. The director himself took on the brief speaking role of a confessional priest. Shot mostly in a succession of tight close-ups, the film is obviously produced on a small budget with no visible sets per se. Its Kafkaesque story involves the interrogation of three members of a theatrical troupe by a sadistic, deceptively calm bureaucrat, Judge Abrahamsson (Erik

Hell), who indulges in subtle cat-and-mouse sessions with the sexually promiscuous Thea Winkelmann (Ingrid Thulin), her patient, older husband Hans (Gunnar Björnstrand), and her neurotic lover, Sebastian Fischer (Anders Ek). The reason for their persecution: an ostensibly obscene performance they are reputed to have given.

Although shown in Sweden on TV, *The Ritual* (or *The Rite*, as it is known in the U.K.) represents the first of a succession of Bergman works for the small screen to have been shown theatrically elsewhere in the world.

The Ritual (1969). Anders Ek and Ingrid Thulin. Svensk Filmindustri.

Bergman on Bergman

"I wrote *The Ritual* quickly and without pretensions. There is not much lighting in *The Ritual*. The film is markedly aggressive and received startled reactions, both within the television's theater department and from the critics. Today when I watch *The Ritual* or read the screenplay, I see how I could have made the film differently."

Critics' Circle

"The Ritual *looks quite diffrent from any other Bergman movie we've seen simply because it is not a movie. It's a seventy-five minute play, in nine scenes, made for Swedish television, a fact that is impossible to forget while watching it projected on a large theatre screen. The film has a tight, almost claustrophobic compactness.*"
—Vincent Canby in
The New York Times

"*The acting is knowing, direct and professionally dazzling, as is Bergman's calm technical prowess. But again the personal symbols, the ritual of art and whether it is necessary or not, and other inferences may engross many or leave others puzzled or somewhat left out of Bergman's constant attempts to communicate with God or mankind, and usually finding it wanting or impossible, but at least making the attempt.*"
—"Mosk' in *Variety*

"*It is characteristic of Bergman that the judge should be killed not by brute force but almost by proxy, by inducing a degree of empathy in him that makes the ritual, for all its contrivance, a deadly weapon. The Bergman artist exerts a ruthless hold over his adversary, a hold that the philistine (i.e. the spectator) cannot combat because he does not have access to the mechanics of art. The Ritual, in the final analysis, embodies Bergman's own hatred of the officialdom—and the critics—that irked him during his years as head of the Royal Dramatic Theater.*"
—Peter Cowie in *Ingmar Bergman*

En Passion
(The Passion of Anna/A Passion)

Svensk Filmindustri/Cinematograph: 1969
(U.S. release by United Artists: 1970)

CREDITS

Director: Ingmar Bergman; *producer:* Lars-Owe Carlberg; *screenwriter:* Ingmar Bergman; *Eastmancolor cinematographer:* Sven Nykvist; *editor* Siv Kanälv; *art director:* P. A. Lundgren; *set decorator:* Lennart Blomkvist; *Costumes:* Mago (Max Goldstein); *music:* excerpts from Bach's Partita No. 3 in A Minor and from Allan Gray's song "Always Romantic"; *sound:* Lennart Engholm; *running time:* 101 minutes.

CAST

Max von Sydow (*Andreas Winkelmann*); Liv Ullmann (*Anna Fromm*); Bibi Andersson (*Eva Vergérus*); Erland Josephson (*Elis Vergérus*); Erik Hell (*Johan Andersson*); Sigge Fürst (*Verner*); Svea Holst (*Verner's Wife*); Annika Kronberg (*Katarina*); Hjördis Pettersson (*Johan's Sister*); Lars-Owe Carlberg and Brian Wikström (*Policeman*); Barbro Hiort af Ornäs, Malin Ek, Britta Brunius, Brita Öberg and Marianne Karlbeck (*Women in Nightmare Sequence*).

Bergman returned to the use of color film, albeit a bleak—at times, almost monochromatic—use of Eastmancolor stock, with this spare study of four unhappy people living in a desolate landscape. Entirely shot on the director's home island of Fårö, *En Passion* (or *A Passion*, as it is most accurately translated) focuses on a mysterious near recluse named Andreas Winkelmann (Max von Sydow), whose past appears to have included a failed marriage and incarceration for forgery and drunken misbehavior. The widowed Anna Fromm (Liv Ullmann) enters his life one day when she asks to use his phone, and he overhears her emotional conversation with an unknown party. When she leaves her purse behind, Winkelmann finds a strange letter addressed to her late husband, also named Andreas, who died in the car crash that left Anna with a crippled leg and that also killed their son. The pair meet again when both are invited to dine with a neighboring couple, Eva and Elis Vergérus (Bibi Andersson and Erland Josephson), whose childlessness has rendered their union meaningless. While Elis is away on business, the lonely Eva visits Winkelmann, and a brief affair ensues. But Winkelmann realizes a mutual attraction to Anna, and *they* begin living together in his sparse cottage, where he works as Vergérus's assistant and she does translations. A subplot involves the senseless killing of animals on the island by an unknown madman, who may or may not be the local loner, Johan Andersson (Erik Hell), who is eventually attacked by islanders and savagely beaten, leading to his suicide. At the same time, Anna and Winkelmann find themselves growing apart, and after each has violently confronted the other with lies and cover-ups, these tortured people effect an unexpected resolution of their relationship.

Along with *Hour of the Wolf* and *Shame*, *The Passion of Anna* (as this was exploitatively called in the United States), continuing the thread of violence intruding on ordinary lives, has been designated as forming the second of Bergman's 1960s thematic trilogies.

The Passion of Anna (1969). Bibi Andersson and Max von Sydow. Svensk Filmindustri.

Bergman on Bergman

"*The Passion of Anna* was made on Fårö Island during the fall of 1968 and carries traces of the winds that were blowing in those days both in the real world and in the world of film. In some respects, therefore, it looks very dated. In other ways it is powerful and shows a break with accepted film practices. I look at it with mixed feelings. *The Passion of Anna* is in some ways a variation of *Shame*. It depicts what I really wanted to show in *Shame*— the violence manifested in an underhanded way. Actually, it is the same story but told more credibly..."

Critics' Circle

"*Few films can have had so many close-ups. Instead of flashbacks, people describe things; Bergman is loosening the traditional film links between sound track and image. The moments when the actors slip out of their parts to talk about their characters are not modish, not neo–Godard, but brilliantly necessary. They have much the same effect as the showing of film stock breaking in* Persona*— it is as though the dramatic medium itself had for the moment snapped under stress.*

—Penelope Gilliatt in
The New Yorker

"*Ingmar Bergman's thirtieth film may well be one of his most austere and yet the clearest and most penetrating. A crucible look at four characters on an island takes on dimensions in dealing with such themes as violence in the world today and man's stand to live with himself and his conscience. This chamber music of the soul should get specialized adherence and critical attention.*
"*It may be his masterpiece.*"

—"Mosk" in *Variety*

"The Passion of Anna *is one of Bergman's most beautiful films, all tawny, wintery grays and browns, deep blacks and dark greens, highlighted occasionally by splashes of red, sometimes blood. It is also, on the surface, one of his most lucid, if a film that tries to dramatize spiritual exhaustion can be ever said to be really lucid. However, like all of Bergman's recent films, it does seem designed more for the indefatigable Bergman cryptologists (of which I am not one) than for interested, but uncommitted filmgoers.*

—Vincent Canby in
The New York Times

"*This superb movie, one the director's rare forays into color cinematography, is beautifully photographed by Sven Nykvist, and its study of alienation, aloneness and insanity in the interrelationships of two men and two women is brilliantly acted, but then we have almost come to take such brilliance for granted from Max von Sydow, Bibi Andersson and the fantastic Liv Ullmann.*"

— *The Independent Film Journal*

Fårö-Dokument
(The Fårö Document)

A Cinematograph production for Swedish TV: 1970
(No U.S. distribution)

CREDITS

Director: Ingmar Bergman; *producer:* Lars-Owe Carlberg; *B/W-Eastmancolor cinematographer:* Sven Nykvist; *editor:* Siv Kanälv-Lundgren; *running time:* 78 minutes.

CAST

Ingmar Bergman (*Reporter*); with inhabitants of the island of Fårö.

Bergman's first documentary, centering on the island of Fårö— the setting for most of his late–1960s films — was conceived for television and not shown outside Scandinavia. Interview segments with Fårö residents were shot in black and white with a handheld 16-mm camera, while landscape photography of the island was filmed in Eastmancolor.

The filmmaker was motivated to create this work because he felt that island conditions needed government improvement if its young people were to have any reason to remain there and inherit the farming legacies of their hardpressed elders. As a result, the telecast enjoyed high viewer interest when it aired on New Year's Day, 1970.

Bergman on Bergman

"Sven Nykvist and I thought we'd make this film about sheep-breeding. I talked to a sheep-owner, Werner Larsson — the man who is interviewed in a bus. We began talking about the slaughterhouse, how, though the slaughterhouse commands high prices, it yields less to the producers than slaughterhouses on the mainland do. We felt there must be something tricky about that.

"Gradually studying things on Fårö and the Fårö peoples' problems became more and more fascinating. I thought to myself: we must look into this slaughterhouse business; and the ferry traffic; and the bus traffic; and road policy. In many respects the island has been allowed to fall damnably behind the times. So I began looking into things and chatting with people, and one thing led to another."

Beröringen
(The Touch)

Svensk Filmindustri release of a Cinematograph/ABC Pictures production: 1971
(U.S. release by Cinerama Releasing Corp.: 1971)

CREDITS

Director: Ingmar Bergman; *producer:* Lars-Owe Carlberg; *screenwriter:* Ingmar Bergman; *Eastmancolor cinematographer:* Sven Nykvist; *editor:* Siv Kanälv-Lundgren; *art director:* P. A. Lundgren; *costumes:* Mago (Max Goldstein); *music:* Jan Johansson; *sound:* Lennart Engholm; *assistant director:* Arne Carlsson; *running time:* 113 minutes.

CAST

Elliot Gould (*David Kovac*); Bibi Andersson (*Karin Vergérus*); Max von Sydow (*Dr. Andreas Vergérus*); Sheila Reid (*Sara Kovac*); Barbro Hiort af Ornäs (*Karin's Mother*); Staffan Hallerstam (*Anders Vergérus*); Maria Nolgård (*Agnes Vergérus*); Åke Lindström (*Doctor*); Mimmi Wåhlander (*Nurse*); Else Ebbesen (*Matron*); Anna von Rosen and Karin Nilsson (*Neighbors*); Erik Nyhlén (*Archaeologist*); Margareta Byström (*Dr. Vergérus's Secretary*); Alan Simon (*Museum Curator*); Per Sjöstrand (*Another Curator*); Aino Taube (*Woman on Staircase*); Ann-Christin Lobråten (*Museum Worker*); Denis Gotobed (*British Immigration Officer*); Bengt Ottekil (*London Bellhop*); Harry Schein and Stig Björkman (*Guests at Party*); Carol Zavis (*Flight Attendant*).

The Touch, Bergman's first film to be shot in English, came about as the result of talks between the filmmaker and ABC Corporation executives Leonard Goldenson and Martin Baum. With that company entering into motion-picture production, an agreement was reached with Bergman, paying him a million dollars for a film which he would write, produce, and direct, and which would feature an American star in the male lead. The director's first choice, Dustin Hoffman, was unavailable, and so Bergman selected Elliot Gould, who was then a popu- lar actor because of 1969's *Bob & Carol & Ted & Alice* and the following year's *M*A*S*H*.

Bergman's screenplay was inspired by the extramarital affair his mother Karin had once enjoyed, although she later returned to the stability of her marriage to his father. Naming his female protagonist Karin, and her husband Dr. Andreas Vergérus, he oddly chose to retain the character name of *The Passion of Anna*'s male lead and compounded the confusion by casting Max von Sydow to portray his *second* Andreas Vergérus, albeit a character totally unrelated to that in the earlier film. With Bibi Andersson as Karin, the wife and mother who strays from her marriage of fifteen years, the story's basis was not unfamiliar for Bergman. What was out of place, in the opinion of many, was the casting of Gould as David Kovac, the Jewish archaeologist who becomes a patient of the doctor, while working on a dig at an old church in the area. Friendship develops into an affair between the wife and the newcomer that turns turbulent and eventually results in Karin's pursuing David to London, where she meets his crippled sister, Sara (Sheila Reid), who informs her that they are inseparable. David now attempts to win her back, but Karin decides to return to Andreas.

The Touch did not go over well with either the press or the public, and Bergman next turned back to Scandinavian subject matter, with which he was more comfortable.

Bergman on Bergman

"The intention was to shoot *The Touch* in both English and Swedish. In an original version that doesn't seem to exist anymore, English was spoken by those who were English-speaking and Swedish by those who were Swedes. I believe that it just possibly was slightly less unbearable than the totally English-language version, which was made at the request of the Americans.

The story I bungled so badly was based on something extremely personal to me: the secret life of someone who loves becomes gradually the only real life, and the real life becomes an illusion."

Critics' Circle

"Ingmar Bergman, master of enigma, surprises us with his first movie in English. The story of a love triangle is so lucid, even conventional, that it should be easily followed and enjoyed by broad audiences. But Bergman is Bergman. Beneath the surface

view are layers of human relationships to be pondered. Gould—the first American Bergman has ever cast—gives a performance matching the other skillful Bergman regulars as the anxious, hostile young man with a terrible private burden. The story may not always be wholly convincing in plot terms, but everything the great director does has such purpose and effect that the movie is a joy for the lover of cinematic technique and intelligence."

—William Wolf in *Cue*

"The trouble with The Touch is not in the situation, or in the ideas, but in the language. The English dialogue that Bergman has given his stars sounds like those early, grammatically perfect, and lifeless translations of Ibsen that Eva LeGallienne used to pump around the American stage. The banality of the language has no visibly ill effect on the performances of Miss Andersson and von Sydow, who, when they are speaking English, must sound a little bit strange and self-conscious. It is, however, fatal to Gould, who doesn't help matters by giving his lines those slightly flat readings that were so funny in M*A*S*H and Bob & Carol & Ted & Alice, but, in The Touch, suggest that the actor is in a different dimension of drama from those of his costars."

—Vincent Canby in *The New York Times*

"If Elliott Gould's David is certainly brooding and strange, it's unfortunate that in the English version of the film showing here (there is another version in which the characters speak English to David and Swedish to one another) he is likely to appear yet more alien to English speakers than to the Swedes. His part is scripted in the slightly archaic, language-primer phrases one accepts more readily in subtitles, and this gives his spontaneous outbursts a misplaced and portentously literary quality. That the bond between him and Karin slowly erodes its way into credibility is almost entirely due to Bibi Andersson's magical performance. Her characterization of a shallow woman suddenly prey to deep emotions is faultless—whether nervously inventorying her physical defects as she begins the affair, scowling at herself in

The Touch (1971). Elliott Gould and Bibi Andersson on the set with Bergman. Svensk Filmindustri.

the mirror, or simply avoiding her husband's eyes. It is probably the most memorable and the most moving portrait of a lady that Bergman has ever given us."

— Jan Dawson in
Monthly Film Bulletin

"The evolution of Bibi Andersson under Bergman has been nothing short of marvelous: from simple, uncomplicated, and shallow (through the trauma of Persona among other things) to simple, uncomplicated, and deep. She is in some ways the most bourgeois and unimaginative of Bergman's women. But if she is the simplest and least neurotic, she is also the strongest and most adult. Never has Bergman so thoroughly penetrated the depths of her emotions through the changing surfaces of that beautiful, wholesome, inquisitive, sensual face."

— Molly Haskell
in *The Village Voice*

"Bergman's new effort is something of a sabbatical. The complexities of his recent movies are missing here; there is less than meets the eye. Nonetheless, symbol hunters may grasp onto the ancient statue of the Virgin Mary which the archeologist unearths in a Swedish church. The statue is being eaten from within by some form of termite hatching from larvae that has survived centuries of being buried. The archeologist's discovery of the statue ultimately brings on its destruction, paralleling the American's disruption of Karin's and Andreas's marriage."

— *The Independent Film Journal*

Viskningar och Rop (Cries and Whispers)

Cinematograph/Svenska Filminstitutet: 1972 (U.S. release by New World Pictures: 1973)

CREDITS

Director: Ingmar Bergman; *producer:* Lars-Owe Carlberg; *screenwriter:* Ingmar Bergman; *Eastmancolor cinematographer:* Sven Nykvist; *editor:* Siv Lundgren; *art director:* Marik Vos; *costumes:* Greta Johansson; *music:* Chopin's Mazurka in A Minor, played by Käbi Laretei; Bach's Sarabande No. 5 in D Minor, played by Pierre Fournier; *sound:* Owe Svensson; *running time:* 94 minutes.

CAST

Harriet Andersson (*Agnes*); Kari Sylwan (*Anna*); Ingrid Thulin (*Karin*); Liv Ullmann (*Maria/Maria's Mother*); Erland Josephson (*Dr. Lakaren*); Henning Moritzen (*Joakim, Maria's Husband*); Georg Årlin (*Fredik, Karin's Husband*); Anders Ek (*Pastor Isak*); Inga Gill (*Aunt Olga*); Linn Ullmann (*Maria's Daughter*); Rosanna Mariano (*Agnes as a Child*); Lena Bergman (*Maria as a Child*); Monika Priede (*Karin as a Child*); Malin Gjörup (*Anna's Daughter*); Greta and Karin Johansson (*Mortician's Helpers*).

Bergman had not had a successful film for some time, which now made it difficult to obtain backing for his next screenplay, *Cries and Whispers*. Again, it was not considered a promising subject for popular consumption, this period piece about a death watch carried out by two unloving sisters of a third sister, who is more appreciated by a devoted young woman servant than by her own siblings. The only solution appeared to be mass concessions on the part of the filmmaker and his longtime colleagues: Bergman financed the picture with his own money, while Harriet Andersson, Ingrid Thulin and Liv Ullmann agreed to forgo salaries, with the agreement that they would share in the movie's eventual earnings. Cinematographer Sven Nykvist participated on a similar basis, and the film was entirely shot on an old country estate in Mariefred, Sweden.

A moving, emotional motion picture, *Cries and Whispers* compels the viewer with its story of a family's efforts to communicate in an hour of crisis — all of which is told with great artistry and, as usual in Bergman's films, beautifully acted. Its importance in the director's canon is signified by the rack of prizes it managed to accumulate: five Academy Award nominations, including Best Picture, Director, Original Screenplay, Cinematography and Costume Design, although its sole win was for Marik Vos's wardrobe. But the New York Film Critics rewarded *Cries and Whispers* for Best Film, Best Screenplay, Best Direction and Best Actress (Liv Ullmann); the National Society of Film Critics gave it their prizes for Best Script and Photography; and the National Board of Review awarded Bergman their Best Director plaque and another to *Cries and Whispers* as the year's Best Foreign-Language Film.

Bergman on Bergman

"All my films can be thought in black and white, except for *Cries and Whispers*. In the screenplay, I say that I have thought of the color red as the interior of the soul. When I was a child, I saw the soul as a shadowy dragon, blue as smoke, hovering like an enormous winged creature, half bird, half fish. But inside the dragon everything was red.

"When four extraordinary actresses are brought together, fatal emotional collisions can easily result. But the women were good, loyal, and helpful. Besides, most important, they were all incredibly talented. I have absolutely no reason to complain. And I'm happy to report that I did not."

Critics' Circle

"*Cries and Whispers is such an intimate examination of the feminine psyche that its*

creator, Ingmar Bergman, seemed to possess a form of X-ray vision. In some extraordinary way he is able to see into the inner recesses of the human soul. In what is obviously a labor of love, Bergman probes the lives of four women. Dissecting them with the expertise and sensitivity of a skilled surgeon, he leaves exposed all their passions, their anxieties, their frustrations and their insecurities until one is face to face with their very souls and the cries and whispers that echo from their souls. The result of this enforced intimacy is an illuminating, sobering and finally devastating film."

—Kathleen Carroll in
The New York Daily News

"Bergman's lean style, his use of lingering close-ups, fades to red and a soundtrack echoing with the ticking of clocks, the rustle of dresses and the hushed cries of the lost gives the picture a hypnotic impact. Sven Nykvist's Eastmancolor camera, working on period sets dominated by warm reds, catches images of lush beauty that complement the stark emotional undertones. Cries and Whispers is naturally not general-audience holiday fare. Viewing it is both a depressing and exhilarating experience. The depression comes from the subject matter, the exhilaration from sheer admiration for Bergman's achievement."

—Addison Verrall in *Variety*

"Cries and Whispers *is like no movie I've seen before, and like no movie Ingmar Bergman has made before; although we are all likely to see many films in our lives, there will be few like this one. It is hypnotic, disturbing, frightening. We slip lower in our seats, feeling claustrophobia and sexual disquiet, realizing that we have been surrounded by the vision of a filmmaker who has absolute mastery of his art.*"

—Roger Ebert in
The Chicago Sun-Times

"Bergman's story-screenplay stands on its own, true; but his genius is in the scarlets of his sets, the vibrant life of his creation of sounds that pierce the vision, of visions that penetrate to the very soul of the observer. But the cumulative moments, the reality of each

Cries and Whispers (1972). **Ingrid Thulin and Liv Ullmann. Cinematograph. Photo: Bo-Erik Gyberg.**

fantasy and the phantasmagoria of existence combine for a work of genius — certainly the most complex, the most perceptive and the most humane of Bergman's works to date."
        —Judith Crist in *New York*

"The movie is Bergman's The Three Sisters, not set in any recognizable provinces but in three overlapping wastelands of the soul. On the occasion of Agnes's dying, the three sisters come together again briefly, each life having already peaked. Each longs for the kind of communion they may or may not have had in childhood, though they remember having had it. Each realizes that it is now impossible.

"Cries and Whispers is not an easy film to describe or to endure. It stands alone and it reduces almost everything else you're likely to see this season to the size of a small cinder."

        —Vincent Canby in
        The New York Times

"Flawlessly acted, filmed with much the same deceptive simplicity and kaleidoscopic intensity as Persona *(gestures and actions reverberating through and beyond each other), and clearly inspired by a haunting personal regret,* Cries and Whispers *is superlative even for Bergman; a laceratingly beautiful attempt to explore the human need not only to draw comfort from the past, but to project love back into its dusty reaches."*
        —Tom Milne in
        Monthly Film Bulletin

"It is style that elevates this masterwork, lends it its incredible intensity of feeling and extraordinary sense of intimacy. Bergman has stated that his films are essentially emotional experiences, and Cries and Whispers *stands as his ultimate argument."*
        —Paul D. Zimmerman in *Newsweek*

"The performances have a soul-deep conviction which appears to transcend the craft

of acting as such. Harriet Andersson, wan and hollow-eyed, her lips parched with fever and pain, conveys the sense of real anguish so tellingly that it is impossible not to be moved. Miss Ullmann gives us still another astonishing portrayal: of a woman who is both shallow and complicated, warm and

cruel, self-centered but unable to be alone. Miss Thulin, bursting out of repression with shrieks of rage and despair, brings off moments which link Bergman's landed gentry with the agonies of Greek tragedy."

—Charles Champlin in
The Los Angeles Times

Scener ur ett Äktenskap
(Scenes from a Marriage)

A Cinematograph production for Swedish TV: 1973
(U.S. release of the feature version by Cinema 5: 1974)

CREDITS

Director: Ingmar Bergman; *producer:* Lars-Owe Carlberg; *screenwriter:* Ingmar Bergman; *Eastmancolor cinematographer:* Sven Nykvist; *editor:* Siv Lungren; *art director:* Björn Thulin; *costumes:* Inger Pehrsson; *sound:* Owe Svensson; *running time:* 282 minutes (TV version); 168 minutes (theatrical version).

CAST

Liv Ullmann (*Marianne*); Erland Josephson (*Johan*); Bibi Andersson (*Katarina*); Jan Malmsjö (*Peter*); Anita Wall (*Interviewer*); Gunnel Lindblom (*Eva*); Barbro Hiort af Ornäs (*Mrs. Jacobi*); Bertil Norström (*Arne*); Wenche Foss (*Marianne's Mother in TV version*).

Bergman returned to television with the lengthy—almost two-character—drama *Scenes from a Marriage*. It began as a miniseries consisting of six 50-minute episodes. Filmed in the summer of 1972, it aired in Sweden in April and May 1973, where it drew unprecedented attention. Shot in 16 mm for TV, it was later blown up to 35 mm for theatrical release in the United States in 1974; for that purpose, Bergman cut his original production almost in half to realize a more palatable length for moviegoers. In 1977, American Public Broadcasting stations aired the full 282-minute original of *Scenes from a Marriage*.

Based on his own considerable experience with marriage, Bergman charted a union

in decline, focusing on the strains, the grievances, and the self-deceptions of a couple named Marianne (Liv Ullmann) and Johan (Erland Josephson), who have been wed for a decade. She's a thirty-five-year-old divorce lawyer; he's a professor and a scientist, seven years her senior. The drama is intentionally episodic, as befits the title: Celebrating their tenth anniversary, they're interviewed by a magazine writer about their "ideal marriage"; when they give a dinner for another couple (Bibi Andersson and Jan Malmsjö), Marianne and Johan are privy to an embarrassing evening of scathing exchanges as the wine flows and their unhappy guests grow ever more hostile; minor problems between Marianne and Johan escalate to a critical confrontation when he announces that he is leaving her for another woman. Later, Johan returns to visit her, having had second thoughts about his extramarital alliance; Marianne, newly confident after living on her own for a while, refuses to take him back. Still later, a scene of physical confrontation between them results in Johan's beating her, after which they sign their divorce papers. A final sequence, occurring some ten years after the opening one, finds Marianne and Johan now married to other partners, to whom both have been unfaithful. At a country retreat belonging to friends, they rendezvous once again, free of commitment. Nevertheless, each of them remains essentially alone.

Because *Scenes from a Marriage* had been created for television, The Academy of Motion Picture Arts and Sciences declined to consider it for any Oscars. But the New York Film Critics recognized the movie by awarding Liv Ullmann 1974's Best Actress citation and similarly recognizing Ingmar Bergman for Best Screenwriting. And the National Society of Film Critics gave it no less than four of their awards that year: Best Picture, Best Actress, Best Supporting Actress (Bibi Andersson), and Best Screenplay.

Bergman on Bergman

"The screenplay took three months to write, forty-five days to shoot, but rather a long part of my life to experience. I'm not sure it would have turned out better had it been the other way around, though it would have seemed nicer.

"I live on a small island, Fårö, in the Baltic Sea, with mostly farmers and fishermen. For the first time they really liked something I had done. They discussed it with me on the ferryboat to the island. Nothing I have done means anything until two other people start talking about it on the basis of *their* experience."

Critics' Circle

"*The precision of the script is perfectly reflected in the two central performances. Johan's evolution from complacent egocentricity to disappointment and a rather phlegmatic resignation is depicted by Erland Josephson in an unselfish performance which allows Liv Ullmann to blossom from an anxiety to please, through stark pain, to radiant self-confidence.* Scenes From a Marriage *shows how habit and conciliatory effort erode communication. But it is ultimately an optimistic film, suggesting that beyond the hell of a return to zero, the knowledge of one's absolute separateness from others can lead through despair to a glowing fulfillment.*"
— Jan Dawson in
Monthly Film Bulletin

"*Couples unsure of their liaison are herewith forewarned. Be prepared to see a marital relationship ruthlessly dissected, with no quarter given and few nuances left unobserved. Ingmar Bergman wields the scalpel, and Liv Ullmann, as the woman lawyer who finds her life suddenly going up in smoke, lights up the screen with one of the most penetrating, truthful performances I've ever seen an actress give. Her husband, a mediocre professor who decides he wants out, is played brilliantly by Erland Josephson.*
— William Wolf in *Cue*

"*Liv Ullmann, when directed by Bergman, is one of the world's best acting talents (she is not so in her American efforts), and even the brutal concentration of the television camera on her face (the entire film is 90 percent close-ups) cannot intimidate the superb parade of emotions. She flushes at a suggestion of eroticism, she smiles, shudders, flirts, sympathizes and in one brilliant moment, upon being told that her friends already know of her husband's outside affair, is the epitome of 'hell hath no fury like a woman scorned.'*"
— "Robe" in *Variety*

"*Although Bergman's overview of marriage is uncompromising and ultimately pessimistic, the film is a far cry from his earlier metaphysical musings and symbolic forays,*

Scenes from a Marriage (1973). Liv Ullmann and Erland Josephson. Cinematograph.

emerging as his most commercially accessible film to date. Liv Ullmann and Erland Josephson are superb as the couple under glass, and Bergman's intense, unerring ear and humanistic eye make Scenes From a Marriage *a uniquely involving film experience and an almost unqualified masterpiece."*
— *The Independent Film Journal*

Ingmar Bergman's Scenes From a Marriage *is the best, most penetrating, utterly fascinating movie ever made on the subject. It's an inclusive look at modern marriage in the upper brackets.*

"The acting is superb, Bergman's handling of revelatory close-ups marvelously pointed. His knowledge of and feel for the emotional overtones, half-tones and explosions of sex-driven quarrels is exemplary. His balance between male and female points of view is extraordinary, as if he himself were androgynous. Both as writer and director he has performed prodigies in this epoch-making film."
— Archer Winsten in
The New York Post

"Ingmar Bergman's masterpiece of compassion and wisdom about human relationships, the need for change, and the heartbreak and inevitable growth that can come from self-recognition. Liv Ullmann gives the performance of her career in this study of the disintegration of a seemingly perfect marriage, and Bergman burns through the viewer's own psyche like Madame Curie discovering radium. This is a film of dazzling courage and personal vision that taught me more about the way we live now than any other film this year."
— Rex Reed in
The New York Daily News

"Most ordinary films made for television seem empty when seen in a theater. There simply isn't enough visual and emotional detail to keep the mind occupied. The absolute opposite is true of Scenes From a Marriage. *Although we seldom see more than two persons at a time, and usually only one, the theater screen is bursting with information, associations and contradictory feelings."*
— Vincent Canby in
The New York Times

Trollflöjten
(The Magic Flute)

A Cinematograph production for Swedish TV: 1975
(U.S. release by Surrogate Releasing: 1975)

CREDITS

Director: Ingmar Bergman; *producer:* Måns Reuterswärd; *screenwriter:* Ingmar Bergman; Based on Johann Emanuel Schikaneder's libretto for Mozart's opera; *Eastmancolor cinematographer:* Sven Nykvist; *editor:* Siv Lundgren; *art director:* Henny Noremark; *costumes:* Karin Erskine and Henny Noremark; *music:* Wolfgang Amadeus Mozart's opera *Die Zauberflöte*, with the Swedish State Broadcasting Network Symphony and the Radio Choir, conducted by Eric Ericsson; *choreographer:* Donya Feyer; *sound:* Helmut Mühle and Peter Hennix; *assistant director:* Kerstin Forsmark; *running time:* 135 minutes.

CAST

Joseph Köstlinger (*Tamino*); Irma Urrila (*Pamina*); Håkan Hagegård (*Papageno*); Elizabeth Erikson (*Papagena*); Ulrik Cold (*Sarastro*); Birgit Nordin (*Queen of the Night*); Ragnar Ulfung (*Monostatos*); Erik Saedén (*The Speaker*); Britt-Marie Aruhn (*First Lady*); Kirsten Vaupel (*Second Lady*); Birgitta Smiding (*Third Lady*); Gösta Prüzelius (*First Priest*); Ulf Johansson (*Second Priest*); Hans Johansson and Jerker Arvidson (*Guards*); Linn Ullmann (*Girl in Audience*).

In the mid–1960s, Bergman had been scheduled to stage a production of Mozart's penultimate opera, *Die Zauberflöte* (*The Magic Flute*), in Hamburg, a project that was canceled by the director's illness. But a similar offer surfaced in the early 1970s, this time as a film for television, a medium in which Bergman was becoming increasingly experienced. And what began strictly as a TV entertainment for Scandinavian audiences realized a large potential when it was decided to make it available theatrically outside Nordic countries.

Opera has seldom been successfully recorded directly on film, due to the nature of the art; filming a work in performance presents numerous logistical barriers that even a genius is hard put to surmount. And there are the occasional ugly mouth movements of the singers required by certain musical passages that might unintentionally amuse an audience when projected in close-ups. As Bergman realized, it was an economic im-

possibility to consider keeping a full orchestra at the ready throughout his customary period of filming, and so the score was prerecorded by the Swedish State Broadcasting Network Symphony and the Radio Choir, under the direction of conductor Eric Ericsson, with the carefully picked cast later lip-synching to the music they had earlier set in the recording studio. With the original German text translated into Swedish, the company worked on deliberately theatrical looking sets, built and filmed in the studios of the Swedish Film Institute.

During the opera's traditional overture, Bergman pans over the grounds of the Drottningholm Court Theater outside Stockholm, since that venue closely resembles the locale of *The Magic Flute*'s first performance in 1791 Vienna's Theater auf der Weiden. And there are shots of backstage activity and of the audience members taking their seats in anticipation of the performance — with glimpses of Bergman family members and cast regulars available to sharp-eyed members of the film's viewers. Indeed, the young girl whose seemingly enchanted expression reappears in rapt close-up from time to time throughout the opera's performance is that of Linn Ullmann, the director's eight-year-old daughter by Liv Ullmann.

Bergman on Bergman

"Since we were not performing *The Magic Flute* on a stage but in front of a microphone and camera, we did not need large voices. What we needed were warm, sensuous voices that had personality. To me it was also absolutely essential that the play be performed by young actors, naturally close to the dizzy, emotional shifts between joy and sorrow, between thinking and feeling. Tamino must be a handsome young man, Pamina must be a beautiful young woman. Not to speak of Papageno and Papegena. I was totally convinced that the three young women must be young, happy and virtuous. Little darlings, dangerous flirts, with a true sense of comedy, but also fiercely sensual. The three young men had to be little rascals, and so on."

Critics' Circle

"As the set of faces that opens this film suggests, The Magic Flute *is an opera that addresses itself to everyone at almost every level. In sheer cinematic terms, what Bergman has accomplished is pure enchantment; as an interpretation of a masterpiece, the production catches the spirit of Mozart's world more truthfully than most stage presentations; as an example of opera's potential in this medium, it sets a standard that few would have dreamed possible."*
                              —Peter G. Davis in
                              The New York Times

"The beauty that flows in abundance from Ingmar Bergman's film of Mozart's The Magic Flute *doesn't look like the kind of beauty we've come to expect from Bergman*

movies: soul-dredging introspection isn't required to appreciate it, and neither is much thought— open eyes and ears will do. The film is a lark, really—it's as accessible as anything the director has done—and you can almost forget that there stands behind it, as there does behind any work of simple beauty, a complex and somewhat mysterious act of creation."
                              —Frank Rich in *The New York Post*

"The opera is done entirely in Swedish (which often sounds remarkably similar to the German original) by native artists. These are of a generally high caliber: one must note Håkan Hagegård's accomplished Papageno, Ulrik Cold's firm Sarastro and Josef Köstlinger's tidy Tamino; Irma Urrila makes a splendidly photogenic Pamina and is heard at her best in the Ach, ich fühl's Act II aria."
                              —Derek Elley in *Films and Filming*

"The trouble with putting opera on film is that even when you do it right, you are wrong to do it at all; you are only reminding us how much better the thing is in the opera house, where it belongs. You just know that the singing has been postsynched and electronically amplified, and that takes the joy out of the affair. It is almost as bad as dubbing foreign-language acting into English: what you hear is not the natural voice of the singer spontaneously and continuously deployed—you cannot trust what you hear."
                              —John Simon in *New York*

"It is a joyous entertainment, testimony to Bergman's contention that 'making the film was the best time of my life.' Only carpers will carp at the minor changes he's made. Bergman moves in and out of his staged performance, making the audience and the backstage areas of the theater an integral part of the production, bringing movie magic and movement to the stage, making us aware of the mechanics of the setting even as the fairy tale captures us completely. It is a tour de force."
                              —Judith Crist in *Saturday Review*

"The incandescent film Ingmar Bergman made of Mozart's opera is a case of a genius

The Magic Flute (1975). Britt-Marie Aruhn, Kirsten Vaupel, Josef Köstlinger and Birgitta Smiding. Cinematograph.

from one century making the fullest use of his art to respond to the genius of another. It is impossible to imagine any production of The Magic Flute *in an opera house giving so complete, so rich a sense of the opera as Bergman's film."*

—Howard Kissel in
Women's Wear Daily

"Ingmar Bergman mixes mood and style to magnificent advantage in his first filmed essay in opera, The Magic Flute. *It is a picture of protean subtlety, as changeable in its form and shape as it is continually fascinating as musical entertainment. And though the dark and brooding atmosphere we know so well from the Swedish director's past work is dominant, this film has so many sunny moments that the confirmed Bergmanite will go to it at the grave risk of being charmed."*

—Bruce Cook in *Newsweek*

"Ingmar Bergman's film version of The Magic Flute *is a blissful present, a model of how opera can be filmed. Bergman must have reached a new, serene assurance to have tackled this sensuous, luxuriant opera that has bewildered so many stage directors, and to have brought it off so unaffectedly. It's a wholly unfussy production, with the bloom still on it."*
—Pauline Kael in *The New Yorker*

"In what was obviously a labor of love, Bergman has injected as much magic as he could muster, and although the performance is intentionally confined to the concert-hall stage, much of it has been directed with a purely cinematic freshness and imagination. Still, although Sven Nykvist's photography is stunningly handsome, The Magic Flute *is ultimately too delicate and insubstantial to sustain its long and overly literal transition to screen."*

— Stephen Klain in
The Independent Film Journal

Ansikte mot Ansikte
(Face to Face)

A Cinematograph production for Swedish TV: 1976
(U.S. release of feature version by
Paramount Pictures: 1976)

CREDITS

Director: Ingmar Bergman; *producer:* Lars-Owe Carlberg; *screenwriter:* Ingmar Bergman; *Eastmancolor cinematographer:* Sven Nykvist; *editor:* Siv Lundgren; *art directors:* Anne Hagegård and Peter Krupénin; *costumes:* Maggie Strindberg; *music:* Mozart's Fantasy in C Minor, played by Käbi Laretei; *sound:* Owe Svensson; *assistant director:* Peder Langenskiöld; *running time:* 200 minutes (TV version); 136 minutes (theatrical version).

CAST

Liv Ullmann (*Dr. Jenny Isaksson*); Erland Josephson (*Dr. Tomas Jacobi*); Aino Taube (*Grandmother*); Gunnar Björnstrand (*Grandfather*); Kari Sylwan (*Maria*); Sif Ruud (*Elisabeth Wankel*); Sven Lindberg (*Erik, Jenny's Husband*); Tore Segelcke (*Woman Specter*); Ulf Johanson (*Dr. Helmuth Wankel*); Kristina Adolphson (*Nurse Veronica*); Gösta Ekman (*Mikael Stromberg*); Marianne Aminoff (*Jenny's Mother*); Gösta Prüzelius (*Jenny's Father*); Birger Malmsten and Göran Stangertz (*Rapists*); Helene Friberg (*Anna*); Käbi Laretei (*Concert Pianist*); Rebecca Pawlo and Lena Olin (*Boutique Girls*).

Produced via an agreement with the independent producer Dino De Laurentiis, who then planned to present and distribute throughout the world additional works by Ingmar Bergman, *Face to Face* was shot simultaneously as both a feature film for theatres and a television miniseries consisting of four one-hour episodes. As a theatrical movie, *Face to Face* represents a tour de force for Liv Ullmann, who gives so forceful and totally committed an emotional performance of a woman who suffers a harrowing nervous breakdown that her acting almost compensates for the shortcomings of Bergman's script. She plays a Stockholm psychiatrist, who's treating a difficult lesbian patient (Kari Sylwan) at the same time she's undergoing personal traumas related to both her absent doctor-husband (Sven Lindberg) and painful memories of her parents, who were killed in an auto crash. Resorting to dream scenes and nightmare flashbacks wherein astute viewers may recognize incidents related by

Bergman in his autobiographical writings, the director offers Ullmann plenty of scope for bravura dramatics; but he fails to explain very much about her, and one cannot help wondering how any psychiatrist—who would surely have had to undergo extensive psychoanalysis herself—could be so devoid of self-awareness. The one man, a gynecologist named Jacobi (Erland Josephson), who appears to bring meaning to her life, turns out to be a homosexual who continues to pursue his own kind, while her husband appears only briefly to attend her bedside before returning to his medical conference in the U.S. And, while many a viewer may wonder what it all adds up to, there remains that outstanding work by Liv Ullmann, who makes *Face to Face* seem so much better than it actually is.

In Hollywood, The Academy of Motion Pictures Arts and Sciences nominated Bergman as Best Director of 1976, but awarded the Oscar to John G. Avildsen for *Rocky*; and while they also recognized *Face to Face* with a Best Actress nod for Liv Ullmann, the statuette went to Faye Dunaway for *Network*. In New York, the voting committees demonstrated lesser leanings toward the popular and predictable; both the New York Film Critics and the National Board of Review named Ullmann the year's Best Actress.

Bergman on Bergman

"*Face to Face* was intended as a film about dreams and reality. The dreams were to become tangible reality. Reality would dissolve and become dream. I have occasionally managed to move unhindered between dream and reality: *Wild Strawberries, Persona, The Silence, Cries and Whispers*. This time it was more difficult. My intentions required an inspiration which failed me. The dream sequences became synthetic, the reality blurred. There are a few solid scenes here and there, and Liv Ullmann struggled like a lioness. Her strength and talent held the film together. But even she could not save the culmination, the primal scream, which amounted to an enthusiastic but ill-digested fruit of my reading. Artistic license sneered through the thinly woven fabric."

Critics' Circle

"'Physician, heal thyself' is the main theme of Ingmar Bergman's Face to Face, which centers on Liv Ullmann's virtuoso performance as a psychiatrist cracking under the pressures of modern living. It is arguably the finest film role for a woman since Jane Fonda did Klute five years ago, and Ullmann scores a stunning career triumph."

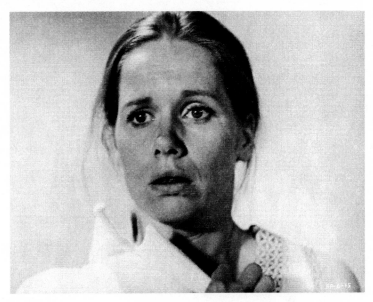

Face to Face (1976). Liv Ullmann as Dr. Jenny Isaksson. Cinamatograph.

"*More than in his six previous films with Ullmann, the writer-director seems to have a deep personal identification with her character.*"

—"Mack." In *Variety*

"Face to Face *is another tour de force for Miss Ullmann, who is nothing short of immense. I know of no other actress today who has at hand the reserves that enable her to move so effortlessly through such multiple levels of mood and feeling. But then nobody today except Mr. Bergman writes such roles for actresses. Erland Josephson, Miss Ullmann's co-star in* Scenes From a Marriage, *is also fine in the much smaller but very affecting role of a man who might have loved Jenny but for one small impediment— his homosexuality.*"

—Vincent Canby in *The New York Times*

"*Although, riveted by another brilliant characterization by Liv Ullmann in the pivotal role,* Face to Face *amounts to an intense but overextended psychodrama, marked by some supremely effective individual scenes, but limited by its relentless focus on one character and a diffuseness— apparently due to cutting— that works against overall involvement.*

"Erland Josephson, who serves primarily as a sounding board for Ullmann's anguished monologue, is enormously subtle nonetheless and like his co-star, survives the soul-searching close-ups of Sven Nykvist's relentless camera with a naked emotional honesty that is truly amazing."

—Stephen Klain in *The Independent Film Journal*

"Bergman's compassion has never been focused so intently on the female psyche, and no 'Bergman woman' has been so thoroughly realized as Ullmann's is here. The entire cast, Bergman's repertory company, is equally fine in the clear focus of familiar scenes and in the strangeness of the extended realities of dreams—all created through Sven Nykvist's camera eye, all underlined by Käbi Laretei's exquisite piano variations on the theme of Mozart's Fantasy in C Minor. *Bergman has probed the universal soul and led us to face ourselves, at last, with love and comfort."*

—Judith Crist in *Saturday Review*

"Like Scenes From a Marriage, *Ingmar Bergman's* Face to Face *is a film of such devastating honesty that there is almost no way of discussing it as a conventional fiction film. Ordinarily, in a film involving emotional breakdown and attempted suicide, the story follows a clear line from 'normality' through crisis to some sort of resolution.* Face to Face *does not admit so reassuring a view of things. It is written and acted from a point of view where the pain of childhood memories and adult inadequacies is tangible and visceral. Nor does the film end, as most such films do, with a new resolve or an understanding that will lead to greater happiness and personal success. The demons have been recognized but not exorcised."*

—Howard Kissel in *Women's Wear Daily*

"In Face to Face, *Ingmar Bergman takes another passionate dive into the turbulent, sometimes muddy waters of his own mental and emotional life. As in many of his other films, he gazes relentlessly and even rudely at a crushingly difficult journey of the human mind.*

"As usual, Bergman ably uses his gifted and committed colleagues in bringing his work to life and warmth—cinematographer Sven Nykvist, stars Liv Ullmann and Erland Josephson, plus a supporting cast headed by Gunnar Björnstrand. Together these artists have created a body of work unduplicated anywhere else in today's movie world."

—David Sterritt in *The Christian Science Monitor*

"Liv Ullmann's performance is shattering. Her attempted suicide is frightening because she does it with such a sweet, mundane practicality. In one long, astonishing take she passes through a hysterical fit into a calm, that disintegrates into another convulsion, subsiding into the pathos of a ravaged peace."

—Jack Kroll in *Newsweek*

"The one incontrovertible splendor of the film is Liv Ullmann's performance. Great art, we know, destroys its scaffolding, hides its artifice; but seldom has an actor been called upon to perform so awesome a set of self-revelations, to cut through to that inner nakedness that is no longer beautiful—mere animality at bay—and executed it so simply, so utterly without self-indulgence or pleas for audience sympathy, with such harsh truthfulness. It is not just sublime acting; it is a piece of great, invaluable daring."

—John Simon in *New York*

Das Schlangenei
(The Serpent's Egg/Ormens Ägg)

A coproduction of Rialto Film and
Dino De Laurentiis Corp: 1977
(U.S. release by Paramount Pictures: 1978)

CREDITS

Director: Ingmar Bergman; *producer:* Dino De Laurentiis; *executive producer:* Horst Wendlant; *screenwriter:* Ingmar Bergman; *Eastmancolor cinematographer:* Sven Nykvist; *additional photography:* Peter Rohe and Dieter Lohmann; *editors:* Jutta Hering and Petra von Oelffen; *art directors:* Erner Achmann and Herbert Strabel; *production designer:* Rolf Zehetbauer; *costumes:* Charlotte Flemming; *music:* Rolf Wilhelm; *sound:* Karsten Ullrich; *choreographer:* Heino Hallhuber; *assistant director:* Wieland Liebske; *running time:* 119 minutes.

CAST

Liv Ullmann (*Manuela Rosenberg*); David Carradine (*Abel Rosenberg*); Gert Fröbe (*Inspector Bauer*); Heinz Bennent (*Hans Vergérus*); James Whitmore (*Priest*); Glynn Turman (*Monroe*); Georg Hartmann (*Hollinger*); Edith Heerdegen (*Mrs. Holle*); Kyra Mladeck (*Miss Dorst*); Fritz Strassner (*Dr. Soltermann*); Hans Quest (Dr. Silbermann); Wolfgang Weiser (*Civil Servant*); Paula Braend (*Mrs. Hemse*); Walter Schmidinger (*Solomon*); Lisi Mangold (*Mikaela*); Grischa Huber (*Stella*); Paul Bürks (*Cabaret Comedian*); Toni Berger (*Mr. Rosenberg*); Erna Brunell (*Mrs. Rosenberg*).

With *The Serpent's Egg*, Bergman continued his association with Dino De Laurentiis, albeit under considerably altered circumstances, for now he was a Swedish exile working and living in Munich. This is a German-American coproduction, based on a Bergman screenplay set in the inflation-beset Berlin of 1923, where the sinister stirrings of Hitler's politics are starting to be felt. Indeed, a quotation from the script explains the odd title: "It's like a serpent's egg. Through the thin membrane you can clearly discern the already perfect reptile."

The focus here is on an unmarried couple named Abel and Manuela Rosenberg (David Carradine — who replaced an ailing Richard Harris — and Liv Ullmann, the only one of Bergman's regulars to join him in his first non–Swedish film, along with cinematographer Sven Nykvist). They are part of a three-person aerial act with a circus, the third member being Abel's brother, who's also Manuela's husband. A wrist injury cancels that brother's participation in the act, forcing the two others to extend their stay in Berlin. At the story's outset, Abel pays his incapacitated sibling a visit, only to discover with shock that the latter has just committed suicide. Questioned about the incident by the police inspector Bauer (Gert Fröbe), Abel is also interrogated about the inexplicable deaths of several other individuals whom he had known. By now, Manuela has found employment as a cabaret performer. Abel then finds refuge at her lodgings. The presence in the city of Nazi strong-arms threatens the guilt-ridden Abel, who's an American of Russian-Jewish heritage. Incidents of minor public destruction signify the rumblings of future events in Germany. Haunting the environs of Manuela's cabaret is a sinister individual named Hans Vergérus (Heinz

Bennent), who's eventually exposed as the one responsible for those mysterious deaths, the result of using human guinea pigs to test dangerous experimental drugs. In a climax more melodramatic than anything Bergman had created heretofore, Vergérus is detected by the police, whose efforts to apprehend him are thwarted when the monstrous fellow ends his own life with a cyanide capsule.

The Serpent's Egg pleased neither the critics nor Bergman's public, for whom little in the material — outside of the faintly reassuring presence of Liv Ullmann — seemed at all characteristic of Scandinavia's most celebrated filmmaker.

Bergman on Bergman

"In *The Serpent's Egg*, I ventured into a Berlin that nobody recognized, not even I. The depiction of time and place might be debatable, but it is hard to deny the care that went into it. Set, costumes and casting were done by experts. If you look at *The Serpent's Egg* in pure cinematographic terms, there are excellent aspects of the film and a good dramatic buildup in the unfolding of the plot. The movie does not tire for a moment; rather the opposite. It is overstimulated, as if it had taken anabolic steroids. But its vitality is powerful on a superficial plane; the failure is hidden underneath."

Critics' Circle

"Ingmar Bergman's new film is a traditional horror movie touched lightly by the filmmaker's genius. The film is an impersonal work and a minor one. 'Minor' Bergman, like 'minor' Fellini, of course, means a major film, one bearing the master's hallmark in its fascinations. But much like Fellini's *Casanova*, this vision of the Germany that incubated Nazism is a chilling exercise that seems alien to the filmmaker and shallow in the context of his work."

—Judith Crist in
The New York Post

"The Serpent's Egg, *Ingmar Bergman's first film made outside his home country, bears the master's stamp right from the beginning in a superior collaboration with cinematographer Sven Nykvist and production designer Rolf Zehetbauer. The latter has re-created a Berlin of a poverty-ridden, fear-stricken early '20s that is much more than paint-deep. Also, Bergman makes his actors, with one fatal exception, work their individualities into the grandest of ensemble playing.*

"The exception is David Carradine, and though Carradine struggles valiantly, all you see is a struggler. His performance has no depth."

—"Kell" in *Variety*

"The Serpent's Egg *is the first film to be made by Bergman after he voluntarily left Sweden to take up residence in Germany following his brush with the Swedish authorities. This information may not be relevant, but it might help to explain the peculiar sense of dislocation within his English-language screenplay, a melodrama that never quite makes any connection to the characters within it...*

"Mostly, The Serpent's Egg *is a movie of beautifully photographed weather and handsome period sets and costumes that encase characters who remain as anonymous as the bodies in a morgue. It's dead."*

—Vincent Canby in
The New York Times

"Gert Fröbe alone is absolutely right as the police inspector who puts his faith in man's desire for order. David Carradine's all–American manner (so right as Woody Guthrie in *Bound for Glory*) never goes beyond superficiality as Abel; Liv Ullmann's role is so ill-defined it has no impact; and Heinz Bennent is asked to play a caricature of an inhuman scientist. As written and directed by Bergman, the film is a story of implacable horror adding up to intellectual and emotional confusion."

—Charles Phillips Reilly in
Films in Review

"Ingmar Bergman's first (German) film since he fled Sweden, and became (temporarily) a tax exile, is powerful and in part

The Serpent's Egg (1977). Liv Ullmann and David Carradine. Rialto Film/Dino De Laurentis Corp.

brilliant (certainly visually so), but ultimately well below his best work for the screen. A story of the distant threatening rumblings in Germany in the 1920s (the time of hyper-inflation) and of the dark menace of the 1930s. Fine performances by several of the cast including Liv Ullmann and Gert Fröbe, but a superficial and unhappy one by David Carradine as the American Jewish circus performer stranded in Berlin and, often, in a drunken stupor."
—F. Maurice Speed in *Film Review*

"The Serpent's Egg *has the most intricate plot and the largest supporting cast of any of Bergman's films. In attending to these and to such things as graphic bloodshed, Bergman failed to extract from his lead actors the performances he usually does. David Carradine is an actor who grows with each performance, but he is short on the intensity that Bergman requires. He is too laconic to be the eyes through which we watch the deteriora-*tion of German society. Liv Ullmann tries to take up some of the slack, giving off an energy that is sometimes close to hysterical.*

"For all the attention lavished on the production, there is not enough paid to characterization. It is a horror film and only that—vivid while it is happening, but too insubstantial to be long remembered."

—Jerry Oster in *The Trib*

Herbstsonate
(Autumn Sonata/Höstsonaten)

Svensk Filmindustri release of
a Personafilm production: 1978
(U.S. release by New World Pictures: 1978)

CREDITS

Director: Ingmar Bergman; *producer:* Katinka Faragó; *screenwriter:* Ingmar Bergman; *Eastmancolor cinematographer:* Sven Nykvist; *editor:* Syliva Ingemarsson; *art director:* Anna Asp; *costumes:* Inger Pehrsson; *music:* Excerpts form Chopin's Preludium No. 2 in A Minor, played by Käbi Laretei; Bach's Suite No. 4 in E Flat Major, played by Claude Genetay; and Handel's Sonata in F Major, played by Frans Brüggen, Gustav Leonhardt and Anne Bylsmå; *sound:* Owe Svensson; *assistant director:* Peder Langenskiöld; *running time:* 97 minutes.

CAST

Ingrid Bergman (*Charlotte*); Liv Ullmann (*Eva*); Lena Nyman (*Helena*); Halvar Björk; (*Viktor, Eva's Husband*); Georg Lökkeberg (*Leonardo*); Linn Ullmann (*Eva as a child*); Erland Josephson (*Josef*); Gunnar Björnstrand (*Paul, Charlotte's Agent*); Marianne Aminoff (*Charlotte's Secretary*); Mimi Pollak (*Piano Teacher*); Arne Bang-Hansen (*Uncle Otto*); Knut Wigert (*Professor*); Eva von Hanno (*Nurse*).

Although he continued to work on his update of the 1970 *Fårö Document*, Bergman's feature filmmaking continued away from his Swedish island home. For *Autumn Sonata*, his first and only film with compatriot Ingrid Bergman, he and longtime cameraman Sven Nykvist went on location to Molde, Norway, and the Norsk Film Studios in Oslo. The film was also somewhat of a "family" affair for Bergman; along with old, familiar faces like Gunnar Björnstrand and Erland Josephson in supporting roles, Liv Ullmann costarred with Ingrid. Bergman's ex-wife (but longtime musical collaborator) Käbi Laretei supplied the important keyboard work, supposedly played by the movie's stars, and the little Linn Ullmann portrayed the silent flashback role of her mother's character as a girl.

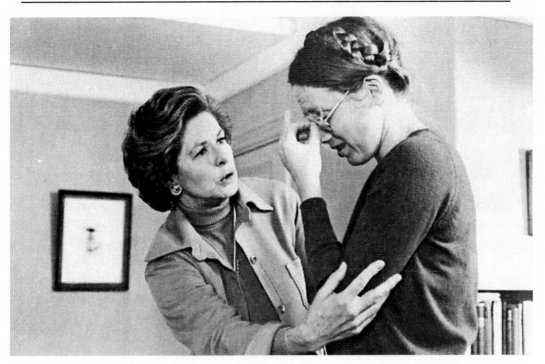

***Autumn Sonata* (1978). Ingrid Bergman and Liv Ullmann. Svensk Filmindustri.**

Autumn Sonata tells an emotion-charged story of the mother-daughter relationship between a celebrated concert pianist named Charlotte (Ingrid Bergman) and dowdy, married Eva (Liv Ullmann), whom Charlotte hasn't seen in seven years, ostensibly due to a busy schedule of touring engagements. Persuaded to visit Eva and her pastor husband (Halvar Björk) in their rural Norwegian parsonage, Charlotte is shocked when told there's another family member present: Helena (Lena Nyman), the once-institutionalized, retarded child Charlotte had hoped never to see again. During her visit, Charlotte manages to put on a false face of smiles for the inarticulate Helena, but she soon finds that what appears to be a happy reunion with Eva develops into an anguished confrontation with a child she never loved and whose youthful adoration she cruelly rejected, turning Eva into a lifelong neurotic. With emotional barriers broken down and false sentiments laid bare, decades of lies and misunderstandings are brought forth in a powerful catharsis.

At the film's close, Charlotte leaves to continue her concert career, but we know that some kind of healing process may perhaps have been initiated between her and Eva.

Ingrid and Ingmar Bergman had long expressed a mutual desire to make a film together, but when they began to do so, theirs proved a difficult, if eventually fruitful, collaboration. Long used to the "star treatment" of Hollywood producers and directors, Ingrid made demands that Ingmar could not accede to; their own confrontations at one point sent Liv Ullmann running from the set in tears, certain that the movie would have to be abandoned. Part of the trouble was Ingrid's discovery of malignant cancer shortly after production had begun on the film. Surgery was performed in London, and her work days were accordingly shortened, along with other accommodations to her condition. During the filming of *Autumn Sonata*, Bergman also filmed a documentary of its making. And although Ingrid later saw it on a visit to the director's Fårö home — and termed it "the best documentary on the making of a movie I've ever seen"—it has, to date, not been shown publicly.

Autumn Sonata won Oscar nominations for Ingrid Bergman and Original Screenplay, but both those statuettes went to *Coming Home* (including Best Actress Jane Fonda). *Autumn Sonata* was more successful with the New York Film Critics, who named Ingrid Bergman 1978's Best Actress, and the National Board of Review, which cited both Bergmans as the year's top actress and director and *Autumn Sonata* as Best Foreign-Language Film.

The film's stars provided their own voices for an excellent English-dubbed version for general release in the United States.

Bergman on Bergman

"The actual filming was draining. I did not have what one would call difficulties in my working relationship with Ingrid Bergman. Rather, it was a kind of language barrier, but in a profound sense. Starting on the first day when we all read the script together in the rehearsal studio, I discovered that she had rehearsed her entire part in front of a mirror, complete with intonations and self-conscious gestures. It was clear that she had a different approach to her profession than the rest of us. She was still living in the 1940s. I discovered early into our rehearsals that to be understanding and offer a sympathetic ear did not work. In her case I was forced to use tactics that I normally rejected, the first and foremost being aggression.

"Once she told me: 'If you don't tell me how I should do this scene, I'll slap you!' I rather liked that. But from a strictly professional point of view, it was difficult to work with these two actresses together. When I look at the film today, I see that I left Liv to shift for herself when I ought to have been more supportive. Liv is one of those generous artists who give everything they have. In a few scenes, she sometimes goes astray. That is because I paid too much attention to Ingrid Bergman.

Ingrid also had some trouble remembering her lines. In the mornings she was often crabby and angry, which was understandable. She lived with constant anxiety over her own illness and at the same time found our way of working unfamiliar and frightening. But she never made any attempt to back out. Her conduct was always extraordinarily professional. Even with her obvious frailties, Ingrid Bergman was a remarkable person: generous, grand and highly talented."

Critics' Circle

"*The center-piece of* Autumn Sonata, *the long duologue that takes place during the hour of the wolf—that magical nocturnal oasis when all defenses are down against both good and evil—is Bergman at his best. Beautifully modulated through the virtuoso performances of Liv Ullmann and Ingrid Bergman, which echo the emotional/intellectual distinction between the two interpretations of Chopin offered by Käbi Laretei in the film, the duologue is also cunningly structured by this same dichotomy.*"
—Tom Milne in
Monthly Film Bulletin

"*The films of Ingmar Bergman have often been compared to chamber music. Taking the analogy literally, the great Swedish director now gives us* Autumn Sonata, *the most ingeniously conceived, brilliantly acted, and deeply moving Bergman film in more than a decade.*

"*Equally central to the film's success are the mighty performances of Liv Ullmann, a regular Bergman actress, and Ingrid Bergman, working for the first time with her near-namesake, Ingmar. Both women do wonders with their immensely challenging roles; Miss Ullmann in particular seems utterly immersed in her character's infinitely poignant emotions, and offers what may be the finest performance of her illustrious career.*"
—David Sterritt in
The Christian Science Monitor

"Autumn Sonata *is a psychodrama about the love-hate relationship of mother and*

daughter, about the egocentricity of a concert artist, about the inability to communicate, about the immutability of any person's
basic character. It raises questions but gives
no answers. Ingmar Bergman is the supreme
realist, and he knows that in life there are
no easy answers. Ingrid Bergman, looking
older and even more beautiful, is superb as
the pianist, and Liv Ullmann is positively
searing as her repressed daughter."
— Harold C. Schonberg in
The New York Times

"As he did in Persona, *Bergman places
two women face to face with each other and
their own inadequacies and, as in* Wild
Strawberries, *there is the painful recognition
that the past cannot be changed. With his
masterly use of the close-up, and the flashback utilized as the subconscious, he creates
a chamber work of almost Strindbergian
intensity. The long night's journey into day
allows the director's namesake to give a remarkable performance, displaying every as-
pect of her screen personality over the years—
naiveté, sophistication, gaiety, and tragedy.
It was, sadly, Ingrid Bergman's last feature
before her death."
— Holt Foreign Film Guide

"As usual in a Bergman drama, night is no
time for sleeping; it's a time for nightmares,
a time to confront old demons, and perhaps
exorcise them. It's a time for truth. In one
long nighttime sequence, resembling a sort of
trial, mother and daughter accuse each other
of past wrongs and then each speaks in her
own defense. The next day, they separate
once more to weigh in their hearts and minds
their feelings of love, hate and forgiveness for
one another.

"In her first appearance in a film by the
master director, Ingrid Bergman has a role
worthy of her talents, not just throwaway
stuff like in* Murder on the Orient Express,
*and she etches an often-moving and always-
commanding performance. Ullmann, in
dowdy dress, braided hair and spectacles, is
equally convincing."
— Edward Perchaluk in
The Independent Film Journal

"The richest surprises of all are contained
in the sequence when mother and daughter
play the Chopin A-Minor Prelude. As Charlotte listens to Eva essaying the piece with
worthy, conventional technique but also a
kind of stunted emotional intensity, she
shrinks back with alarm and suspicion. She
recognizes, perhaps, that had she spent time
with Eva as a child she might have ironed
out the flaws in her playing and allowed that
emotion to flower in a more rewarding and
fulfilling interpretation of life. By contrast,
when Eva watches Charlotte embark on the
prelude, she is amazed at her mother's ca-
pacity for feeling and recognizes that she has
poured that feeling exclusively into her career and her music. That is where she was
during Eva's lonely youth."
— Peter Cowie in
Ingmar Bergman

Fårö-Dokument 1979
(Fårö Document 1979/Fårö 79)

A Cinematograph production for Swedish TV: 1979
(No U.S. distribution)

CREDITS

Director: Ingmar Bergman; *producer:* Lars-Owe Carlberg; *screenwriter:* Ingmar Bergman;
color cinematographer: Arne Carlsson; *editor:* Sylvia Ingemarsson; *music:* Svante Pettersson,

Sigvard Huldt, Dag and Lena, Ingmar Nordströms, Strix Q. Rock de Luxe, and Ola and the Janglers; *sound:* Thomas Samuelsson and Lars Persson; *production assistants:* Peder Langenskiöld, Robert Herlitz, Siv Lundgren, and Daniel Bergman; *narrator:* Ingmar Bergman; *running time:* 103 minutes.

CAST

Richard Östman, Ulla Silvergren, Annelie Nyström, Per Broman, Irena Broman, Inge Nordström, Annika Liljegren, Arne Eriksson, Adolf Ekström, Victoria Ekström, Anton Ekström, Valter Broman, Erik Ekström, Ingrid Ekman, Per Nordberg, Gunilla Johansson, Herbert Olsson, Rune Nilsson, Joe Nordenberg and Jan Nordberg (*themselves*).

Again made for Swedish television, this was a ten-years-later follow-up to Ingmar Bergman's original documentary about Fårö, his island home. The movie was two years in production, shot in color by cameraman Arne Carlsson, who photographed the island and its people. Bergman eventually faced some twenty-eight hours of footage that was then edited down to an hour and forty-three minutes, which he also narrated. *Fårö Document 1979* aired in Sweden on Christmas, 1979. In the United States it had no regular release, but was shown twice at New York's Museum of Modern Art in October 1980 as part of a series called "Scandinavia: New Films."

Critics' Circle

"*The earlier Fårö document ended on a somewhat downbeat note, with most of the young people interviewed indicating that their departure for bigger and grander locales couldn't come soon enough. Ironically, those youngsters interviewed ten years later seem to have decided to stay home after all and today's kids, while curious about the world, sound and look more content with life on Fårö, despite its limited resources and (as the film was shot during the winter and the nontourist season) its rather bleak look.*"
— "Robe" in *Variety*

"*The discretion with which he treats the tourists extends to his own residency on Fårö, a subject the film virtually ignores. Mr. Bergman's presence on this tiny island, where he*

filmed some of his greatest works and lived for many years, cannot have failed to affect the simplicity of the place; it may even have contributed to making the island so well-noticed by outsiders. A T-shirt worn casually by one farmer's wife, with a "Fårö" logo, says more about the island's popularity than anything Mr. Bergman cares to say. It's too bad he doesn't address his own impact upon the place."
— Janet Maslin in
The New York Times

"*Colored with affection and sympathy is this Ingmar Bergman portrait of the Swedish island of Fårö, east of Stockholm. If Bergman has heeded the Flaherty dictum and captured the essential story of the people of this island, it is a far different story than he told of the island in 1969. And an even farther perspective from the grim* Through a Glass Darkly, *which he filmed on the same isle.*"
— Duane Byrge in
The Hollywood Reporter

"*Given Fårö's special significance in Bergman's affections, he makes an admirably detached reporter. Much of the island speaks for itself—the changing colors of sea and sky, the drifts of light snow over trees and barns, the reflections of stone walls and cattle, the uncluttered pastures. The people, too, need little prompting. The interviews with the younger generations are less rewarding. Cutting between his 1969 film and the same faces today, Bergman enjoys—as one might expect—the shock effect of cheating real time, but the kids don't have too much to say. There's nothing much to do on Fårö, but nothing much anywhere else, either.*"
— Philip Strick in
Monthly Film Bulletin

Aus dem Leben der Marionetten
(From the Life of the Marionettes)

ITC release of a
Personafilm production for German TV: 1980
(U.S. release by ITC/Associated Film Distribution: 1981)

CREDITS

Director: Ingmar Bergman; *producer:* Horst Wendlandt; *executive producers:* Lord Grade and Martin Starger; *screenwriter:* Ingmar Bergman; *Eastmancolor and black-and-white cinematographer:* Sven Nykvist; *editor:* Petra von Oelffen (English-language version: Geri Ashur); *art director:* Herbert Strabel; *production designer:* Rolf Zehetbauer; *costumes:* Charlotte Flemming and Egon Strasser; *fashion show:* Heinz A. Schultze-Varell Couture; *music:* Rolf Wilhelm; *song:* "Touch Me, Take Me" (in English; singer uncredited); *sound:* Peter Beil and Norbert Lill; *assistant directors:* Trudy von Trotha and Johannes Kaetzler; *running time:* 104 minutes.

CAST

Robert Atzorn (*Peter Egerman*); Christine Buchegger (*Katarina Egerman*); Martin Benrath (*Mogens Jensen*); Rita Russek (*Katarina Krafft, known as "Ka"*); Lola Müthel (*Cordelia Egerman, Peter's Mother*); Walter Schmidinger (*Tomas Isidor Mandelbaum, known as "Tim"*); Heinz Bennent (*Arthur Brenner*); Ruth Olafs (*Nurse*); Gaby Dohm (*Secretary*); Karl-Heinz Pelser (*Police Interrogator*); Toni Berger (*Peepshow Doorman*).

In *Scenes from a Marriage*, Bergman had dealt secondarily with a quarrelsome couple named Peter and Katarina (portrayed by Jan Malmsjö and Bibi Andersson). Apparently, theirs was a relationship the filmmaker could not get out of his system, for in *From the Life of the Marionettes*, he resurrects them, surnames them "Egerman" and allows them to virtually destroy one another. Originally, this dangerously restive couple was to have been the center of a Bergman screenplay he called *Love Without Lovers*, which was never realized. Reworking their story into the present scenario. Bergman took several innovative steps: filming the script in Munich, he employed an entirely new-to-the-screen cast of stage actors from the Residenztheater and made what's essentially a black-and-white movie, with only the opening and closing segments filmed briefly in color by the enduring Sven Nykvist.

Opening with the murder of a prostitute (Rita Russek) by a businessman, Peter Egerman (Robert Atzorn), with deep-rooted neuroses and a beautiful wife (Christine Buchegger) who's a successful fashion designer, the story is told in cryptic segments, each beginning with an explanatory legend. Each section, in turn, reveals where it is in relation to the crime, as *From the Life of the Marionettes* moves oddly back and forth, both before and after the killing. In the secondary character of the wife's gay business associate (Walter Schmidinger), Bergman depicts his most in-depth portrait ever of a homosexual male who, in one prolonged murder-interrogation sequence, reveals his inner soul to a government official.

Bergman on Bergman

"The film is based on concrete observations and memories surrounding a theme that had haunted me for a long

From the Life of the Marionettes (1980). Martin Benrath and Robert Atzorn. ITC/Personafilm.

time: how two human beings who are insolubly and painfully united in love at the same time try to rip themselves free of their shackle...

"I found it was fascinating not only to work with actors who had not been before the camera before, but also to have a film without a plot. Just to make an investigation, like an operation: very, very clear, very simple, very sterile, but not to find the truth."

Critics' Circle

"*Ingmar Bergman has long been fascinated with the psychological dilemma of modern man struggling to exist in an increasingly alienated society. He continues this exploration with astonishing force and impact in* From the Life of the Marionettes, *which ranks alongside his best work. On the surface, it is a very bleak and unrelenting*

film. But it is developed with a very subtle sense of humor and irony.
—Ron Pennington in
The Hollywood Reporter

"*Robert Atzorn, as Peter, is a visibly desperate man. Christine Buchegger, as Katarina, is vibrantly attractive, but irritatingly remote. In contrast to the upper-class arrogance of the rest of the characters, Rita Russek arouses complete sympathy with her total lack of pretense as the prostitute.* From the Life of the Marionettes *is a depressingly austere film which, with its talky scenes, is infuriatingly static at times. But it remains a devastating comment on the problem of alienation in a world where spiritual values have been replaced by materialistic ones, leaving everyone feeling helpless and alone.*"
—Kathleen Carroll in
The New York Daily News

"*Its construction is a special intrigue, the narrative switching back and forth in time* around the climactic killing to demonstrate that the old rules of chronological sequence need never be heeded again. Instead, each switch in time contributes to an underlying linear development that reaches its logical destination in the film's closing shot and completes one of the most detailed portraits in all of Bergman's work."

—Philip Strick in
Monthly Film Bulletin

"The characters in Ingmar Berman's bracingly angry From the Life of the Marionettes aren't like the people in other Bergman films. They're just as talkative, but much less articulate or analytical.

"And yet around such blank, lost characters, Mr. Bergman has fashioned his most forceful film in a long while. From the Life of the Marionettes isn't a delicate work, or even an especially clear one, its violence and bitterness create an undeniable urgency."

—Janet Maslin in
The New York Times

"With this formal analysis of a man's psyche under excruciating sexual pressure, Ingmar Bergman, thirty-five years a director

and possibly the world's best-known minority-appeal filmmaker, gives the impression of a master holding his cinematic artistry in check.

"Sven Nykvist's cinematography, hallmark of many of Bergman's films, is in stunning form here for the dream sequences—minimal dark shapes in limbo on a bled-white background."

—"Simo" in *Variety*

"A bleak film that is more interesting to analyze than to attend."

—Richard Schickel in *Time*

"Bergman, a stupendous director of actors, gets forceful, perfectly calibrated performances from them. Especially brilliant is Walter Schmidinger as Tim, Katarina's homosexual business partner. It is the aging, anguished Tim who most deeply articulates Bergman's vision of man as a spiritual double agent. Marionettes is one of Bergman's most powerful and troubling explorations of this atomic fission in the human soul. He should be the first filmmaker to win the Nobel Prize."

—Jack Kroll in *Newsweek*

Fanny och Alexander
(Fanny and Alexander)

Sandrews release of a coproduction of Cinematograph, the Swedish Film Institute, Swedish TV, Gaumont, Personafilm, and Tobis Filmkunst: 1982 (U.S. release by Embassy Pictures: 1983)

CREDITS

Director: Ingmar Bergman; *executive producer:* Jörn Donner; *screenwriter:* Ingmar Bergman; *Eastmancolor cinematographer:* Sven Nykvist; *editor:* Sylvia Ingemarsson; *art director:* Anna Asp; *costumes:* Marik Vos-Lundh; *music:* Daniel Bell, with excerpts form Benjamin Britten's Suites for Cello, Opera 72, 80 and 87, played by Frans Helmerson; and Robert Schumann's Piano Quintet in F Major, played by Marianne Jacobs with the Fresk Quartet; *military band conducted by:* Per Lyng; *sound:* Owe Svensson and Bo Persson;

assistant director: Peter Schildt; *running time:* 315 minutes (TV version); 197 minutes (theatrical version).

CAST

Gunn Wållgren (*Helena Ekdahl*); Allan Edwall (*Oscar Ekdahl*); Ewa Fröling (*Emilie Ekdahl*); Bertil Guve (*Alexander Ekdahl*); Pernilla Allwin (*Fanny Ekdahl*); Börje Ahlstedt (*Carl Ekdahl*); Christina Schollin (*Lydia Ekdahl*); Jarl Kulle (*Gustav Adolf Ekdahl*); Mona Malm (*Alma Ekdahl*); Maria Granlund (*Petra*); Emelie Werkö (*Jenny*); Kristian Almgren (*Putte*); Angelica Wallgren (*Eva*); Majlis Granlund (*Miss Vega*); Svea Holst-Widén (*Miss Ester*); Siv Ericks (*Alida*); Inga Ålenius (*Lisen*); Kristina Adolphson (*Siri*); Eva von Hanno (*Berta*); Pernilla Wallgren (*Maj*) Käbi Laretei (*Aunt Anna*); Sonya Hedebratt (*Aunt Emma*); Erland Josephson (*Isak Jacobi*); Mats Bergman (*Aron*); Stina Ekblad (*Ismael*); Gunnar Björnstrand (*Filip Landahl*); Anna Bergman (*Hanna Schwartz*); Per Mattson (*Mikael Bergman*); Nils Brandt (*Harald Morsing*); Heinz Hopf (*Tomas Graal*); Åke Lagergren (*Johan Armfeldt*); Lickå Sjöman (*Grete Holm*); Sune Mangs (*Mr. Salenius*); Maud Hyttenberg (*Mrs. Sinclair*); Kerstin Karte (*Prompter*); Tore Karte (*Administrative Director*); Marianne Karl-Beck (*Mrs. Palmgren*); Gus Dahlström (*Set Decorator*); Gösta Prüzelius (*Dr. Fürstenberg*); Georg Årlin (*Colonel*); Ernst Günther (*Dean of the University*); Jan Malmsjö (*Bishop Edward Vergérus*); Kerstin Tidelius (*Henrietta Vergérus*); Marianne Aminoff (*Blenda Vergérus*); Marrit Olsson (*Malla Tander*); Brita Billsten (*Karna*); Harriet Andersson (*Justina*); Lena Olin (*Rosa*).

At the time of its production, Bergman declared that *Fanny and Alexander* would be his farewell to theatrical filmmaking. And so it has proved to be, despite the theatrical showing of subsequent TV films. Like *Scenes from a Marriage* and *Face to Face*, *Fanny and Alexander* was also produced in a longer, TV-miniseries version. Indeed, the television edition of the latter offers some two hours of additional material—which undoubtedly accounts for continuity gaps and unanswered questions about the big-screen release. *Fanny and Alexander* is also reputed to be, at a cost of $6 million, the costliest film produced in Sweden up to that time. In fact, it required a conjoining of various production companies, including the Swedish Film Institute, to make it all possible; fortunately, the result became Bergman's biggest box-office success in his native land.

In every way, *Fanny and Alexander* marks a imajor turnabout from Bergman's previous film, the austere, mostly monochromatic, psychological drama *From the Life of the Marionettes*, for this rich, sprawling family saga details a year in the lives of an extended theatrical clan, the Ekdahls, in 1907

Uppsala, Sweden. Beginning with a lengthy Christmastime celebration, the movie introduces almost too many characters for the average viewer to keep track of—especially in the theatrical version, which may eliminate details which would tend to make certain of the characters more vivid. It is a wealthy household of servants and traditions, looked over by the weary, aging Helena Ekdahl (Gunn Wållgren), a retired actress whose family owns the town's theater, where some members continue to perform. Fanny and Alexander (Bertil Guve and Pernilla Allwin) are Helena's beloved grandchildren by her son Oscar (Allan Edwall) and his actress-wife Emilie (Ewa Fröhling), and it is through their preadolescent eyes that much of *Fanny and Alexander* is seen. However, neither child plays much more than a subsidiary role in this large ensemble, and one is liable to come away from a viewing questioning the use of their names as the film's title. Eight-year-old Fanny, in particular, is little more than an occasional wide-eyed presence in the relatively few scenes in which her ten-year-old brother is briefly the center of attention.

Fanny and Alexander (1982). Bertil Guve, Ewa Fröhling, Gunn Wållgren and Pernilla Allwin. Sandrews.

Fanny and Alexander reiterates bits and pieces from many of the themes which have consumed Bergman's interest throughout his long career, and readers of *The Magic Lantern* will also recognize references from his childhood. The director's fans will also find interest in the casting of two of the film's supporting roles, for her vinegary portrayal of the turncoat servant Justina renders the once-sensual Harriet Andersson to all but unrecognizable in a wonderful character performance. By the same token, Gunnar Björnstrand's brief but effective bit as an elderly member of the Ekdahl theater troupe displays the then-ailing actor in his final role. Similarly, *Fanny and Alexander* records the last performance of the wonderful Gunn Wållgren, who had played the title role in 1947's *Kvinna Utan Ansikte* (*Woman Without a Face*), directed by Gustaf Molander from a Bergman screenplay. Like Ingrid Bergman during *Autumn Sonata*, Wållgren was battling cancer amidst the making of *Fanny and Alexander*.

Released in the United States in 1983, *Fanny and Alexander* garnered a truckload of prizes, including Academy Awards for Best Foreign Film, Cinematography, Costumes, and Art Direction. And the New York Film Critics named it the year's Best Foreign Film, as did the National Board of Review.

Bergman on Bergman

"There are two godfathers to *Fanny and Alexander*. One of them is E. T. A. Hoffmann. Toward the end of the 1970s, I was supposed to direct *Tales of Hoffmann* at the opera house in Munich. I began to fantasize about the real Hoffmann, who sat in Luther's wine cellar, sick and nearly dying. In a short story written by Hoffmann there is a gigantic, magical room. It was that magical room I wanted to re-create on stage. There is also an illustration from E. T. A. Hoffmann's stories that had haunted me time and time again, a picture from *The Nutcracker*. Two children are quivering close together in the twilight of Christmas Eve, waiting impatiently for the candles on the tree to be lighted and doors to the living room to be opened. It is that scene that gave me the idea of beginning *Fanny and Alexander* with a Christmas celebration.

"The second godfather is Dickens: the bishop and his home, the Jew in his boutique of fantasies, the children as victims; the contrast between flourishing outside life and a closed world in black and white."

Critics' Circle

"*Watching an Ingmar Bergman film is like settling in to a sumptuous feast. You're never quite certain what the dishes will be, but you know that everything will be scrupulously prepared, surprising in its variety, and substantial. If this has been true in the past, it applies even more specifically to* Fanny and Alexander, *the latest and certainly the richest of his creations. It is also his most personal, most accessible and, with the possible exception of* Smiles of a Summer Night, *his sunniest. Often in the past, his films have been bitter, vain protests against what he once called 'the silence of God.' Here, the underlying philosophy is positive, a celebration of the joys of life, love, kindness, procreation, and the kind of illusion and illumination that the theatre can bring to our lives.*"

— Arthur Knight in
The Hollywood Reporter

"*Even as you watch Ingmar Bergman's new film,* Fanny and Alexander *it has that quality of enchantment that usually attaches only to the best movies in retrospect, long after you've seen them, when they've been absorbed into the memory to seem sweeter, wiser, more magical than anything ever done in its own time. This immediate resonance is the distinguishing feature of this superb film, which is both quintessential Bergman and unlike anything else he has ever done before.*"

— Vincent Canby in
The New York Times

"Fanny and Alexander *offers us a glimpse of earthly paradise, which is not what we've come to expect from Ingmar Bergman, that master of private hells. Its highly theatrical pleasures are right there on the surface: it's a fairy tale, a ghost story, a family epic, a portrait of the artist in the making. There's a little something for everyone in this swan song.*"

— David Ansen in *Newsweek*

"*In attempting to sum up his amazing career, Bergman may have failed to make an authentic masterpiece, if only because he* seems to be trying too hard. *But* Fanny and Alexander *is a joy to experience, for in it Bergman demonstrates his love for all things human, creating a fairy tale of such cozy warmth and good-natured whimsicality that one wishes it would last forever instead of a mere three hours.*"

— Kathleen Carroll in
The New York Daily News

"*The picture is an almost sustained flight of Victorian fantasy, and it may win Ingmar Bergman his greatest public acceptance. Coming from Bergman, banality is bound to seem deeply satisfying—wholesome. It can pass for the wisdom of maturity.*"

— Pauline Kael in *The New Yorker*

"*Ingmar Bergman was once asked why, since he found life so exciting, he made such serious, dark movies? Bergman's reply may be* Fanny and Alexander, *a magical, mystical, metaphysical tapestry celebrating the mysteries of life, tinged with brooding, solemn overtones.*

Bergman has said that this is his last theatrical feature. If so, he has gone out in style."

— Rod Granger in
The Film Journal

"Fanny and Alexander *is a surprisingly optimistic work from a director known for his portrayals of the hells people create for each other on earth. As critics are sure to note, the film is a deliberate summing up of Bergman's past work: It's as if the characters from* Smiles of a Summer Night *had been kidnapped by the characters from* Winter Light, *only to be rescued at the last minute by* The Magician. Fanny and Alexander *will do very well in art houses, and could reach a wider audience with its tale of childhood wonder and terror, permitting Ingmar Bergman to bow out with the kind of last testament all great filmmakers should have: a hit.*"

— Bill Krohn in *Boxoffice*

Efter Repetitionen
(After the Rehearsal)

A Cinematograph/Personafilm production
for Swedish TV: 1984
(U.S. release by Triumph Films: 1984)

CREDITS

Director: Ingmar Bergman; *producer:* Jörn Donner; *screenwriter:* Ingmar Bergman; *color cinematographer:* Sven Nykvist; *editor:* Sylvia Ingemarsson; *art director:* Anna Asp; *running time:* 72 minutes.

CAST

Erland Josephson (*Henrik Vogler*); Lena Olin (*Anna*); Ingrid Thulin (*Rakel*); Nadja Palmstierna-Weiss (*Anna at Twelve*); Betril Guve (*Henrik at Twelve*).

Since Bergman remained adamant that his last theatrical feature be the edited version of *Fanny and Alexander*, he was opposed to this TV movie being shown in American cinemas. But his efforts to prevent its distribution here proved fruitless, and what is essentially a three-character chamber drama, set in a close-quartered backstage locale with little use of scenery or props, appears little more than what it essentially is — a claustrophobic television drama. Having enjoyed its U.S. theatrical run in 1984, *After the Rehearsal* appears far more effective as it was intended, viewed on videocassette on a small-sized screen.

Characteristically bearing echoes of Bergman's past works, much of *After the Rehearsal* concerns a production of Strindberg's *Dream Play*, a work that figured in the final scene of *Fanny and Alexander*, where two of the leading characters discuss Strindberg's then-newly-published work. As its title suggests, this film begins following a rehearsal of that work, as its director, Henrik Vogler (Erland Josephson), rests alone on the empty stage, soon to be distracted by the appearance of his young leading lady, Anna Egerman (Lena Olin), who has returned on the pretext of having lost her bracelet. In a way, what follows is a dream play of its own as the two discuss and argue over the production, their relationship, and the young woman's heritage (Anna's late mother, Rakel, had played an important part in Vogler's earlier life). Amid their scene, Rakel (Ingrid Thulin) enters, and since her exchanges are confined exclusively to Vogler, we can assume that she remains a figment of his memory — until we notice that Anna is still present. However, at second glance, it isn't the adult Anna at all, but rather her teenaged self. Where does reality end, and where do dreams take over? What in this film is real, and what is imagined? Typically, Bergman doesn't tell us; his enigmatic mind-tricks prevail.

Noting Lena Olin's charismatic intensity as Anna, one recalls the tradition of Harriet Andersson, Liv Ullmann, Bibi Andersson and Ingrid Thulin, as well as earlier echoes of the heritage of Ingrid Bergman and Viveca Lindfors. One can only regret that Bergman's filmmaking years cannot play a part in Olin's talented future. However,

she was cast by Bergman as Cordelia in his stage version of *King Lear* following the completion of *After the Rehearsal*, which led, in turn, to her leading role in the film *The Unbearable Lightness of Being* with Daniel Day-Lewis and to subsequent leads in *Havana and Enemies — A Love Story*. Her performance as *Miss Julie* in the Bergman stage production, seen at New York's Brooklyn Academy of Music in the late spring of 1991, was a revelation of skilled emotional acting.

Bergman on Bergman

"*After the Rehearsal* was meant to be a pleasant little episode on my road toward death. To my surprise, the shooting was completely joyless. Seeing *After the Rehearsal* now, I find it much better than I had remembered. When you have struggled with a bad shoot, the dispiritedness lingers. It makes you remember the film with greater distaste than necessary…

"The editing was another wretched experience: there was so much cutting and pasting. *After the Rehearsal*, in the final edited version, ran one hour and twelve minutes. I had been forced to cut at least twenty minutes of the finished material. Today it is hard to believe that *After the Rehearsal* was actually written as a bit of a black comedy with dialogue in harsh yet comedic language. The film itself is lackluster, with none of the vitality of the original screenplay."

Critics' Circle

"*Ingmar Berman's first love has always been the stage. And it has been an ambivalent, passionate love. In* After the Rehearsal, *Bergman darkly and unsparingly confronts the problems of being an artist. Less expansively, he reveals the joys. For Bergman worshippers (and they are certainly the only ones who will see this film), this seventy-two-minute production offers little further insight*

After the Rehearsal **(1984). Conferring on the set: cinematographer Sven Nykvist, Lena Olin, Erland Josephson and writer-director Bergman. Cinematograph/Personafilm.**

into the contradictory Swedish director than the body of his work already has."
— Duane Byrge in
The Hollywood Reporter

"Although it's a very different kind of film, After the Rehearsal *is as passionate, knowledgeable and funny about the stage as Francois Truffaut's* Day for Night *is about movies. The Bergman characters aren't that different from the rest of us, but the eccentricities of their profession make demands on them that produce insights that most ordinary folk don't have to face."*
— Vincent Canby in
The New York Times

"While After the Rehearsal *is minimal in every respect, it is remarkably compelling. The film is talky but the talk is interesting. The director also achieves an almost embarrassing intimacy by resorting to emotionally-charged close-ups — a Bergman trademark."*
—Doris Toumarkine in
The Film Journal

"I found After the Rehearsal *numbing — deeply humorless and both overwrought and weary, an unsettling combination of qualities. Bergman made the movie for television, and has been at pains to speak of it publicly as a TV movie, but the stiffness and banality of his filmmaking style in this work cannot be blamed entirely on the restrictions of the tube.* After the Rehearsal *would work better, I think, in the theater, where its superheated confrontational dialogue might serve as the basis for a juicy acting exercise."*
—David Denby in *New York*

"The new work, though only seventy-two minutes long, seems interminable and almost as unsuited to TV as to the cinema. It is an example of talking heads where neither the talk nor the heads are very interesting. Aside from being static almost to the point of rigor mortis, it features characters and situations — even dialogue — that we have encountered in previous Bergman films in fresher, more penetrating and pertinent form."
—John Simon in *National Review*

"No other filmmaker of the first rank has devoted himself so fully to another medium as Ingmar Bergman has to the stage. Now he has distilled his forty years' theater experience into a 'small' film — one simple set, three speaking parts, seventy-two minutes — that is as direct, serene and human as any he has made.
—Richard Corliss in *Time*

"Word from Cannes preceded the first screening here of Ingmar Bergman's After

the Rehearsal, *stating in no uncertain terms that Bergman was annoyed that this 'minor work was being touted as a motion picture.' It had been made as a TV play in Sweden.*

"However, the long and short of it (mostly the long) is that the picture talks itself to death, even Sven Nykvist's eloquent photography notwithstanding."
—Archer Winsten in
The New York Post

Dokument: Fanny och Alexander (The Making of Fanny and Alexander)

A Cinematograph production for Swedish TV: 1986 (No U.S. theatrical release)

CREDITS

Director/screenwriter: Ingmar Bergman; *color cinematographer:* Arne Carlsson; *editor:* Sylvia Ingemarsson; *running time:* 110 minutes.

Bergman's final theatrical feature, *Fanny and Alexander*, was filmed on location in Uppsala and at the Svensk Filmindustri studios in Stockholm from early September 1981 to late March 1982. During that time, the production's stills photographer, Arne Carlsson, had the director's full cooperation in also shooting an abundance of 16-mm behind-the-scenes footage that was eventually edited (by *Fanny's* editor, Sylvia Ingemarsson) into this feature-length documentary. Shown publicly at the 1986 Berlin Film Festival, it has also aired on Scandinavian and U.S. television.

Critics' Circle

"Bergman at work helming is seen as an endlessly patient, but relentless, meticulous

and demanding artist who maintains an atmosphere of easy camaraderie with everybody around him. He acts out movements and nuances in dialog for his actors, but rarely engages in discussions with them as he does, gladly, with cinematographer [Sven] Nykvist. It is obvious that everybody is in loving awe of him and ready to do their damndest to heed his advise and admonitions."
—"Kell" in *Variety*

"Here is filmmaking as the vision of a single artist. Beginning on the day before shooting for this 1983 film and continuing until the wrap, the documentary quietly and methodically follows Ingmar Bergman as he works his way through many of the film's key scenes. Splashy effects are unthinkable as Mr. Bergman strives constantly for subtlety."
—John J. O'Connor in
The New York Times

Larmar och Gör Sig Till (In the Presence of a Clown)

An SVT production for Swedish TV, in collaboration with DR (Denmark), NRK (Norway), RAI (Italy), YLE 1 (Finland), and ZDF (Germany), with support from the Nordic TV Coproduction Fund and the Nordic Film & TV Fund/1997 (No U.S. release)

CREDITS

Director: Ingmar Bergman; *producer:* Pia Ehrnvall; *screenwriter:* Ingmar Bergman; *Eastmancolor cinematographer:* Per Sundin; *editor:* Sylvia Ingemarsson; *art director:* Goran Wassberg; *costumes:* Mette Moller; *running time:* 120 minutes.

CAST

Börje Ahlstedt (*Carl Åkerblom*); Marie Richardson (*Pauline Thibault*); Erland Josephson (*Osvald Vogler*); Pernilla August (*Karin Bergman*); Anita Björk (*Anna Åkerblom*); Agneta Ekmanner (*Rigmor the Clown*); Anna Björk (*Mia Falk*).

In 1997, after a prolonged absence from filmmaking, Bergman returned to direct this characteristically uncommercial TV movie. Its inspiration was a story found among the papers of a late uncle already memorialized by the director in *Fanny and Alexander* and in his screenplay for *The Best Intentions*, and portrayed (as here) by actor Börje Ahlstedt.

Set mostly in an Uppsala psychiatric hospital in the mid–1920s, *In the Presence of a Clown* centers on middle-aged Carl Åkerblom, an eccentric inventor obsessed with the death of composer Franz Schubert, whose recorded music entertains him at the asylum. Åkerblom had attempted to kill his young fiancée, Pauline (Marie Richardson), and was consequently institutionalized. In collaboration with another patient, Prof. Osvald Vogler (Erland Josephson), Åkerblom devises a plan to create the world's first live talking-picture with actors stationed behind a screen to synchronize their speech with the film's silent images. Its subject: an imag-

ined encounter between Schubert and a notorious 19th–century courtesan. The first showing of their movie proves a technical fiasco, but is rescued from complete disaster by the actors, who stage a candlelight reading of the screenplay.

Screened at 1998's Cannes Film Festival, *In the Presence of a Clown* also had four showings at that year's New York Film Festival.

Critics' Circle

"In the Presence of a Clown, *Ingmar Bergman's latest telepic, doesn't rank high in the filmmaker's pantheon, but it reps a solid piece of work that will delight aficionados of the vet director.*"
—Emanuel Levy in *Variety*

"*When great filmmakers reach old age, their work tends to grow sparer and more austere, the texture stripped away so that the core themes of a lifetime's output jut out like bones under crumbling flesh. In the Presence of a Clown,* Ingmar Bergman's two-hour 1997 made-for-television movie is such a film. A gloomy, murky, static work laced with an absurdist gallows humor, it doesn't try very hard to entertain or to look beautiful. But the movie is still a must-see for Bergman aficionados."

—Stephen Holden in
The New York Times

Appendix

Bibliography

Bergman, Ingmar. *Bergman on Bergman: Interviews with Ingmar Bergman by Stig Björkman, Torsten Manns and Jonas Sima*. Translated by Paul Britten Austin. New York: Simon and Schuster, 1973.

_____. *Four Screenplays by Ingmar Bergman*. Translated by Lars Malmström and Davis Kushner. New York: Simon and Schuster, 1960.

_____. *Images: My Life in Film*. Translated by Marianne Ruuth. New York: Arcade Publishing, 1990.

_____. *The Magic Lantern*: An Autobiography. Translated by Joan Tate. New York: Viking Press, 1988.

_____. *The Marriage Scenarios*. Translated by Alan Blair. New York: Pantheon Books, 1978.

Cook, Davis A. *A History of Narrative Film*. New York: W. W. Norton, 1981

Cowie, Peter. *Ingmar Bergman: A Critical Biography*. New York: Scribners, 1982; updated: New York: Limelight Editions, 1992.

_____. *Scandinavian Cinema*. London: Tantivy Press, 1990.

_____. In collaboration with Arne Svensson. *Sweden 1: An Illustrated Guide to the Work of the Leading Directors, Players, Technicians and Other Key Figures of the Swedish Cinema*. New York: A. S. Barnes, 1970.

_____. *Sweden 2: A Comprehensive Assessment of the Themes, Trends and Directors in Swedish Cinema*. New York: A. A. Barnes, 1970.

Crist, Judith. *The Private Eye, The Cowboy and the Very Naked Girl*. New York: Holt, Rinehart and Winston, 1968.

Donner, Jörn. *The Personal Vision of Ingmar Bergman*. Translated by Holger Lundbergh. Bloomington: Indiana University Press, 1964.

Gilliatt, Penelope. *Unholy Fools*. New York: Viking Press, 1973.

Kael, Pauline. *5001 Nights at the Movies: A Guide from A to Z*. New York: Holt, Rinehart and Winston, 1982.

Katz, Ephraim. *The Film Encyclopedia*, 2nd ed. New York: HarperCollins, 1994.

Kauffmann, Stanley. *Living Images*. New York: Harper & Row, 1975.

Lloyd, Ann, and David Robinson, eds. *Movies of the Fifties*. London: Orbis, 1982.

_____. *Movies of the Sixties*. London: Orbis, 1983.

_____. *Movies of the Seventies*. London: Orbis, 1984.

Long, Robert Emmet. *Ingmar Bergman: Film and Stage*. New York: Abrams, 1994.

Maltin, Leonard, ed. *Leonard Maltin's 1996 Movie and Video Guide*. New York: Penguin, 1995.

McBride, Joseph, ed. *Filmmakers on Filmmaking: Volume One*. Boston: Houghton Mifflin, 1976.

Mekas, Jonas. *Movie Journal: The Rise of a New American Cinema, 1959–1971*. New York: Macmillan, 1972.

Osborne, Robert. *65 Years of the Oscar*. New York: Abbeville Press, 1994.

Quinlan, David. *The Illustrated Guide to Film Directors*. Totowa, N. J.: Barnes & Noble, 1983.

Reed, Rex. *Big Screen, Little Screen*. New York: Macmillan, 1971.

Samuels, Charles Thomas. *Encountering Directors*. New York: Putnam, 1972.

Sarris, Andrew, ed. *Interviews with Film Directors*. New York: 1967.

Shipman, David. *The Story of Cinema*. New York: St. Martin's Press, 1982.

Simon, John. *Ingmar Bergman Directs*. New York: Harcourt, Brace, Jovanovich, 1972.

_____. *Private Screenings: Views of the Cinema of the Sixties*. New York: Macmillan, 1967.

Steinberg, Cobbett. *Film Facts*. New York: Facts on File, 1980.

Ullmann, Liv. *Changing*. New York: Alfred A. Knopf, 1977.

Wood, Robin. *Ingmar Bergman*. New York: Praeger, 1969.

Young, Vernon. *Cinema Borealis: Ingmar Bergman and the Swedish Ethos*. New York: David Lewis, 1971.

Index

Italicized page numbers refer to illustrations.
Entries for films not by Bergman show the director.

175